# ADVENTURES IN TIBET

# ADVENTURES IN TIBET

SVEN HEDIN

GYAN

*Published by*

Gyan Publishing House
5, Ansari Road
Daryaganj, New Delhi-110002
Phone: 011-47034999, 9811692060
E-mail: books@gyanbooks.com

*Distribution Network*
gyanbooks.com
India, USA, Canada, UK, Australia



ISBN: 978-93-7097-476-0 (HB)
First Published, 1904

2nd Impression 2025

*Printed at:* Gyan Press, Delhi.



**ADVENTURES IN TIBET**
Author SVEN HEDIN

# ADVENTURES IN TIBET

# ADVENTURES IN TIBET

BY

SVEN HEDIN

AUTHOR OF

"Central Asia and Tibet," "Through Asia," etc.

*Illustrated with Drawings and Photographs, mostly by the Author*

LONDON

HURST AND BLACKETT LIMITED

1904

# PREFACE.

THE favourable reception accorded to my book, *Central Asia and Tibet*, has emboldened me to prepare a cheaper and more popular edition. This, although of course based upon the longer work, has been entirely re-written from beginning to end specially for the present issue.

The halo of romance and the magic of the unknown which have for so long drawn the adventurous as by a magnet to the mysterious land of Tibet have now been in great part dissipated. I am the last traveller who penetrated into the Land of Snow trusting to my own resources alone. When the future traveller enters Tibet, and especially if he is an Englishman, it will be under the protecting ægis of the cannon and the stern safeguard of treaty; but no reflection of the romantic will envelop him as he treads in all security the last hermit "kingdom" of the world, the revered Holy Land of Lamaism and the Sacred Books. I will confess that, in the events which have happened in that country during the present summer, my sympathies have been entirely on the side of the Tibetans—not, I hasten to add, for any political reason, but because I am a lover of freedom. And, in saying this, I trust I shall not offend any, for I have experienced too many and too great proofs of friendship and hospitality in both England and India for me to contemplate such a contingency with anything like equanimity. But I am bound to admit, that with me freedom goes before friendship, and I should be untrue to myself were I not to testify thus publicly my sympathy with the Tibetans.

This book has, however, nothing whatever to do with politics. It is simply the narrative of my own journeys in that lofty region where the wild yak and the kulan browse amid the hailstorms and the driving sleets of summer. And if it teach no other lesson, it will perhaps serve to remind the reader of the difference that exists between the life of activity spent among the powers of Nature and the sedentary and stationary life of the great city.

SVEN HEDIN.

*Stockholm,*
20th September, 1904.

# CONTENTS.

# LIST OF ILLUSTRATIONS.

# ADVENTURES IN TIBET.

## CHAPTER I.

### EASTWARD BOUND.

FAR away to the East, on the other side of the mountains and the deserts, there lies, hidden in the heart of the earth's greatest continent, a region which even at this late period of time has been visited by only a few travellers. And yet there are associated with that distant region a greater number of puzzling and unsolved problems than are to be found in perhaps any other part of the earth. Forty years ago the inquirer who sought information with regard to the heart of Asia had to have recourse to Marco Polo, the adventurous merchant of Venice, who, more than six hundred years ago, travelled across the continent, and left a description of his journey, which, meagre though it is, nevertheless constitutes an enduring monument of human enterprise. When, towards the end of the '70's, a new era dawned in the history of geographical discovery, the centre of Asia could no longer escape the attention of Europeans. The great Russian traveller, Przhevalsky, was the first who, in modern times, seriously attempted to lift the veil behind which hitherto so many secrets of the region beyond the deserts had lain hidden.

Whilst still a schoolboy I was fascinated by the travels of Adolf Nordenskiöld, and later of Przhevalsky, and dreamed of some day following in their footsteps, and in those of Marco Polo. It is now nearly twenty years since I first travelled in Persia, and stretched myself to rest under the date-palms of Basra and Bagdad. Nine of the winters which have passed since then I have spent on Asiatic soil, and during the same period have had to strike out of my life nine of the bright summers we enjoy in my native home.

With respect to the broad features of its geography, Asia is now pretty well known, but in the matter of details there is an endless amount of work to be done before we learn all there is to be known about it. I was always drawn by an irresistible attraction towards that continent of lofty mountains and vast arid wastes. You may imagine the delight which attends geographical discovery whereby human knowledge is increased; you may imagine the fascination of the endless desert, engulfing the traveller amid its giant waves of sand! Conceive, too, the peculiar joy and pride of being the first to stand 16,000—17,000 feet above the cares and anxieties of life, to be the first to behold the stupendous mountains of Tibet, and to know that their fields of everlasting snow have never before been seen by human eyes, but have only been shone upon by the sun and been bathed by the softer glow of the luminaries of the night. And when you return home to houses and streets, to steam-boats and railway trains, to newspapers and telephones, and think back upon the free untrammelled life in the saddle and the tent, and recall the solemn processions of the camels, silent save for the tinkle, tinkle of their bells, a thousand pictures of the past flit before you as in a dream; you see them again like memories of the time when you sat entranced in Cooper's romances, *Robinson Crusoe*, or Jules Verne, and you long to get away from the prosaic life of Europe, and to return to the poetry and glamour of

Asia. There creeps over you a longing for the stillness of the desert and its great loneliness, where you are free to meditate upon the chances and changes of human life. Do not, however, imagine that the explorer is the first visitant in every region he visits. If fortune is with him—and fortune was with the explorer whose wanderings are described in this book—he may happen to discover traces of a civilization which disappeared 1,000 years or more ago, and light upon evidences of races whose destiny is unknown, except that they were swept away from off the earth as the dust haze is blown off the face of the desert. And do not imagine that the rewards which fall to the successful traveller are reaped by a summer-day dance upon the soft petals of roses. No; the traveller has to take many a heavy and weary step before he reaches the goal of his desires, and many is the gloomy and dreary hour he spends in his smoke-reeking tent whilst resting at the end of an arduous day.

It was a bright and beautiful midsummer day when I said good-bye to those at home and set out for Finland and St. Petersburg. All who have ever left their home, and those dear to them, having no prospect of seeing them or hearing from them again for a long time—nay, in actual uncertainty as to whether they will ever see them again—such will readily understand what my feelings were as the last lingering hand-shake was exchanged. Many and many a time since then have I seen that last glimpse of Stockholm and those I loved standing on the quay, waving their final farewells to me, their hearts too full for utterance.

Shrill whistles the engine and at a giddy pace I fly across Holy Russia, through Moscow, and over the majestic Don, rolling its muddy waters down to the Black Sea. Like shooting stars the towns disappear one after the other. The bulb-shaped spires of the churches peep up above the horizon, grow bigger on the view, and disappear again, while the engine-crank thud-thuds unceasingly along the gleaming metals. We turn our backs upon Vladikavkaz, the little town up and down whose dusty streets I sauntered, a newly-fledged student, in 1885. It was a dark, warm night when we sped down to the greatest inland lake of the earth, the Caspian Sea. The only sounds that broke upon the stillness of the steppe were the groaning of the engine and occasionally the shrill chirping of the crickets. Meanwhile lightning was playing round the summits of the Caucasus as though a host of volcanoes were hidden in the range, which the seas on either hand had not yet availed to quench.

At Petrovsk we stepped on board a smart little paddle-steamer, lying within the double piers, which clasp the harbour like the claws of a Brobdingnagian crab. We were not long in getting across the bright salt water to Krasnovodsk, the terminus of the Trans-Caspian railway. The blue-green waters of the Caspian are, however, very treacherous. Storms burst upon the lake from the deserts of Asia, or swoop down from the summits of the Caucasus, even when the sky is calm and bright, and with incredible fury churn it into wildly-tossing waves. Not long ago a steamboat started from the one side, but was never seen on the other. Of its fate nothing is known with certainty ; it disappeared, leaving not the slightest trace behind it.

Do not imagine, however, that it was with any feeling of pleasure, after a boisterous voyage across the sea, that I set foot on land at Krasnovodsk, or the Red Water. Anything but that. Krasnovodsk is the very opposite of an earthly paradise. It is a little hole of a place, with white one-storied flat-roofed houses, and a couple of unpretentious churches, girdled round by a ring of barren, crumbling mountains and yellow sand-dunes—not a tree, not a blade of grass, not even a drop of fresh water ! All the water to drink is brought in in huge barrels laden on creaking carts. To have to live in a wretched place like that, baking as it was in the hot sun, would be sheer transportation.

General Kuropatkin, Minister of War, the same who is now fighting in the Far East, the eyes of both the white and the yellow races fastened upon him, had kindly telegraphed to Krasnovodsk, ordering the railway authorities there to place at my disposal a special railway carriage right through to Andijan, the terminus of the line. It was a delightful way of travelling. The conductor provided me with cold water for douches—most refreshing with the thermometer at 106°.5 Fahr. in the shade. My *salon* was furnished with couches, chairs, and a writing-table. My carriage was the last on the train, so that it might be readily uncoupled should I wish to stop anywhere. I used to sit under the sheltering roof of the back platform and study the scenery, and watch the metals converging to a pin's-point in the far distance.

On we sped eastward bound. The hot air flickered on the tops of the burning hot dunes, and when I put my head outside it was like thrusting it into a baker's oven. Never a glimpse of an oasis, never a whiff of flowers, nor the crisp murmuring of a brook. It was only at the stations that I got glimpses of plant-life, all burnt up by the sun.

With a hollow rumble the train, slowing down, rolled across the long pile-bridge of the Amu-daria, though the wooden bridge has since been replaced by one of iron. How I longed to fling myself into the fresh, though turbid, waters of the big river. High is their ancestry, for they descend from the "roof of the world," and are the offspring of the blue blood of glaciers, which carry down with them into those stifling deserts a little of the coolness of their ancestral home.

How I longed to see the sun sinking below the horizon! and with what a sigh of relief did I wish god-speed to the last golden ray that it suffered to linger for a moment upon the crests of the dunes. In those regions the twilight is short; the deserts are soon clasped in the shades of night. and it gets very dark. Although the temperature dropped but a few degrees, the air seemed to be decidedly cooler, I woke up as from a swoon, unlocked my carriage door, and walked to the dining-saloon at the other end of the train for a late dinner. Upon returning to my *salon*, I used to take off every stitch of clothing, and stretching myself on one of the couches, read *The Three Musqueteers;* not that I was preparing for an adventurous robber's life, but simply because this book happened to have fallen into my hands.

At length we arrived at Samarcand, classic ground in the history of the world. Whilst we are feasting our eyes for a few minutes upon the magnificent mosques of the time of Tamerlane, amongst which I spent a couple of weeks, sketch-book in hand, 14 years ago, let me recall in a few words some of the claims which Samarcand has to be called the queen amongst the cities of Central Asia. According to the local tradition, this city was founded by the hero Afrasiab, but it is first known to history under the name of Maracanda (Strabo, XI. ii.), and as such was the capital of Sogdiana when Alexander the Great conquered that country. Leaving a part of his army in Bactria, to keep that country in check, Alexander (Arrian, IV. 16) crossed the Oxus and invaded Sogdiana. Then, dividing his forces into five divisions, he "put himself at the head of the fifth and so marched across the country to Maracanda." Alexander's fame still lives indelibly in the traditions of Central Asia, and many of the chieftains along the banks of the Amu-daria trace their lineage back to one or other of the great warriors who stood about his throne. There is a little lake in the vicinity of Samarcand which for 2,200 years has borne his name—Iskander-kul. How strange that a man who died so young should thus powerfully impress his memory upon the consciousness of all ages! The only great ones who can, in point of renown, compete with Alexander are the great teachers of religion, all of whom sprang from Asia.

In the year 711 Samarcand was conquered by the Arabs,

**Islam Bai.**

and in 1219 was plundered by the great Mongol conqueror, Jenghiz Khan. But a fresh era of greatness came to the city under Tamerlane—that is, Timur the Lame—who wrote in his famous memoirs: "It is the duty of a victorious king to subject to his power every kingdom that is oppressed by its rulers; it is for that reason I have freed

Khorasan and purged the kingdoms of Fars, Irak, and Shaum "—the same warrior who, after having crushed the army of the Seljuk Bayazid I., is said to have shut up the Turkish Sultan in an iron* cage and exhibited him wherever he went as though he were a wild animal. Tamerlane was on the point of invading China when he died, 17th February, 1405, at the age of 69, leaving behind him an empire of immense extent and an imperishable name. Embalmed with musk and rose-water, and swathed in fine linen, the body of the world-conqueror was placed in a coffin of ebony, and deposited under a monolith of nephrite, underneath the dome of the burial-mosque which he himself had built. Its magnificent green cupola is visible from the station. Amongst pious texts of the Koran and his many royal titles and boastful deeds are to be read in alabaster relief these words: "If I were still alive men would tremble."

After the stifling heat of the desert the fresh and luxuriant greenery around Samarcand is perfectly delightful. Seven hundred years ago Sadi, the flower-loving poet of Shiraz, wrote to his beloved: "If the maiden in Shiraz held my heart in her hand, I would give her Samarcand and Bukhara in exchange for the mole on her cheek"; meaning that these two cities were the most precious possessions a man could give to his mistress.

But there goes the station bell! Good-bye, dreams! It is time to return to colourless prose. Behind us in the west we leave Samarcand buried amid its thick orchards, the greenness of which vies in vividness and purity with the inlaid tiles of the cupolas; and behind us, too, we leave the proud memories of the past.

At length we reach Andijan, the terminus of the railway, the furthest point to which steam will carry us. There on the platform awaiting me stands my old faithful servant,

* It really was a sort of palanquin, in which the captive sovereign travelled.

Islam Bai, tall, confident, calm, wearing a blue *khalat* ("long Turkestan coat"), and with King Oscar's medal on his breast. Our mutual pleasure upon meeting again found expression in a hearty hand-shake, and we very soon found plenty to talk about; nor was it long before my Turkish, which had rusted for two years, was flowing as fluently as ever. Poor Islam Bai! Little did I foresee in that glad hour the unhappy destiny which was to overtake him before we parted for good and all.

## CHAPTER II.

### THROUGH THE MOUNTAINS AND DESERTS TO THE YARKAND-DARIA.

THE distance between Osh, the most eastern town of Fergana, and Kashgar, the most western town of China, amounts to 270 miles. An easy and picturesque road, which can easily be traversed in a fortnight on horseback, connects the two over the Alai Pass of Tong-burun. After the heat of the deserts, the cool mountain air was doubly welcome. I had with me seven men and 26 horses. Islam Bai was *karavan-bashi*, or "leader of the caravan." I also took from Osh two active little pups. One was called Dovlet, or the Happy; the other, with the blood of Asiatic wild animals in his veins, rejoiced in the name of Yoldash, or the Travelling Companion. They lived and ate in my tent, and were my acknowledged favourites; and when I lost them I missed them as much as if they had been human beings. Yoldash, who held out for 2½ years, was one of the most important members of our caravan.

We crossed the frontier between Russia and China at the little fort of Irkeshtam, and then rode down into the beautiful glen of Nagara-chaldi, with its forest of poplars, willows and smaller bushes. In this beautiful oasis, with the cooling tinkle of its waters echoing against the perpendicular cliffs, we rested more than a day. It was delightful to be in the forest during the day, and the night breathed deep solemnity, especially when the big camel caravans, carrying wool from Kashgar, tramped silently past. I used to lie and listen with indescribable pleasure to the hollow ding-dong of the leader's bell in the distance. The sound grew more and more distinct, the

A Camel Caravan Fording an Arm of the Kizil-su.

solemn echo keeping time with the calm, majestic stalk of the camels. Peeping out of my tent, I saw the huge black forms flitting past like spectres. Their soft padded feet made no sound, though the rocky walls flung back again and again the harsh echoes of the caravan bells. Then, creeping back into my bed, I heard the sound slowly die away amongst the mountains. Perhaps it may seem strange that such a simple thing as the sound of bells should exercise such a hypnotic power upon the nerves, and that the recollection of them should awaken such bright and happy associations in my memory. But it is 20 years since I heard them for the first time, and since then they have echoed like an undertone through my life. It was to the sound of bells that I rode away from Bagdad up through the mountains of Kurdistan, when the march of the Arabs was too slow for my impatience, and I ran away from them, but was received with hospitality by Aga Muhamed Hassan, and was given unlimited credit on the strength of my being a countryman of Charles XII. The sound of bells was in my ears when I travelled through Khorasan and Turkestan, and again when I made my dash across the Desert of Takla-makan; though on this last occasion their echoes were funereal, for the whole of the caravan perished of thirst except myself and two of my men. I have also travelled through the land of the Mongols, and through Northern China, always with the cling-clang of the camels' bells in my ears. The various vicissitudes of joy and sorrow which inevitably attend a long journey have always in my case been accompanied by the same penetrating music. No wonder, then, that these bells of the desert have such a weird fascination for me.

At length we reached the bank of the river Kizil-su, or the Red Water, and down its bed immense volumes of water were pouring as red and thick as tomato soup. After several of the other men had in vain attempted to find a ford, it was Kader's turn to try his luck. Resolutely digging his spurs into the flanks of his shaggy little Kirghiz horse, he rode straight down into the sullen stream. Down, down, sank the horse; the water came up to the pommel of the saddle; in a moment horse and rider disappeared in the muddy waters, their heads alone being visible. Kader flung his arms around the horse's neck, and away they both went swirling down stream,

Nagara-chaldi.

and disappeared like corks behind the next bend. Somehow or other Kader managed to get through all right, for, after a good long interval, he made his appearance wet and dripping like a drowned cat, leading his horse by the bridle. Strange to say, having found a passable ford, we managed to cross the river tolerably dry-shod.

Fording the Kizil-su.

The caravan with which on the 5th September, 1899, I left Kashgar consisted of 15 magnificent camels, 12 horses, and a whole retinue of servants. Of the horses, none survived the journey, of the camels only two. I must now introduce two of my Mussulman attendants, Turdu Bai and Faisullah, a couple of white-bearded old men from Russian Turkestan, who during the whole of the time they were with me served me with exemplary fidelity. On the other hand Nias Hadji, notwithstanding his pilgrimage to the Prophet's grave, turned out a thorough-paced rascal.

A word or two to explain how the two West Siberian Cossacks, Sirkin and Chernoff, came to take part in this journey. In an audience which I had with the Emperor Nicholas II., in April, 1899, His Majesty told me that he wished to send with me an escort of Cossacks, "that I might have all the protection and security that human power could give me." When I ventured to express some hesitation on the ground that I was only accustomed to Mohammedan servants, and had never had Cossacks under my command, and at the same time pointed out that the presence of Cossacks in my retinue might give rise to difficulties when I approached the frontier of India, the Czar laughed, and said that I should never regret having followed his advice, "for," he added, "in my journey through India, Japan, and Siberia I was accompanied by Cossacks, and I know from experience what useful fellows they are." I expressed my thanks for this signal mark of imperial favour. That same day about two o'clock the Imperial Horse Guards were celebrating the memory of their patron saint, and the Emperor and all the Grand Dukes were present. An hour later I received a letter from General Kuropatkin, asking me to call upon him if possible at once. At the banquet, His Majesty the Czar had ordered the General to make arrangements for my Cossack escort. The Czar proposed to send ten Cossacks, but I thought that two would be enough, and begged General Kuropatkin to let them meet me in the vicinity of Lop-nor on the 1st December (O. S.). They were to be requisitioned from the Cossack army of Trans-baikalia. By the Czar's express order they were to be Buriats, of the Lamaist faith, "for they will be useful to you in Tibet." When I was leaving Kashgar, intending after a few days to separate from my caravan, and make my way by a different and unusual route to the country of Lop-nor, how convenient it would have been had I then had my Cossacks to act as a guard to the caravan, with which I was sending the greater part of my baggage, including between 600 and 700 lbs. weight of Chinese silver money. It was eventually arranged that two of the Cossacks of the Consular guard should be at my disposal until we met the Buriat Cossacks.

The Two Cossacks—Sirkin and Chernoff.

It was a piece of rare good fortune for me that I was able to secure these men. Seldom or never have I been served with such fidelity and such ready obedience as during the years they were in my employ. Like their Buriat comrades, who joined us later on, these two Orthodox Russians were distinguished for their military discipline; and their courage and capability exceeded my most sanguine wishes. Next after Divine Providence, which has never deserted me during my journeyings, I owe it to these

*From a photograph by*] [CONSUL-GENERAL PETROVSKY.

The Start from Kashgar—In the Foreground, from Left to Right, the two Cossacks, Kader, the Author, and Islam Bai.

2

Cossacks that everything passed off so successfully; in the hour of danger the knowledge that I had them at my back always made me feel confident and safe. Moreover, they did not cost me a penny—such was the order of their supreme commander. They were to receive their pay when they got home, and each man brought with him his own horse and accoutrements, and his own new magazine rifle of the Russian army pattern, together with a sufficient supply of ammunition.

It was a close hot day when our long caravan defiled through the Sand Gate of the town-wall of Kashgar. Heavy black clouds, with hanging draperies, began to close in upon us from the mountains. A violent gust of wind, and a second following it, drove the dust along the road in trailing clouds. Then the tempest burst upon us with incredible fury. The inky black sky was slashed with zig-zag lines of glittering blue-white fire, the thunder crashed deafeningly, the rain came down like a shower of slanting arrows, and within a few minutes the road and its surroundings were converted into a splashing puddle of clay. The horses and their riders, the camels and their loads, were all alike drenched; the rain ran down us in torrents, dripping from every projecting angle. At every step our boots went squelch, squelch, and every bend of the arm was like wringing out a dishcloth. The road became slippery and treacherous; the camels, with their flat soft padded feet, slipped and slid in every direction. First one and then another of the huge brutes lost its footing, out flew all four legs side-ways, and down the poor beast thumped with its heavy load on the sloping hill-side, making the sloppy mud fly for yards. This caused great confusion; the men ran and shouted, and set to work to lift the camel up again. When at length the beast stood upright on his own legs, he was plastered all along one side with a thick coating of yellow clay, and scarcely had the rain got it all washed off, when down the camel would go again. Fortunately, my photographic plates were all securely stowed away in metal cases, hermetically sealed, and all my instruments were well packed; as for the rest of the baggage, it was of less consequence.

Perhaps I ought to say a word or two about the contents of my cases which were being thus drenched with rain and flung about so unceremoniously in the mud. They included sketch-books and drawing-materials for a good three years, clothes and felts, a bed, a canvas skiff, preserved foods, cooking utensils, all sorts of implements, provisions (consisting of flour, vegetables, bread, rice), sufficient for the entire caravan, a quantity of *khalats*, of cotton goods, of caps, and of various other small articles intended as gifts for the natives. My photographic equipment formed a heavy load for one camel. I had sufficient tobacco to last, not only myself, but my Cossacks, for the whole of the journey. On the other hand, though you had searched from the one end of the caravan to the other, you would not have found a single drop of either wine or spirits. To make yourself dependent upon alcohol is under all circumstances a serious mistake; but to do so during a journey, which is in itself sufficiently exacting, is absolutely reprehensible. Those who abstain from them, both in civilised countries and in uncivilised, are the best; while those who are slaves to them are bodily and mentally pitiful creatures. In my caravan there was nobody who missed these things; I never heard the Cossacks even hint at them. In this respect they were, I am glad to say, characterized by the self-restraint and discipline which are absolutely necessary if any great undertaking is to be carried through to a successful issue.

As we were to be for so long a time cut off from the outer world, and to be thrown entirely upon ourselves, we naturally had to take a great variety of things with us. I cannot enumerate everything; but just think of such things as ropes, buckets, spades, axes, poles, and all the implements and appliances we required for mending anything that got broken. Tents, the men's sleeping-carpets, sporting rifles and the ammunition for them—all these made up a considerable weight. Nor must I forget my medicine-chest. Fortunately, I never wanted it myself, but the Mussulmans always had the blindest confidence in it, and when any of the men of the caravan died, the rest fully believed, at the least, that every remedy had not been tried that might have been tried to save him.

My travelling library was not very extensive; I should so seldom have time to read. Beyond a few scientific works, dealing with physical geography, and some on Buddhism, it consisted only of a few novels, two or three of our great Swedish poets, a history of Sweden, and the same Bible and Psalm-book which have accompanied me in all my journeys, though they are now getting a good deal worn.

The Chinese paper lanterns were already lighted in the bazaars when we tramped along the wet road round the northern town-wall of Yanghi-shahr, or New Town of Kashgar, and shortly afterwards we encamped in a caravanserai by the road-side.

A few days more sufficed to take us across the desert that stretches between Kashgar and the Yarkand-daria. There we made our camp on the left bank of the river, near the little village of Lailik.

In the Desert near Lailik.

## CHAPTER III.

### BOAT-BUILDING.

ALL the water which gathers from the glaciers and melting snow-fields, from the springs and rains, on the high plateaus of Western Tibet and the Eastern Pamirs, gradually stream together into a magnificent transverse valley, and form the great river which, in the upper part of its course, is variously known as the Zerafshan, Raskan-daria, or Yarkand-daria. Augmented by several tributaries, it acquires sufficient power to force its way across the whole of the East Turkestan desert, a distance of 900 miles, and to empty its waters into the Lake of Kara-koshun.

And now for the plan of my journey. Why should I traverse again the roads through the desert or alongside it, which I already knew so well? Why should not this river, which for thousands upon thousands of years has expended its power to no purpose—why should it not be compelled, late though it was, to render me service? Its muddy current streams at all events due east. Why, then, should it not convey me, seeing that I want to go in the same direction? Prudence—though over-much prudence is not my pet failing—might have warned me of the dangers ahead. "Do you not understand," Prudence might have whispered, "that there are cataracts in which your craft may be capsized; that there are sand-banks upon which it may repeatedly run aground, and that if from any cause you are prevented from proceeding further you will be helplessly stranded in an unknown region, where there are no inhabitants, and no horses to be obtained." To this I replied, "All you say is quite true. All that might very well happen; but I always find that life is best when it has just a spice of risk and danger attaching to it; so that, notwithstanding your good advice, Mr. Prudence, I intend to drift the 1,200 miles down to the point where the river finally succumbs in its desperate struggle against the sands of the desert."

Lailik had never before presented such a bustling scene as when our big caravan encamped on the left bank of the river. Of course, all the inhabitants of the neighbourhood had to come and look at what the wonderful strangers were doing, though of the real nature of our proceedings they had only the vaguest notions. The very first morning after our arrival I requested the chiefs of the place to procure me a big ferry-boat of the kind which is employed in the vicinity of the city of Yarkand for transporting caravans and wares across the river—and to lose no time about it if they did not want to be honoured with the unwelcome attentions of my friend Dao-tai, the Chinese governor of Kashgar.

Meanwhile, taking Sirkin to help me, I tried my little canvas skiff. Light as a feather and silent as thistledown it floated down the stream, and very strange was the sensation it produced. In comparison with the greyish muddy water the little skiff appeared to be absolutely motionless, while it was the bushes on the banks that raced past us at a giddy speed. Silence, the stillness of the grave all around! On we went at a glorious pace—a splendid foretaste of the journey that awaited me! At length, however, it occurred to me that we were getting a long way from home, and would somehow have to get back to camp. We pulled to shore, and Sirkin hurried into the forest, and after a while returned leading a horse. Having yoked it to the skiff he jumped into the saddle, and guiding the horse into a side-arm of the river, began to tow me back to camp. But the water grew deeper and deeper; soon it reached up to his waist. Then all at once the horse lost his footing, and away he went, carried down by the current. Sirkin, flinging himself off into the water, tried to swim to the boat, but after a few strokes disappeared. I turned pale, and felt an icy shiver run down my back. "Is he going to drown just when everything is so promising? Am I to lose my fine Cossack before the journey has really begun? Thank God, no!" Two or three seconds later up came Sirkin and began to struggle towards the skiff. I reached out an oar towards him; he seized it and was saved.

When we at length reached camp we found it a scene of the liveliest bustle. There was the ferry-boat all ready. She was being punted across to the right bank, where we were going to rig up a boat-building yard. But to get the heavy monster up the steep bank was easier said than done. However, after laying down a sort of wooden track, we managed, with the help of a hundred men or so, to draw her up. Meanwhile, the men sang as they hauled, and Hakim Bek, the chieftain, stationed himself in the middle of the ferry-boat; not that he lightened the load, but that he might by his distinguished presence facilitate matters, and keep order, which he did with all the *aplomb* of a circus director, vigorously flourishing the long rod he held in his hand, and whacking and shouting with the greatest gusto.

Without loss of time men were soon swarming all over the ferry-boat, hard at work re-shaping and re-fitting her in accordance with my instructions. She would have to serve me for a dwelling, and I wanted to have her both comfortable and serviceable. Carpenters hammered away all day, and sang merrily as they drove the rasping saw-blades through the planks. We rigged up a small tem-

Traffic Between the Building-slip and the Camp.

porary smithy among the bushes, and there the sparks flew to right and to left as the men forged the iron clamps to hold the planks together. Little caravans kept arriving one after another, bringing planks and beams, and what other timber we needed. Meanwhile, relays of sightseers succeeded one another incessantly all day long. They generally brought with them fruit, bread, rice, eggs, sheep —presents for us, which we always paid for. At length, however, their generosity grew too expensive. We were supplied with more stores than we could consume for a long time to come, so I had to get up and formally announce that, grateful though we were for their kindness, we could not receive any more presents.

When duly finished and upholstered, my ferry-boat looked something like this: in the fore-part she was provided with a deck, on which the tent was erected. Amidships was a square cabin, made of thin planking, and covered with double black felts. On the after-deck we piled up the greater part of our provisions, and there, too, my native servants had their quarters. During the long days we were drifting down the river those of the men who were not immediately engaged in navigating our craft used to sit round a little fire-place of brick, whereon they cooked their breakfast, and where in the late autumn and winter, when the cold began to nip, a huge fire was kept constantly blazing.

The black cabin served as my laboratory; it was there I developed photographic plates. Round the walls ran tables and shelves, covered with all sorts of bottles, jars, boxes, and various other things. On the floor lay several wooden trays filled with water, and on the roof stood a big tub, from which water was conducted by a rubber tube into a samovar, or urn, under the tap of which I washed my plates. In the walls of my cabin I had three glass windows fixed, in case the cold in autumn should drive me indoors.

Building the Black Cabin.

In the fore-part of the tent I made a writing-table by placing two boxes one upon the other, while the case of the camera served as a stool. There I sat glued to my seat during the whole of the long journey, mapping the great river, all its banks and islands, and the forests and hills of drift-sand that ran beside it. The floor—that is to say, the deck on which the tent stood—was covered with a magnificent Khotan carpet. The rest of the furniture consisted of my comfortable tent-bedstead, and two or three boxes filled with valuable instruments.

At Lailik we also knocked together a smaller ferry-boat to carry our heavier baggage, principally provisions, such as bags of flour and bread, vegetables and fruit, sheep and poultry. As it floated down the Tarim, this little ferry-boat looked for all the world like an idyllic farm-yard. The hens provided me with eggs for breakfast. The cock awoke me every morning by crowing "To work!" and did it with as much cocksureness as though he were the Lord High Admiral of the entire flotilla.

Before leaving Lailik I invited all the distinguished men of the neighbouring villages, as well as all our workmen, to a magnificent banquet, at which mutton, steaming rice-pudding, and smoking-hot tea were handed round without stint. In the dusk of the evening Chinese paper lanterns were hung up amongst the tents, while an orchestra, consisting of drums and stringed instruments, filled the still bright evening air with their monotonous and melancholy music. To me their melodies were sympathetic, although they awakened saddening recollections, for four years before the same men who were then thundering away on their goat-skins for all they were worth had in a similar way celebrated my departure on that awful journey across the desert. How different were the conditions under which we were now about to travel! This time we should certainly not perish of thirst; day and night we should always have the sound of rippling water in our ears. Nor would our lungs be choked with drift-sand and dry powdery dust; the air we should breathe would be as pure as could be after filtering through the thick woods that line the banks of the Tarim.

Then lovely dancers stepped forward, and in the subdued light of the lanterns began to circle round with curtseying, though not very graceful, steps, swaying their

Musicians and Dancing-girls at Lailik.

bodies as they moved. They wore long white garments, and had heavy black plaits of hair hanging down their back. Their movements were silent, and as light as the footsteps of fairies, but slow and solemn. Now they vanished like dark shadows, then again they glided into the light like white spectres, swaying from side to side, with their arms outstretched. Above-head was the immense vault of heaven, pricked with glittering stars. Not a breath of wind came whispering through the thickets.

Music, song, dance—transitory, yet ever affording renewed pleasure!

Beautiful? Certainly—dancers are always beautiful. At least, I thought so as I saw them circling under the soft lamp-light. Wishing to perpetuate their loveliness, I begged politely that they would allow me to photograph them the next morning. But grim and shameless, the sun ruthlessly lifted the veil with which the twilight had beautified them; they were three old hags who never ought to dance except in moonshine.

The 17th September was the day fixed for our start, a really great day that I shall never forget; for the journey I then began was so idyllic and so pleasant, so crowded with agreeable recollections and important discoveries, that I despair of making anyone realise it who has never imagined to himself that the deserts in the middle of Asia could ever be traversed by water. And yet it was not without a certain degree of anxiety that I started upon it, for, for the next three months, I was going to be separated and cut off from my caravan, the greater part of my baggage, almost all my money, and my servants, including the two Cossacks. With me I had only Islam Bai and a Kashgar lad named Kader, who, being able to write, I appointed my Turkic amanuensis.

Having issued my final orders to the caravan-men and their leader, Nias Hadji, and having bid them and their escort of Cossacks good-bye, and waited until the sound of the camels' bells had died away in the forest, I turned and went on board my proud Viking ship, as she lay pulling at her cables beside a sand-bank. The day was already far advanced by the time we got all the knots unloosed, and the ferry-boat, feeling the force of the powerful stream under her keel, glided out upon the majestic river.

And what did we do on board, and how did we spend our time? In the bow, in front of my writing-table, stood

The Author at Work on the Ferry-boat.

Palta, a tall, sinewy Turk, with his strong hands clasped about a 20-feet pole, to keep us off the bank in case the current should bear us down upon it too swiftly. At each corner of the stern was another man with a pole. The crew was completed by Kasim, who travelled alone on the provision-boat, his duty being to take frequent soundings and warn us of the shallows. The passengers consisted of Islam and Kader, who sat and talked on the after-deck—that is, when they were not standing craning their necks to look down the river, lost in wonder at this strange mode of travelling. After a few days, when they became more accustomed to it, they took the matter quite calmly. On the list of passengers I ought not to forget the names of Yoldash and Dovlet, who bore me faithful company in the tent, except when it grew too warm, and then they took refuge under the fore-deck, seeking the cellar-like coolness below.

On my writing-table lay in admirable confusion mariner's compass, field-glass, watch, telescope, geometrical compasses, and pens, with a big sheet of white paper in the middle, the first sheet of the map which I was going to make of the Tarim, plotting down its various windings one after another as they came into sight; and there I sat like a spider in its web, watching every object on the banks, vigilant that no mud-bank in the river escaped my observation.

Before we had gone very far we saw groups of countrymen standing on the banks, with their arms full of melons, bread, eggs, and similar good things; but we had plenty of provisions and would not stop. A deep current separated them from us and on glided our ferry-boat, leaving them crestfallen behind. But we were not to escape thus easily, for at the next bend of the river there stood another group of people, also laden with provisions. In vain we tried to avoid their ambiguous benevolence by keeping the ferry-boat out in deep water ; but before we knew what we were about they had waded out into the stream, had met us, and were on board the ferry-boat, depositing their possessions on the deck in front of my writing-table. After being well paid for their trouble they plunged back again into the water and returned the same way they had come, laughing and jesting at the success of their little stratagem.

After rounding a couple more bends of the river, we thought it time to prepare for camping, especially as the sun was dipping to the horizon. As compared with pitching camp on a land journey with a big caravan, when you have to unload and arrange all the baggage, put up the tent, and furnish it, and then get your supper ready, camping by the river side is mere child's play. As soon as I saw a suitable site on the bank, I commanded halt. In went Palta's pole to the bottom, and propping his feet against the fore-deck for better leverage, he forced the huge craft to describe a half-circle with her stern in towards the bank. Then one of the other men leapt on shore with a rope in his hand, and in a trice we were anchored to a tree stump. A couple more ropes made us perfectly secure against drifting off in the night.

Our encampment soon became the scene of busy life and bustle. Boxes containing provisions and cooking utensils were carried on shore. Axes and spades were speedily at work, making a clearing in the young forest, where the men spread out their sleeping-carpets in a ring round the fire, which was very soon blazing away merrily in the twilight. Copper saucepans, filled with water for the tea, were soon spluttering on the embers, with an iron tripod fixed above them for our cooking-pot. Meanwhile, the first sheep was being slaughtered. After its legs were tied together with a piece of rope, the butcher seized it by the nose with his left hand, and with the other cut its throat. As soon as the poor beast had ceased to struggle he set about skinning it. First he cut off a piece of skin on the inner side of one of its hind legs, making a hole; then, applying his mouth to the hole, he blew with all his might, until the sheep's body became plump and round as a ball. This greatly facilitates the operation of skinning, because it makes the skin part from the flesh with the utmost ease.

Then the sheep was cut up, and some of the choicest pieces were sliced into little strips and lumps, ready for being made into *ash* pudding, a dish which formed my daily fare for close upon three years. Hence it deserves a few words of description. After the cooking-pot is cleaned and placed on the tripod over the flames, a few pieces of fat from the freshly-slaughtered sheep are dropped into it, and when the fat, after making a tremendous spluttering, is at length melted, the pieces of meat are added to it, followed by the vegetables, especially garlic, carrots, and white beet, all cut up fine. Meanwhile, the cook has steeped rice in a wooden bowl; this he also pours into the pot, which he finally fills up to the brim with water. Then a lid is placed on the pot, to prevent dust and other rubbish from falling in. When the water has all boiled away, and the individual grains of rice have properly swelled, the pudding is ready; and I can assure you, it is very tasty—in fact, it was the only dish I never grew tired of. As soon as it was cooked, Islam brought me a piled-up plate, and put it on my writing-table amongst my maps and compasses. I finished off the meal with bread, tea, milk and eggs, pears and melons. Dovlet and Yoldash watched my proceedings with the liveliest interest, their heads on one side and earnest petition in their eyes, as they wondered and wondered at my amazing appetite. As soon as I was finished and had lighted my evening cigar, it was their turn. One of the men brought me some choice tit-bits and pieces of bone, and with these I used, out of my own hands, to feed my faithful travelling companions.

Meanwhile, an unwonted silence reigned around the fire on the bank. The Mussulmans were seated in a ring round a common dish, out of which each man helped himself with his fingers. They began the meal with "Bismillah, Rahman Errahim" (=In the name of God the Merciful, the Compassionate!), and when they had finished they stroked their beards or their chins, and cried all together "Allahu Ekbar" (=God is great!).

Natives of the Tarim Region.

Very soon after that the day's labours were brought to an end, by the men stretching themselves almost naked on their felt carpets round the blazing fire.

Sunburnt and copper-brown as they were, lying there in the red fire-shine, they put me in mind of Indians resting after a day's foraging. But for some time after they started their distant "saw-mills," I sat writing away at my table, entering up in my diary the experiences of the day. The tent canvas was flung back so that the night, dark yet sublime, was able to penetrate freely into my solitary floating dwelling. The only sound that broke the deep and solemn silence was an occasional avalanche of sand plunging down into the stream from some overhanging eave of the terraced bank. The gnats, which had celebrated a bloodthirsty bacchanal at sunset, had now all gone to bed. The moon poured her silvery light across the broad bosom of the stream, which stretched like a street before me towards the north. I could not tear myself away from the absorbing beauty of the scene. Hour after hour I sat and steeped myself in it. It was as though in those moments the angel of holy peace were passing over the earth. Then from afar off there came through the silence of the night the barking of a dog. My pups began to growl threateningly in answer. Aroused out of my dreams and speculations as to the future, I would jump up and hasten to close the tent, and creep to bed. The pleasure of rest was greatly enhanced by the consciousness that on board I was safe from the attentions of scorpions and similar inquisitive creatures, which infested the river-banks.

## CHAPTER IV.

### A GLORIOUS FOREST.

However, we had not been many days on the journey when it became evident that the summer was over. At home in Sweden the lilac blossoms had long since wilted, and now the plentiful vegetation on the banks of the Tarim had begun to follow their example. When we rose at sunrise on 20th September the sky was threatening. The night had been cool, and the air was full of the premonitory indications of autumn that cause the leaves to yellow. A light haze hung over the landscape, and through the thick fine dust, which had been whirled up by an easterly storm, the tamarisks and reed-thickets on the banks adjacent were only faintly discernible. The wind was too violent to allow us to continue our drift; accordingly we lay up by the bank and waited patiently. When we at length resumed our journey, the waves broke in melodious music against the prow of our ferry-boat—where Palta sat with his long pole, singing a melancholy ballad about the adventures of some king and his faithful followers. When Islam Bai began to find the time wearisome, he used to have himself put ashore in the skiff, and then, rifle in hand, he roamed through the forest; and when he came back in the evening, he often brought wild-duck and pheasants in his hands. As he had no need to follow all the endless windings of the river, he generally got ahead of us. Sometimes we used to see him sitting on a headland, patiently waiting for us, until I sent the skiff to fetch him off.

Day and night, it being now autumn, great flocks of wild-geese flew on overhead, making their way *viâ* Yarkand to their warmer winter quarters in India. They generally kept at an altitude of between 600 and 700 feet, and filled the air with their anxious screaming; but when they intended to stop for the night, we would see them gradually droop downwards, until they almost seemed to brush against the crowns of the poplars, and soon after they would disappear amongst the trees. They find their way—do these wonderful, hurrying pilgrims of the air—with the same unerring certainty that the brooks from the melting glaciers find theirs to the terminal basin of the Tarim. They are a striking sight, as, in strictly-ordered phalanx, and on unwearied wing, they drive on, on over the earth towards their distant goal. In October these flocks were so numerous and so frequent that we no longer paid any attention to them.

We were now approaching a part of the river known as the Kötäklik-daria, in which, according to rumour, there was an alarming waterfall eight fathoms high. But the nearer we came to the critical point the less grew the height of the cataract, until, by the time we got quite close to it, it had dwindled to about only three feet. However, the velocity of the stream was increased to such an extent that our ferry-boat was sucked at a tremendous pace into a narrow, irregular passage, beset with stranded drift-wood and islets. Very often her prow would run against a sunken poplar-trunk, and she would be swung completely round by the current. I used to feel a slight jerk, and in a minute or two the scenery before me became entirely changed. These whirligig movements used to make me quite giddy. In a trice all the men would be overboard in the river, pushing and hauling to get the vessel free, and

A Camp beside the Yarkand-daria.

then off we went again, racing between the islands. I confess my heart was in my mouth; I began to wonder whether we should have time to pull up or should plunge headlong over the cataract.

At length I heard a distant roar. Louder and louder it grew as we advanced. Before we knew where we were, we were in the middle of the first of the rapids, with the water foaming and thundering about us in an alarming way. Stopping was out of the question. I ran to the bow, and surveyed the situation. If there was no treacherous whirlpool boiling at the foot of the "threshold," we should get through all right. "Let her go, straight over the fall!" I cried; and bringing her head straight with the current, the men let her go, and over the boiling water she glided at dizzying speed.

Hardly had we passed this "dangerous" place when a score or so of men on horseback and on foot appeared on the bank. They were countrymen sent from two or three of the neighbouring homesteads to help us over the rapids. But they were more amazed at the sight of our floating monster than at the information that we had already navigated the falls without mishap. And yet these men appeared very opportunely for us; because a little bit further down, where the river widened out and became exceptionally shallow, we got stuck helplessly fast in the blue clay at the bottom. I and all the men dropped into the water and floundered about barefoot for an unconscionable time, trying to find a navigable channel; nine inches of water were quite sufficient to float us.

"There!" thought I to myself. "Is my proud river-journey to come to an abrupt termination here? No, it shall not; we must, we will go further." All our baggage, down to the very smallest case and package, was transferred to the bank. Then, uniting all our forces, we began to push the ferry-boat like a sledge over the blue clay; but the only result was, that she bit deeper and deeper into it, until at last she looked as though she were cased in plaster of Paris. Despite our utmost efforts, she refused to budge. What was to be done? We were only about ten or twelve yards from deep water. Luckily the old ferry-boat turned a few points in her muddy bed, softening the clay; and after floundering about her again, we managed by the most desperate efforts to get her once more afloat.

After drifting for about another hour we came to the lowest cataract. It was considerably higher than the first, and it really looked as if we must unfailingly capsize. All the men voted unanimously for putting the baggage on shore again. We did so, and all the Mussulmans without exception begged to be excused from participating in the shipwreck. For my own part I could not resist the temptation of such a magnificent "tobogganing hill." By means of a rope fastened to the ferry-boat's stern, some of the men, wading out into the river, let her glide down gently and bravely to the edge of the fall. I took my stand on the fore-deck with the boiling, thundering water immediately in front of me. "Let go!" I shouted, and like an eel the vessel glided over the "threshold." "Bang!" down went the prow crash upon the water below, and immediately afterwards it was followed by the stern; and so that danger was safely passed.

Karaul-dung, a solitary hill by the river-side, affords from its top an extensive view of this grey winding stream, which bores itself so deeply into the silent woods of Turkestan. Looking south-east, we saw beyond the greenery a sort of yellow gleam. The telescope showed it to consist of immense yellow waves—the drift-sand of the desert "ocean," the terrible, suffocating Desert of Takla-makan.

Below that point the river contracts until it resembles a narrow canal, sometimes only about 20 feet wide; but then it has before that lost the greater part of its water, it having been drawn off north to irrigate the cultivated lands of Maral-bashi. Here the men with the punting-poles had to keep a very sharp look-out, for the current was swift and our vessel was constantly threatening to come into collision with the bank. One day she did drive so swiftly upon the low bank that, upon being struck by the full force of the current, she came within an ace of capsizing,

But the river soon widened out again. In rounding a curve, where the current is always most powerful, our ferry-boat was drawn close in to the right-bank, at a spot where a decaying poplar, rooted in the very bed of the river, was leaning a long way across the water. The men did not perceive the obstacle in time to avoid it. Its strong branches brushed along the side of our craft, and did their best to sweep my tent from the deck. I succeeded just in the nick of time in saving my precious instruments by flinging them on the cabin-roof, so that after all we lost nothing more than a very small piece of the tent-canvas.

Towards the end of September we reached a region in which the river, after picking up some tributaries from the north, again assumed noble proportions. But the current was slow, its surface being ruffled by nothing more than gently circling eddies. In the otherwise smooth surface the veterans of the forest were mirroring their russet crowns. It was a beautiful, a magnificent scene! Not a breath moved. Nature was in a Sabbath mood, an invisible organ that could not be heard, only felt, was pouring a solemn flood of music through the woods in praise of the Eternal. There was no trace of human beings, no sign of human dwellings. Not a dry stick crackled under the foot of the solitary wanderer. At intervals in the dense thickets, which form the forest undergrowth, appeared the dark mouth of a tunnel, marking the tracks by which the wild boar came down to the river to drink, and so dark are those leafy tunnels that never a ray of sunshine penetrates into them. The sun was baking hot, and we kept an eager look-out for the deep river-bends through which we floated as it were through a park-avenue, a leafy vault above and cool, delicious shade below.

Thus, hour after hour we drifted down the broad bosom of the stream, clasped in the arms of the sleeping woods.

A Shepherd's Hut near the Masar-tagh.

It was like a journey through fairyland. I often fancied I was being drawn along by invisible elves and other ministering spirits in a triumphal car, along a pathway of gleaming crystal, which wound through enchanted woods, where eternal silence reigned undisputed queen. My thoughts fell involuntary captive to the magic, the witchery of the scene. I was in a mood in which I should not have been surprised at anything happening. As I sat there, drifting and dreaming, I believe I verily expected any moment to see a virgin huntress of the forest draw aside the curtain of greenery, step forward and make a charming curtsey to our prosaic procession, and then turn and with a merry silvery laugh disappear behind the thickets. But she never came. The woods were silent; not even a shepherd's pipe was heard. I scarcely dared to speak for fear of breaking the spell. The effect it had upon my men was to send them to sleep. Turn about they nodded over their punting-poles, and on we drifted—drifted—drifted with the river.

When the sun set and the lurking-places of the forest grew darker, the gnats began to dance for their supper, and I was the supper they danced for, for of course they preferred Christian blood to Mohammedan!

Upon reaching the mountain of Masar-tagh, we had a change in the scene—the rugged terraced flanks of holy Ali's mountain, its foot washed by the stream. A little lake, lying immediately west of the mountain, discharges through a deep-cut channel into the river, forming a tiny waterfall that was a tossing plume of white foam as we passed it. The broken water at the foot of the fall was a favourite spot for *asmans*, fine whopping fish. Here Kasim was in his element. Before leaving Lailik he had provided himself with a long flexible rod, at one end of which a hook was fixed, with its barbs pointing downwards. Upon striking its object, the hook became loosened, but not separated from the rod, for it was fastened to it a little higher up with a cord. Kasim, taking his station like a harpooner on the edge of the boiling cataract, waited with his eyes intently fixed and his weapon poised until a peculiar movement of the water told him a fish was there. Then, flinging his rod with all his might, so that it whistled through the air, and the shaft vibrated, and the spray flew, he the next moment had a big *asman* dangling and writhing at the end of his harpoon. Our fisherman was so successful that he supplied us with fish enough to last for several days.

On 4th October we saw peeping up above the horizon the two detached mountains of Choka-tagh and Tuzluk-tagh, with which I had become acquainted during my desert journey in 1895. These two elevations are separated by the small lakes of Sorun-köl and Chöl-köl. These I thought of sufficient importance to warrant a closer

Kasim Fishing.

examination. Accordingly, I had my little canvas skiff carried to the northern shore of the former lake and got ready for sailing. Islam Bai went with me to look after the sounding line and velocity instrument. For my part I had my hands full, having to manage the sail, the rudder, the compass, the watch, and the map, to say nothing of a note-book, thermometer, field-glass, pipe and tobacco-pouch. But we had no difficulty; the wind was favourable and steady, so that I was able to tie the sail and could fill my pipe comfortably between the compass observations. The lake formed a beautiful open sheet of water, with reeds nodding all round it. A flock of 14 snow-white swans got up from time to time in front of us, and after flying on a little way ahead, dropped into the water again with a noisy splash.

My little skiff behaved beautifully, skimming gracefully and easily over the crystal surface, gently rippled by the wind. After a four hours' sail we approached the end of the Sorun-köl. It is connected by a narrow channel with its sister-lake to the south, the Chöl-köl, which means the Desert Lake—a significant name, for on its southern shore the sand-dunes are piled up mountain-high. The connecting channel between the two lakes, only six to ten feet broad, was bordered by reeds, extraordinarily dense and tall. Their yellow plumes met overhead, so that for considerable distances we seemed to be traversing a dim-lit watery tunnel.

Entering the mouth of the reedy tunnel before a crisp breeze, our little craft swept like a swan along the picturesque water-way, the reeds either bending complaisantly under her keel or rustling sideways out of her path. After a while the channel widened out, and in the expansion were hundreds of wild-duck. They must have known that Islam had forgotten to bring his gun with him, or else they took our little skiff for some unknown, but peaceful, member of their own species, for they were not the least bit disturbed. It was only when we got quite close to them that they took wing; but so great were their numbers that the water was white with froth after they rose. Yet they soon settled again, and began to dive and swim and chatter to their heart's content.

Our dim-lit water-way soon began to lighten. We caught a glimpse of the southern shore of the next lake, as straight as if it had been drawn with a ruler, so great was the distance. Brushing aside the last of the reedy curtains with her spread sail, our little craft leapt out of her prison, and began to dance across the blue waters of the Chöl-köl.

Close by on the shore we saw Palta and a shepherd waiting

Kasim with his Catch.

for us, so we pulled in and took our simple breakfast, consisting of bread and wild-goose, and very good it was. But now a mad idea seized me. I had been sailing long enough, and for some hours, nay for some days, for some weeks, had had but little exercise. I wanted a thorough good walk to stretch my legs. Well, there on the east was the rugged crest of the Choka-tagh, cutting the sky-line like a gigantic hog's back. I made up my mind I would walk right over it. I had to cross it anyhow in order to complete the map I made in 1895. The shepherd mumbled something about the distance being "a vast sight greater than it looked; we should not be back at our camp before the following morning." But I did not hear him; my resolve was already taken, and when it is talking is useless. Besides, when it really is necessary, I do know how to walk. But we should have to get back to camp before midnight, else my chronometers would stop, and that would be serious.

It was already three o'clock in the afternoon, and the evening star was showing bright above the summits of the Tuzluk-tagh. Leaving Islam to look after the boat, I set off at a round pace, followed by the other two men. We made straight for a low pass or saddle in the crest of the range. We walked for one hour, we walked for two hours, before we came to the gravelly scree which stretches down from the outermost foothills. The wind had died away, and it was perfectly still. A couple of roe-deer fled up the mountain side, as lightly as a dream, taking long agile leaps, so that their feet scarcely seemed to touch the ground. Our shadows were already portentously long when we breasted the final slopes leading to the summit of the range. Upon reaching it we thought we were entitled to a few minutes' rest.

The thoughts which here crowded upon my mind recalled the saddest and most sorrowful days I have spent in Central Asia. It was from the southern shore of the lake at my feet that on 23rd April, 1895, I set out with a strong and first-rate caravan to cross the terrible desert of Takla-makan, a caravan destined to perish amid the most horrible suffering that it has ever fallen to the lot of an Asiatic traveller to witness.

The summits of the high dunes were now bathed in the strong and brilliant hues of the setting sun, and under its vivid purples and reds they resembled a gigantic lava-stream. It was in their cruel arms that my faithful servants and patient uncomplaining camels lay dead, having perished for want of water! It was five years since that happened and their corpses were long ago engulfed by the sand in its pitiless march across the desert. When twilight spread its mantle over the scene of these painful memories, I fancied I could see shadowy spectres gliding between the sand hills, threatening vengeance upon me, the involuntary cause of all their suffering and torment.

But the sun is sinking, and it is time to be moving again. On the other side of the mountain the descent was exceptionally steep, leading down over a continuous succession of rocky crags; but down them we must go at all costs. It was a wonder we did get down, however; but, somehow, we slipped, we stumbled, we staggered down the rugged slopes. Then sitting down we slid bodily into the hollows to the no little damage of our nether garments and our skin. I had the advantage of "sledging" last, so that I could not be killed by the stones which the others sent flying with their heels. Fortunately, however, my companions managed to reach the gentler slopes at the foot of the mountain with unbroken crowns and without serious hurt.

Then we set off upon what appeared to be a never ending tramp towards our camp by the river side. It was already night. I had instructed Islam Bai when evening came to light a fire on a crag at the northern end of the mountain. Hour passed after hour, and still we looked in vain for our welcome beacon-light. Unaccustomed to forced marches of this description, I had to stop and rest after every 2,000 paces—I was counting our steps with the object of calculating the distance. And how I did look forward every time to stretching myself full length on the sand, for the heat of the day had gone out of it, and the night had made it cool.

At length, however, after a long, long tramp we caught sight of the faint reflection of a fire. Have you ever tried to walk towards a bright fire on a dark night? It keeps drawing you on in a most expectant way; you always imagine you are quite close to the goal. Hour after hour passes, and yet you seem to get no nearer. At length you begin to doubt whether it really is a fire you see. So it was now; but at length, after surmounting a little hill, we were able to see the bright flames quite distinctly. We raised a shout; but no answer came. We quickened our steps, yet once more we had to rest for a few minutes. Then we shouted again, and this time we were heard.

As soon as my men heard that we were coming, they got up a brilliant illumination in our honour. They had halted in a part of the forest where there was an abundance of dead dried-up trees still standing upright on their roots. Some of these they set fire to. A long time before we reached them we could hear the dry timber crackling and bursting with noisy vigour. After a while we made our state entry into camp; the tree-trunks, all of a red glow, were leaning over in every direction, threatening to fall, and the heat was unbearable. Then, guided by two or three of the men carrying torches, we reached the ferry-boat at a very late hour, and thus brought to an end a long hard march, and oh! we were tired!

## CHAPTER V.

### THROUGH AN UNKNOWN COUNTRY.

MEANWHILE autumn was coming on apace; the forests were showing predominantly shades of yellow and russet and red. The slow drift began to be trying to our patience, especially when the river wound so very much as to describe fifteen-sixteenths of a complete circle. On one occasion, after drifting 1,575 yards, we found we had only advanced 197 yards of lineal direction. Very often it happened that towards noon we came back to the same clump of forest that we had started from in the morning.

Upon reaching the forest-tract of Moreh, I suffered a heavy loss. Dovlet, my favourite dog, jumped ashore, ran off amongst the bushes, yelping as if he were searching for something, then began to stagger about and behaved in a very odd fashion. We caught him and gave him all the attention we could beside the fire; but all our efforts were in vain, though I sat up all night with him myself, and watched him until the last breath had fled. We buried him on shore, and even the Mohammedans were depressed the whole of the following day, as though it were a real friend they had lost.

That peaceful region appeared to abound in game. We sometimes caught sight of shy antelopes and deer on the banks. Once we saw a deer swimming across the river in front of us, and Islam and Mollah, our new guide, came to the front with their rifles. But with a bound the animal leapt up the bank and disappeared in the underwoods, Yoldash barking himself hoarse until the animal was out of sight. Further on we surprised a herd of wild-boar wallowing in the mud by the river-side. When they became aware of us, they rose to their feet, stared at us a minute or so, and then galloped off like a whirlwind into the nearest thicket of reeds. A wild-duck, which sat and coolly regarded us without moving, made an excellent dish for supper.

As the season was getting on and we had still a long way to go, we continued to drift even after the sun had set. In order to keep up the spirits of my men, I brought out the musical-box and appointed Islam to look after it. The men listened in a spirit of devotion, and Kasim, in the little ferry-boat, kept as near as he could. Then the echoes of the Asian forests were awakened to the clear but plaintive strains of *Cavalleria Rusticana*, to the joyous music of *Carmen*, and the varied notes of Swedish popular songs. And when at length the instrument struck up a thrilling march, it was as though we were making a triumphal entry to the crash of regimental music. It was a still and peaceful evening, the air full of the scents of the forest and of vapours arising from meadow and reed-patch. The stillness of the wilderness, like that of a holy temple, was undisturbed except for the occasional quacking of a wild-duck or the stealthy movements of a fox prowling amongst the *kamish* (reeds).

Early on the morning of the 11th October the mirror-like surface of the Yarkand-daria was veiled with a moist haze; the belt of forest on the opposite bank was only discernible as a faint dark line. Kasim, who still continued to navigate the little ferry-boat, made a sharp-cut, yet faint, silhouette against the misty veil, which still hung like a spider's web outspread from bank to bank. But up rose the sun and scattered its showers of morning gold over the river ; the mist disappeared, and a fresh day began, bright and clear, but cool, after the first frosty night of autumn.

A couple of days later the forest had everywhere turned from green to gold, and once, after a fresh breeze, the river was littered with fallen leaves, so that it was not unlike a park avenue when the leaves begin to fall in autumn.

As it grew colder, I sometimes exchanged my station in the tent-opening, where I generally sat in the shade, for a more sunny position in the canvas skiff, after it was made comfortable with felt carpets and cushions. There, pipe in mouth and drawing-materials on my knee, I thoroughly enjoyed myself. As a rule, I kept a good bit in front of the ferry-boat, so as to ensure perfect quietude. In this way I glided round one river-bend after the other, an occasional pull with an oar sufficing to avert a collision with the bank.

On 17th October, we at last saw, after a long interval, signs of human beings. A good bit ahead we perceived a column of smoke and tongues of flame leaping up amongst the trees on the bank. Now, thought I to myself, I shall get information about the country on both sides of the river here. Mollah declared that the fire was made by shepherds to frighten the tigers and wolves away from their flocks. When we drew nearer, we saw that there was a big flock of sheep guarded by a couple of dogs and some shepherds. But as for getting speech with the men, the moment they caught sight of the ferry-boat, with its spectral white tent and coal-black cabin, they turned sharply to the rightabout, and, making the dust fly from their sheepskin sandals, fled for dear life, leaving their flocks to their fate. We shouted, we even sent out a patrol to look for them, but it was all no use, we never saw a glimpse of them again. And I don't wonder at them. Simple children of nature that they are, what must they have thought when they saw our floating monster gliding noiselessly as a panther down the stream? Some evil spirit of the desert, no doubt, coming to disturb them in their peaceful forest-haunts!

During the two following days the wind proved very troublesome. A regular desert storm was in progress, for the fine dust drifted in dense clouds across the river and its forests.

The sun was only visible when directly above-head, and then as a faintly-blurred, yellowish-red disk. The air was full of dry, rustling leaves, and in some of the bends of the river they had accumulated until they formed actual sargasso seas. In the reaches in which the wind was against us our progress was painfully slow; but when we turned, so that we had the wind behind us, our vessel flew past the banks until the water foamed off her bow. But the wind dropping on the 19th, we resumed our steady drift, and continued far on into the night. The moon glittered on the surface of the river, throwing up the figures of the men in front of me in sharp-cut outline. The woods on the bank were as if etched in ink, the moon's rays only piercing through the thickets at the rarest intervals. Two or three times we ran aground on the sand-banks, not very pleasant for those who had to jump into the water and push us off again, for the night was cold. However, they got some compensation at the fire we kindled when we stopped; and a grand fire it was, made up of no less than four gigantic *toghrak* (spreading poplar) trunks, crackling and blazing away at once.

Not far from the bank at that spot stands the burial-place of a saint called Hazret-i-Akhtam Rezi Allahu Anhu. The holy place was marked by a mosque, constructed of beams and dry timber, and by a number of

An East Turkestan Burial-place.

poles hung about with streamers and antelopes' skulls. We landed and paid a visit to the peaceful sepulchre, and our honest Mollah (priest) offered up a solemn prayer at the shrine. "La illaha il Allah" (There is no God but God!) rang out his deep voice with earnest conviction, the echo being repeated afar off in the solemn silence of the poplar woods.

During our absence, young Kader acted as watchman on board the vessel, and when we got back he begged permission to go alone to the shrine. But very soon afterwards we saw him running back as though there were a score of wolves at his heels. The young hero frankly explained that he had been so terrified by the loneliness and uncanniness of the place that he had lost heart and had no desire to go further.

On 22nd October we had a pleasant break in our monotonous, but glorious, life on the river. A horseman appeared amongst the bushes on the bank, but no sooner did he catch sight of us than, wheeling his horse about, he disappeared again. Evidently he had been on the watch for us, for after a while we saw a whole cavalcade of horsemen gallop up, dismount, spread carpets on the ground, and deposit upon them grapes, melons and bread. It was a chieftain from the village of Avvat who adopted this agreeable method of welcoming us. We invited him on board, and then continued our drift, the attendant cavalcade marching beside us along the bank.

Shortly afterwards, another band of horsemen appeared in sight, dressed in gay-coloured festal *khalats* (coats of honour), and once more we had to stop and partake of their gifts of welcome. These were West Turkestan merchants, living in Avvat, led by their principal bai. I invited the last-named on board, and set Islam to work to dispense hospitality—tea and so forth—around the glowing fire on the after-deck.

A Chinese Bek and his Attendants Waiting to Receive us.

Before we had gone very far we perceived a third troop of mounted men awaiting our arrival on a projecting headland. It was the Bek of Avvat himself come to bid us welcome to the region he ruled over. In this way the members of our mounted escort were gradually increased, and fresh horsemen kept appearing above the thickets. The forest, recently so silent, now echoed with lively conversation, the riders eagerly discussing the object of our strange journey. Our ferry-boat in particular was the object of their keenest attention.

In the red rays of the setting sun our double procession made, I am sure, a very striking object. On the after-deck Islam was pouring out tea to the Beks, who kneeled in their gay holiday attire around the fire, looking both important and anxious, although the current was quite moderate. I was, as usual, tied to my writing-table, for for no ceremonies in the world would I have allowed a blank to appear in my map of the river. On the banks the dust rose in clouds from the thud, thud of the horses' hoofs on the hard ground. Never before had such a spectacle been seen beside the muddy waters of the Yarkand-daria. Eight falconers, mounted on active little ponies, were conspicuous in the company; two of them carried royal eagles, the others hunting-hawks. The fierce eyes of the birds were hidden under a hood, and their talons were tightly clasped about the thick skin gloves of their bearers. These wonderful, but bloodthirsty, birds of prey are indispensable on all ceremonious occasions in that part of the world. Later in the day they gave me proofs of their skill, and their prey, four hares and a deer, were handed over to my cook, Islam Bai. To see a hawk attack a hare, a pigeon, or a pheasant once is quite sufficient. You admire, you are amazed at, the precision, the swiftness, the strength developed by their elastic, and yet so fragile, wings. Like a knife their sharp curving claws pierce the back or head of their victim. With a few careless movements of the head and violent jerks they pluck fiercely at the feathers or hair of their prey, but only in one little spot. Then, shifting their claws, they take another sure grip, and pick away first

A Hunting Eagle.

on one side and then on the other, and in this way they devour their victim alive, strip by strip.

The 27th October was to be our last day on the Yarkand-daria, for in the evening our guides assured us we should reach the mouth of the Aksu-daria. It is below the confluence of these two streams that the name Tarim is given to the united river. For the last portion of the journey our old ferry-boat moved with exasperating slowness. But we were resolved, at all costs, to reach our goal that night. "Out with your punting-poles!" I cried, and the men pushed, and whistled, and sang as they worked together. The pole of one of the men, Alim, stuck fast in the mud at the bottom, and was left behind. Alim, nothing daunted, flung off his clothes and swam back to it, and then turning swam after the ferry-boat. And yet the temperature of the water was only 48° Fahr. For my own part, I no longer had any passionate desire for a bath. The air had, however, that day been as warm as in summer. I even sat in my shirt-sleeves and thoroughly enjoyed watching the changing perspectives of the uniform, but ever varying, scenery, my senses drinking in the scent of apricots, grapes and pears, a dishful of which always stood beside me.

At length the curtains parted and a new act began in our fairy spectacular play. The side scenes of the forest setting moved wider and wider apart, the drop-scene at the back was pushed back to a great distance, and before us appeared, in the centre of the stage, the boiling, seething waters of the Aksu-daria.

Our big clumsy craft was just beginning to feel the force of the treacherous, but powerful, suction which was drawing her into the eddy of the actual confluence, when we managed to check her in the very nick of time. I wanted to stop there and examine the meeting of the waters. Next morning there was a very earnest ring in the "Bismillah!" ("In God's name!") of my Mohammedans, as, planting themselves firmly at their posts, feet wide apart, muscles tense, they gripped their poles so tightly that their knuckles turned as white as cubes of ivory. Having taken my bearings from a distant promontory, I put my instruments away carefully into my pocket just in case the water in

Our Landing at the Confluence of the Aksu-daria.

the eddy should prove too rough. One push and off we glided, with all too easy a motion into the middle of the mælström. For one second our craft swung round on her axis, but in the next she was safely past the point of danger; nevertheless, the swiftness with which she spun round was enough to make one giddy. It was as though the entire horizon, the banks and the dark lines of forest, now distant, now close at hand, were rivetted fast on a gigantic merry-go-round, which all at once began to revolve at terrific speed before the spectator's eyes. But thanks to Palta's presence of mind and strength of arm, our boat was checked in time, and after that she floated along smoothly, and even with dignity, down the broad bosom of the open river.

Upon reaching our camp that evening, which we had more difficulty than usual in doing, we were no longer alone. A flock of wild-geese settled close beside us, making a tremendous splashing and clatter; but when we started at daybreak they were already gone, except one solitary laggard, which was apparently exhausted by the long flight of the day before. But when we began to move, he, too, spread his wings in the morning sun, and followed along the invisible pathway taken by his companions.

## CHAPTER VI.

### AT RACING SPEED DOWN THE GREAT AND LONELY TARIM.

AFTER passing, on 30th October, the mouth of the Khotan-daria, we left the last of the great tributaries of the Tarim behind us. The mouth of the tributary just mentioned was at that time dry; but that its bed does contain water, sometimes flowing, sometimes stationary, I had the very best reason in the world for knowing, for on 5th May, 1895, it had saved me from the horrible fate of dying from thirst.

Next day we had not gone very far when a furious tempest sprang up in the east. The river was perfectly straight, broad, and open, and the wind, driving up it unimpeded, churned the water into foam-tipped waves, which struck with great force against the bow of our vessel, making her timbers quiver from end to end. A yellowish-grey haze swept above both banks, while a mass of fine dust hid the forest from our view. My tent threatened to blow away bodily, and for several hours we stood perfectly still, marking time, while the tempest howled above us.

At last the gale grew so bad that we thought it better to lie up under the shelter of the forest, and wait until the weather improved. Although it was broad daylight the forest was as dark as twilight. We made up a huge fire amongst the trees and most welcome it was, for the air was decidedly cool. I had been sitting for weeks on end with my eyes rivetted on the minute figures and signs on my map, I hailed this as a splendid opportunity for a most delightful diversion—a sail. We rigged up the canvas skiff, bamboo mast, shrouds, sail, steering-oar. But I took nobody with me. The men were almost seasick when they saw me skim off like a flying wild-duck, barely touching the surface of the water. The mast creaked ominously. But what would it have mattered even if it had sprung, when there was a whole forest of slender young trees close beside me? All I cared for just then was the glorious motion of skimming along before the tempest. With the mast bent like a bow and the sail blown out like a ball, the banks shrouded in the dust-haze, the river broad and tossing with foam-crested waves in front of me, I had a delightful sail. The wind howled and whistled and roared all around. The elements were in uproar, celebrating the wildest of autumn carnivals, with yellow chaplets in their hair! I could hear nothing but the sound of winds and waters. Yet when I heard the dry branches snapping, I knew that I was getting dangerously close to the bank, and made haste to steer farther out into deep water. What are all the theatrical spectacles in the world compared with one such day as that! To be absolutely alone in the midst of a devastating storm, especially in the forest wilderness of the Tarim, is at once an impressive and a sublime experience such as is not readily forgotten.

At length, thinking I had gone far enough, I put in to the bank, drew up my little craft into a sheltered position, furled the sail, kindled a fire, boiled water for tea, and took my simple breakfast in solitude. Then I drifted back with the current to the ferry-boat, and having made the black cabin comfortable, I proceeded to develop the photographic plates which I had recently taken.

At length the tempest exhausted itself, and we were able to continue. Beside a hut on the bank we saw a man watching us with his mouth open in amazement; but as soon as he saw that he was observed he took to his heels in a great hurry. We traversed the Kara-toghrak, or the Black Forest, at great speed. The river here was shallow, and the water frothed and foamed over the thresholds or ledges at the bottom. At one point we were driving straight down upon a projecting headland, and a catastrophe seemed inevitable, but just at the right moment the stream itself came to our assistance, and we only grazed the overhanging thickets, our ferry-boat carrying along with her a few tamarisk branches. It was an exceedingly near thing. Yet what a pleasure it was to see the banks hasten so trippingly past.

On the other side of the Black Forest the river stretched away, away to the north-north-east. The belts of yellow reeds thinned out to a fine point on each side of the stream, and in the far distance the river itself seemed to melt with the sky, or rather to diffuse itself through the endless spaces of the world. Just as we, suspecting no danger, were gliding quietly past a huge overhanging, undermined section of the terraced bank, the entire mass broke off and plunged into the river, drenching the starboard side of our vessel, and the men who were working there, and at the same time setting up such a wash that for a time we rolled like a derelict in the trough of the sea.

Some distance farther on we saw a solitary woman standing amongst the reeds. She showed no signs of alarm, and shouted that she wished to make us a present of half-a-score eggs. We manœuvred the ferry-boat so as to bring her stern close in under the reed thicket where the woman stood; and then Islam received the packet of eggs and flung a few coppers to the unknown lady. Who was she? She was like the wind; she came we knew not whence and went we knew not whither.

It was, as I have said, autumn, and was beginning to

grow decidedly cool. The navigators on the after-deck kept up a brisker fire than before, and there they sat in turns and warmed themselves. Meanwhile, Kader read aloud to them stories of the adventurous doings of the old Mohammedan missionaries in East Turkestan centuries ago.

But soon they had something else to do. The velocity of the stream increased very considerably, and every man had to be alert and ready at his post. The immense masses of water rolled swiftly on from one river-bend to another, and we had to keep a very sharp look-out, so as to be able to head off our vessel in time. On one occasion all our efforts were of no avail; our heavy craft ran full tilt against the perpendicular bank, and swung sharply round. But, fortunately, no misfortune happened—a couple of somersaults on board and a basketful or two of earth on the bow, that was all.

But the river grew wilder, more impetuous, and more uncontrollable, contracting to a narrow sharp-cut passageway, its banks being 15 or 16 feet high, but perfectly barren and destitute of vegetation.

It was getting exciting. I expected a mishap every moment. Our floating domicile shot at a giddy pace through the weirdly moving ravine. It was as though we were being sucked helplessly into a whirlpool; but of this we had little time to think, for all our energies were required to avoid a collision.

Kasim, as usual, was leading the way in the provision-boat. All at once we heard him shout: "Stop! stop! stop!" in a tone of desperate anxiety. A poplar tree was grounded in the middle of the stream, which was here only 60 to 70 feet wide, and around it had gathered a quantity of driftwood and rubbish, making an awkward island amid-stream, around which the water was foaming and chafing itself white. At once the greatest excitement arose on board; everybody shouted and screamed at the same time. The men tried to stop the ferry-boat, but the punting poles were not long enough to reach the bottom of the river. Yet we were close upon the obstacle. A few seconds more, and we should infallibly have been capsized had it not been for Kasim. He, flinging off his clothes, scrambled ashore with a line, and by desperate efforts managed to check the ferry-boat in time. Then we swung safely past the treacherous obstacle, and thereafter continued our dizzy race of nearly four miles an hour. That evening when we encamped we fell in with shepherds, and bought some sheep from them. Close by was the *masar*, or "grave," of a saint. Him my Mussulmans hastened to thank sincerely for having protected them through the perilous passage from which we had just escaped, as well as for having brought them safe and sound all the long way from their homes.

Where in the world did all those countless flocks of wild-geese come from which day after day flew unceasingly westwards? Even at night we heard their hoarse quackings as they passed on, on over the tops of the poplars. Did they come from Siberia, or was it Jungaria or Kulja? I never grew tired of watching those arrow-headed, dragon-shaped arrangements of little black dots speeding through the sky. There was always one bird acting as leader. On, on he flew, without a moment's hesitation, the two wings of the phalanx following him with marvellous fidelity, obeying every movement of their leader with the ready ease of streamers fluttering in the wind. How wonderful is the life of these birds ordered! Twice in every year they cross Asia all the way from Siberia to India and back again. And here was I taking 39 years to traverse the continent four times only; but, then, when I made my first journey I was already 27 years old, and therefore older than most wild-geese.

In one place, where the river described an almost complete circle, we saw sitting on a silt peninsula 12 dark-brown vultures, big, heavy, ruffled birds. They had just gorged themselves upon the carcase of a white horse which lay at the water's edge. They merely followed us with their eyes as we drifted round the promontory, but beyond that they took no further notice of us.

On 6th November we passed the sheep-station of Bostan, and the shepherds gave us some vegetables and a big white cock. No sooner was the new passenger put down on board than, like an arrow from a bow, he flew upon our old cock and without more ado drove him into the river, where he lay flapping his wings, struggling and screaming until fished out again. After that we had to keep the two on separate boats, and so long as they had the water between them, they remained the best of friends. When one of them crowed, the other was sure to answer him. Funny creatures—cocks! The only things to be compared to them for comicality are camel-foals.

We were now approaching more inhabited regions; the reed-huts were growing more numerous, and every now and again we saw a canoe on the bank, hewn out of a single poplar trunk. After one of these had been calmly appropriated by my men, Kasim gave a water pantomime display in the coggly-wobbly thing, to the intense amusement of his comrades. And although my men were unable to understand why I should do so, I afterwards honourably paid for the stolen canoe. They were clearly of opinion that stranded goods are common property.

Upon reaching the village of Terez, which I had visited before, we were received with gladness and hospitality by my friend Khalil Bai, an old man of seventy-three, who brought us all sorts of nice things—pears, pomegranates, vegetables, hares, pheasants, sheep, poultry and eggs, and, best of all, several big bowlsful of milk. This was a most welcome replenishment of our stores, and happily we might pile as much as we liked upon our "camel"; he never murmured as the caravan camel sometimes does.

When we started again at daybreak on 10th November, the river and country adjacent were veiled in a damp mist. The night previous it had been unusually cold, and our ferry-boat and black cabin were white with rime frost; but after a crisp breeze got up from the south-west, the air soon cleared, and we renewed our delightful journey down the great river. Our flotilla now numbered four craft, a guide leading the way in a canoe. A nice bek of Terez gave me a new dog, which I called Dovlet, after the one I had lost. He was a little reddish-brown, short-legged pup, fat and round, and from the very first moment on board played the maddest pranks you can think of. He very soon made himself the prime favourite of all the two-legged passengers, the cocks alone excepted.

The more sheltered parts of the river now began to be gradually covered with thin sheets of bright pure ice. By the middle of November the ice was strong enough to bear the weight of our dogs. All along, when they grew tired of the monotony on board, they used to jump over, swim to land, and follow the ferry-boat on the bank. Then, when they again wanted a change, they just swam back and once more scrambled on board.

The ice reminded us that we had still a long, long way to go to reach our goal, and if we did not wish to get frozen in we should have to make very great haste indeed. For if we did get frozen in what would happen to us? Should we have to leave all our belongings in the lurch, and tramp on foot through these never-ending silent woods? To obviate such a possibility as that, we now made it a rule to travel 12 hours every day. These cold mornings, as soon as I had got my clothes on, I used to hurry up to the men's camp-fire to thaw myself, and get a cup of smoking hot tea. As I appeared I was greeted from all sides with a friendly "Salaam aleikum!" (Peace be with you!). A few minutes later I used to issue the command, "Cast off!" and on we went again on our long journey. The navigators' song echoed sympathetically through the woods, and used to be kept up until the evening, when their thoughts began to turn towards the welcome camp-fire. But in order to spare time, we continued long after sunset. These lonely regions were lit up by no fires except our own. The reflection of the moon was broken into a thousand trembling ripples around every eddy, and the fire on the after-deck shed a faint gleam upon the reeds that lined the margin of the river. One of our guides, who was ordered to keep in his canoe about 100 yards in front of the ferry-boat, carried a gigantic Chinese lantern, with an oil lamp inside it, hanging from the end of a sloping pole. This made the canoe look like a Venetian gondola, as the gleam from its lamp rippled unceasingly behind on the water.

Our Pilot-canoes.

The natives in this neighbourhood were inconceivably shy and difficult to get into communication with. Sometimes they would stand stock-still and stare at us without moving; then all of a sudden they would disappear, and we would never see them again. In one place we made certain of getting hold of somebody, for there was a cooking-pot boiling over the fire; the sheep were grazing round about, and the dogs were kicking up a fearful din. We scoured all the thickets in the neighbourhood, and at length got hold of a solitary boy; but he was so frightened that he was quite unable to open his mouth, still less to give us any information. He simply stood like a log, with his eyes glued to the ground. Next day, however, we instituted an energetic hue and cry, and managed to capture a shepherd, whom we took on board with us and kept in mild captivity for as far as his geographical knowledge extended.

In the forest of Dung-kotan we looked in upon a rich hunter and shepherd, who had killed many tigers and sold the skins to the Chinese. He told me how he used to kill his prey. He had to do it by craft, for, with the clumsy muzzle-loading blunderbuss which is commonly in use in that country, to go near the fiercest and most dangerous creature that haunts their woods and thickets would have been fatal.

When a tiger seizes a horse, a cow, or a sheep, he drags it into the reeds, and after making a good meal leaves the rest for another occasion. When he goes away he nearly always follows a well-trodden shepherds' path. His track shows in which direction he has gone, and from which direction he may be expected to come back. In his path the natives place a trap over a hole about half-a-yard deep, and cover it all up with branches and leaves. If the tiger has the ill-luck to tread on the trap, it goes off and holds him fast. The trap is made of iron, and is so heavy that the prisoner is only just able to drag it after him. Once caught in it, it is impossible for him to escape, for its grip is tremendously strong, and it is provided with long sharp teeth. Nevertheless, the hunter leaves him alone for at least a week before he ventures to approach. The tiger, thus deprived of his freedom of movement, and no longer able to get anything to eat, grows thin and weak. At length the hunter approaches him on horseback, with his weapon loaded, and fires several shots at the beast, still keeping his saddle, so as to be able to escape more easily in case the tiger, with a last desperate effort, should leap upon him.

Further down the river tigers are more numerous. Yet they hardly ever attack human beings, and seldom show themselves by day, but prowl about the shepherds' paths by night.

## CHAPTER VII.

### FROZEN FAST.

IN the bright autumn atmosphere the sun at setting often gave rise to magnificent displays. On the evening of the 19th November the steppe all around us was lit up with an intense fiery yellow glare, as though the reeds which encircled us on all sides were in flames. Dark and silent wound the river through the dense thickets in which the royal tiger had his lair. The sheet of ice, which covered all the lagoons, gave out whistlings and whinings unceasing. Sometimes it was as though a flash of lightning had struck the dark water in front of us; yet it was but a disk of drift-ice, to us hitherto invisible, becoming tilted on edge in an eddy and lifting above the inky black water a corner as bright as glass, against which the rays of the setting sun struck, broke, and were shivered into a thousand fragments, as if scattered by a prism. Black and bare stood the poplar trees and stretched their gnarled, dry branches out over the life-giving stream.

The next afternoon we arrived at Ketchik, at which point the river had deserted its old bed two years before, and made a new path for itself through the desolate wilderness of the sandy desert. As this part of the river's course was considered to be dangerous, we found some of the native beks assembled with canoemen to give us help. For the news of our journey by river had spread far and wide through the interior of Asia; but the natives never knew where we came from or what was the object of our journey. All they knew was that I was a strange and most remarkable person. More than two years afterwards I was asked by some Indian merchants in Ladak, whether I had heard of a white man who for several months had sailed down a big river a long way to the north; they assured me that a similar journey down the Indus would be impossible. The 21st November was our first day on the new river. This was extremely irregular, in that the current was repeatedly divided by small islands, upon which we should unfailingly have run aground had not an entire fleet of native canoemen gone on in advance, sounding and testing the depth with their paddles.

Every now and again we came to a dead poplar sticking up in the middle of the channel, its branches extended menacingly over the water. For safety's sake we had to take down the tent and carry our instruments inside the black cabin. On both sides the stream was shut in by high sand-dunes, and the belts of vegetation grew narrower and narrower.

We shot down the cataracts at a dizzy pace, nearly four miles an hour. As it was just turning dark when we entered the sandy desert proper, we thought it better to halt for the night. But as soon as day broke we were off again, yellow sand-dunes on both sides of us fully 150 feet high. A dreary, dreary region, dead cold, not a human being, not an animal, not even a crow or a vulture, the usual denizens of the wilderness. It was everywhere as silent as a churchyard, no sound reached us from the desert, all we could hear was the rippling song of the river, and that would now soon be silenced.

It was a totally unknown country through which the river had here carved its path. Even our canoemen had never been there before; but they did royal service with

Our Way Stopped by a Fallen Poplar.

their canoes as despatch-boats. With their broad-bladed paddles they would sound the depth of the stream; then they would slip round the next bend, be gone a little while, and come paddling back again as soon as they found anything like a critical passage. In one place the river was split into five branches, and between the islands of rubbish and driftwood the water was churned white. Straight into the gaping throat of one of these we drove at full speed. It was as much as ever our ferry-boat could do to scrape through, indeed, the passage was so narrow that she crashed against the obstacles on both sides. But she did just manage it, amid the excited shouts and cries of the natives.

On the 24th November we had a more than usually exciting experience. As it happened, the big ferry-boat was leading the way, all the small craft being behind her. We were travelling rapidly. The river, though regularly formed, was narrow, and all was going gaily; but all at once the stream made a sudden bend, and we had to exert our every effort to prevent the rapid current from carrying us into disastrous collision with the high vertical bank. Immediately below the bend, Palta caught sight of a fallen poplar tree, which lay in a horizontal position, reaching out across the river just where the current ran. Its crown was trailing in the water, but the trunk hung about a yard above it; and it was straight against this treacherous bridge that we were being carried down so swiftly. Palta shouted a shrill cry of warning. In went all the punting-poles; but the river was too deep. Where are the new poles we have had made—those of extra length? These the boatmen now seized upon, two men to a pole, and they began to pull at them with desperation. Meanwhile we were approaching the ill-omened poplar alarmingly fast. A minute or so more, and all our top hamper would be swept overboard, or if our craft went broadside on she would be capsized. The water was foaming under the poplar immediately in front of us. Another moment and we should be shipwrecked, and all our belongings lost in the ghastly whirlpool. The men were working with frenzied energy; some of the smarter canoemen clambered on board our ferry-boat, leaving their own frail vessels to their fate, and planted themselves bare-legged in the prow beside Islam and myself, ready to seize hold of the poplar and try, at any rate, to break the force of the collision. But once more fortune was with us. My Lailik boatmen pulled like galley-slaves and, just in the very last moment, succeeded in forcing the ferry-boat into an eddy under the opposite bank. There we spun half-round the circle, and should, of course, have once more drifted down upon the poplar, had not Alim jumped into the ice-cold water with a line and towed us past the point of danger.

Whilst we were being whirled round in the eddy, Kasim and Kader went spinning past with the provision boat and my little sailing-skiff hung on behind her. Fortunately they had sufficient presence of mind to give the latter a sharp push, so that she was caught in the eddy, and we managed to get hold of her. But their own craft swept straight upon the poplar, and came within an ace of being upset, only Kasim contrived to hold on to the tree-trunk.

Had this happened on a dark night we should never have seen the poplar, and a serious catastrophe might have resulted. My Lailik boatmen were now beginning to feel dispirited. They thought this winding, curling river would never come to an end, but we should go on drifting, drifting, day after day, farther and farther towards the east. Twelve hundred miles away from home! Were we never going to stop? Would they never return to their families in Lailik? They grew sick at heart as they thought of the constantly growing distance behind them.

We had not gone very far when we heard anxious cries

for help from higher up the river. Kasim and Kader had dropped behind again after their recent narrow escape. General consternation! What had happened now? I instantly gave orders to push to shore, and sent all the men back through the thickets and underwoods. It appeared that the two men with the little ferry-boat and the canvas skiff had got caught in an eddy, and just in the very worst part of it had run upon the stump of a poplar that was grounded in the bottom of the river and reached barely above the surface. It was the skiff which received the full force of the impact, and its canvas was rent as with a knife in the fore part. Kader, however, succeeded in getting to land with the "wreck." The provision-boat, on the other hand, was not injured, but she heeled over to such an extent that everything she had on board was pitched out. Some of the things, such as lanterns, axes and spades, saucepans, and copper utensils, sank to the bottom, while others went dancing down the river, until all the eddies were full of bobbing buckets, baskets and boxes, filled with flour, loaves of bread, and so forth. These, however, were mostly picked up again by the canoes. As for the skipper, Kasim, he clung like a wild-cat to the tree-stump, and yelled blue murder in the middle of the whirlpool. He was at length taken off by a canoe. The rest of the afternoon was spent in fishing our belongings out of the river and drying them.

Next day our escorting flotilla was still further augmented, and we now had a company of ten vessels, and made quite a stately procession as we wound down the sinuous Tarim. The scene which unfolded itself before us at Tokuz-kum, or the Nine Dunes, was grand and imposing. Sand-dunes, nearly 200 feet high, overhung the right bank of the Tarim, and the yellow, impassive masses of powdery sand contrasted most sharply with the lively movements of the transparent water at their base. Simple

Gigantic Sand-dunes on the Right Bank of the Tarim near Tokuz-kum.

though the elements of the scene were, they nevertheless impressed me with a feeling of solemnity. As we glided in under the steep slopes of the dunes, it was as though we were making our entry into a Gothic cathedral of simple, but none the less sublime, architecture. Upon climbing to the top of them, I saw the river winding away eastwards like a ribbon of ethereal blue, until it melted out of sight in the far distance; and then, turning, I let my eyes sweep across the barren and awful desert of sand which stretches miles upon miles to the south.

Immediately below this point we received a hospitable welcome in a little village where ten families of Loplik race were living in airy *kamish* huts. Their bek invited us to go with him fishing. At the edge of the ice, in the throat of a long narrow creek or bay, he put down his nets. Then a couple of canoes were driven at full speed against the ice until it broke. Thereupon, a fresh net was let down at the edge of the broken ice; and so on, turn and turn about, until the fishermen reached the innermost end of the creek. Thither the fish, terrified by the noise and uproar, had gradually retreated, and were easily taken, while those that tried to escape became entangled in the nets. On the present occasion we caught 26 fine fat fellows.

It was evident that our days on the river were now numbered. During the night the temperature fell to 3.2° Fahr., and the water was very near the freezing-point. The Lop-men prophesied that, after the first drift-ice appeared, it would be only ten days before the river was frozen throughout. It was with anxious expectation that we looked forward to that happening. It came on the 28th November. In the morning, when I looked out of my tent, the surface of the river was dotted all over with round disks of soft ice, each with a snow-white chaplet of ice-needles at its edge. It was our first warning, a harbinger of the long winter sleep, during which the fish seek refuge in the clear water of the creeks and side-lagoons. All the Lop-men were now out with their canoes, busy catching fish for the winter.

Of a morning we had to chop out our boats with axes and iron bars, and the ropes and cables were frozen stiff. The frost was very keen, for although we had fires both fore and aft, we nevertheless froze. Pushing out amongst the drift-

Drift-ice on the Lower Tarim.

ice, we continued our journey amidst its dancing, whirling disks. Watching them gave us a new occupation. They were always most numerous in the current. They were drawn into the eddies, where they whirled round and round until they became so crowded that some of them were pushed back again into the current. They grounded on the sand-banks just below the surface and thus gave us timely warning of them. They swam merrily down-stream like small islands, grating noisily one against the other. They struck against our ferry-boat, and were broken to pieces; became consolidated again and collided with the frozen banks, which set them spinning like tops.

The next day the drift-ice was even denser. The river wore a very strange appearance, just as though it had frozen and a shower of snow had fallen upon it, only the white mass was in unceasing movement. When we watched it steadily for some time, we began to fancy it was the ice that was motionless, and it was we who were floating up-stream.

That evening we chose an unfortunate camping-ground, a quiet, sheltered creek, which in the morning was frozen so hard that the men were easily able to walk all round every vessel of our flotilla. It was as though these were embedded in lava, and it took a long time to hew out a canal by which to get them back to the river. Meanwhile the ice-disks were clattering together like the breaking of pottery. All day long we had, as it were, this fluvial carillon playing round about us, and the millions of ice-crystals glittered and sparkled in the sunshine. The unceasing noise, coupled with the blending of the lights, produced a deafening and somnolent effect upon the senses. These endless snow-white rings were wreaths of immortelles that the Tarim was putting on in token of the cold shroud under which it was about to be buried.

After that we took care to avoid the quiet creeks, but halted in the very middle of the stream. In the evening, when I sat writing up my diaries, every disk of ice that went past bumped, bumped against the ferry-boat, making her groan and shiver from end to end. I worked 14 hours a day. No sooner did we get our clothes on than off we went. I had a brazier standing beside my writing-table, over which I occasionally warmed my hands. I ate my breakfast, generally of boiled fish, whilst under way, and now had my dinner as well on board.

The Ferry-boat at the Confluence of the Ughen-daria with the Tarim.

On the 2nd December the sky was covered with thick clouds, as heavy as a pall, but never a snowflake came from them. In the evening, however, the sun gleamed like a ball of golden fire from underneath their dark canopy. The entire expanse of the atmosphere was as if filled with inflammable gas which had caught fire; and the reed-thickets were flooded with purple. The lower borders of the firmament were stained with various shades of intense violet, and the outspread arms of the poplars seen against them at once arrested attention. But the magnificent spectacle lasted only a few minutes. Dusk came, and gathered everything into its pitiless, iron-grey embrace, and the reeds, which had lately stood in serried ranks like life-guards on parade, became converted into mere dry flagged stalks.

When it grew so dark that we could no longer see, I gave the order to stop. On this occasion there was no dry wood to be found for firing. But the men, not to be beaten, set fire to the inconceivably dense reeds which clung to the shore. The dry stalks crackled and whistled, and burst like bamboos; the wild, reddish-yellow glare spread across the dark water, and lit up with an intense illumination the thousands upon thousands of disks of drift-ice which were dancing restlessly past.

At Karaul I met another old acquaintance, my honest, faithful servant, Parpi Bai, who had accompanied me in 1896. When he came on board, and saw me and Islam Bai, his old comrade, the tears started to his eyes; he looked remarkably well, with his grey-sprinkled beard, dressed in a dark-blue *chapan* (long coat) and cap, edged with fur. After he had told me all that had happened to him since we last parted, I engaged him again at a fixed salary.

On the 7th December the natives came to tell me that we were getting quite close to the place where the river was

The Meeting of Parpi Bai and Islam Bai at·Karaul.

frozen over from side to side. By a stroke of rare good fortune my caravan happened to have arrived there simultaneously, and was in the immediate neighbourhood, so that I was able to send a message to the Cossacks to stop at Yanghi-köl. This 7th December was our last day's drift down the river. We were travelling due south-east, having on our left immense steppes of grass and *kamish* (reeds), and on our right high, barren sand-dunes, the bases of which were undermined by the river. This last was now everywhere frozen over, except for a small strip of water in the middle, and *it* was choked with drift-ice. In that confined water-way we were carried along at an uncomfortable speed, the edges of the ice crunching and ringing like broken glass as we brushed against them; nevertheless, it was fine to see our ferry-boat cutting her way through it like a sugar-saw.

Early in the day we became aware of some horsemen approaching on the bank. They were Chernoff, Faisullah, and Nias Hadji. They confirmed the report that within another two hours we should reach the spot where the river was frozen across from side to side, and beyond that point it would not be humanly possible to advance. Although the sun had already set, I determined to push on. I was resolved we would not stop until we were literally forced to do so. By the light of lanterns, and of torches fastened to long poles, held up in the canoes, we made our way through the huge ice-mill, where the ice-disks were being ground to powder. But at length silence fell. The ferry-boat stopped, the ice-disks glided in under the firm ice. A gigantic fire was burning on the bank, the signal that our long river-journey was at length ended. Thus far were we to drift on the broad bosom of the Tarim, but no farther. And it was here that my caravan awaited me.

Ördek in his Canoe, and Palta and two other Men in a Double Canoe, on the Ughen-daria.

# CHAPTER VIII.

## A PERILOUS DESERT JOURNEY.

I WAS now able to get a good sound sleep, for we were no longer in a hurry. After ordering my camp beside a small natural harbour, I dismissed my excellent boatmen from Lailik, doubling every man's pay, so as to carry him home free of cost, and when they said good-bye to me the tears stood in their eyes. Parpi Bai, whom I put in charge of the horses, at once set about building stables for them of *kamish* sheaves. Turdu Bai and Faisullah, both Russian subjects from West Turkestan, were appointed to look after the camels. Kurban, a fine, frank, happy old boy of sixty, hailing from Aksu, was made man-of-all-work to the Mussulmans; while Ördek, a Loplik, whom we found at the camp, performed the coarser labour, such as carrying water for cooking, fetching wood from the nearest forest, getting in provisions, and so on, in which he was assisted by a number of other Lopliks. Islam Bai was chief of the Mussulmans. The Cossacks were my own immediate attendants. Khalmet, an *aksakal* (merchant) from Korla, an old friend of my 1896 journey, came to visit me here for a few days. I commissioned him to buy me in Korla mules, Mongolian felt *kibitkas* (tents), and silver change, besides a quantity of provisions of all sorts.

The caravan had brought with them from Kutchar and

Our Winter-quarters at Yanghi-köl. The men, going from left to right, are Kader, Turdu Bai, Kasim, Chernoff, Parpi Bai, Sirkin, Niaz Hadji, Khalmet Aksakal, Islam—the last five kneeling—and behind them Faisullah, Palta, Musa, and others.

Korla five dogs, amongst them two handsome greyhounds. These I called Mashka and Taigun, and from the first day they were my declared favourites. Both were tall, and had thick coats of short white hair, and for this reason they were fond of being by the fire in winter. Then I had felt bags made for them, in which they slept at night inside my tent. It was very comical to see how quickly they learned to creep inside their bags, and how they sighed with contentment when I tucked them in. But on the warpath they were invincible; all the dogs in the neighbourhood went in terror of them. They waged war in a very cunning way did Mashka and Taigun, for they manœuvred round their opponent, until they were able to seize hold of him by one of his hind legs, and then swung him round and round until the poor beggar tumbled head over heels, whereupon they would let him go, and off he would run, howling and limping on three legs. When we threw food out to the dogs, none of the others dared look at a piece of meat until Mashka and Taigun had done eating. After their arrival in the camp, Yoldash, whilst not exactly falling into disfavour, withdrew himself from my company, and never dared to peep into my *kamish* hut when the two newcomers were there. One attempt which he made to do so proved disastrous; it was vain for me to intervene between them, for I have found that dogs have their own ways of settling such affairs. But Yoldash still continued to sleep faithfully outside my hut, and I often delighted him by stepping out and patting and caressing him.

Yolbars, or the Tiger, was a gigantic black-brown animal, a son of the jungle, with the blood of the wolf in his veins, a perfect terror of a watch-dog; I called him "the knight of the murderous fangs." He was usually kept fastened to an iron chain, and nobody except myself and a couple of the men durst go within reach of him. He was the terror of thieves, for he was always loose at night. During the months that followed he had various adventures. Once his flank was literally ripped open by a wild-boar, so that his intestines hung out of the wound; nevertheless, after the place was sewn up, he recovered again. On another occasion he ran off into the burning desert, and we thought he was lost, but he turned up again at the end of six months. His memory is especially dear to me, because he accompanied me on my forced and perilous ride towards Lassa, and protected us at night.

Around the "market-place" in our village, where the men had their open-air kitchen and their "club" beside the fire—which I may add was never allowed to go out until May of the following year—our huts, stables, and tents were built and piles of provisions were stacked. The natives came from far and near, partly out of curiosity, partly to sell us goods, so that there was a perpetual coming and going, and an incessant murmur of voices as from an actual crowded market-place.

Here at our head-quarters at Yanghi-köl I allowed myself a few days' rest. These I partly employed in making a reconnaissance into the sandy desert to the south, with the idea of learning something of its characteristics, for I had made up my mind to travel right across the desert to the village of Tatran on the Cherchen-daria, a distance of 170 miles. The natives did all they could to dissuade me from my purpose; for they regarded the enterprise as sheer madness, and me as one going to deliberate suicide. Nobody had ever been into that terrible desert, and anybody who did venture in need never hope to come out again. All they knew about it was that, several hundred years ago, there lived far away in the south-west a heathen people, under the rule of one Atti Kush Padishah. Holy Imams had gone there to spread the faith of Islam, and when the people refused to accept the new teaching, the Imams called down upon them the wrath and vengeance of Heaven, and for several days it rained sand, until all that country, and all its people, were buried underneath it.

They almost made it a matter of conscience, did these honest people, at seeing me fling myself, as they thought, wantonly away to destruction, and suggested that it would be better if I started from the south, and went round the desert, and then made direct for Yanghi-köl. By way of helping me to find my way out of the desert they proposed to kindle every evening a big beacon-fire on the top of a high dune. But, tempting though their project was, I thought it better to start from a known point, and with animals that were fresh and rested. And so that settled the matter.

The caravan consisted of the following: Islam Bai, who had already shared with me the horrors of the desert, Turdu Bai, Ördek, and Kurban. We took with us seven camels only and one horse, besides the two dogs, Yoldash and Dovlet; the greyhounds would have been unable to stand the midwinter cold under the open sky.

My preparations were made with the greatest care. Not a single unnecessary article was taken; the camels must have light loads to carry through the heavy sand. We took with us rice and flour enough to last ten days, enough ready-made bread for a fortnight, and for the same period a little tea, *talkan*, or "roasted wheat flour," which is simply mixed with water and eaten just as it is. For my own use I had some tins of preserved food, tea, coffee and sugar, and the men were provided with a huge packet of cube tea. We were provisioned only as far as the little town of Cherchen, where we should easily be able to renew our supplies. In addition I carried with me the necessary instruments. Our heavier baggage consisted of winter clothing and fur coats, as well as felt carpets to sleep upon at night. On the other hand, we were not cumbered with tents; but during the whole of the winter, a period of more than two months, I slept, like my men, in the open air, and I can assure you it was sometimes pretty cool when the thermometer registered 54° of frost.

Early on the morning of 20th December I was awakened by Islam, who came to ask if I meant to start, for a violent

A Loaded Camel.

storm was raging from the south-west; but the day of departure having been once fixed could not be altered, and I gave orders to start. I said good-bye to the Cossacks and the rest of the men, who were to stay behind at Yanghi-köl, and take care of our belongings, and especially keep guard over our piles of baggage. The camels having been led across the frozen river on a sanded track, we set about loading up. Two of the camels carried the baggage and provisions, a third maize, for the animals' own use, a fourth was laden with thick logs of wood, and the three others with huge blocks of ice, wrapped in goat-skins, for in the desert we could not hope to find either fuel or water. Three other camels, which were to accompany us for four days, under the charge of three men, were likewise loaded with ice and wood. This little supplementary caravan was put under the charge of Parpi Bai.

When Islam reported that all was ready, our heavy caravan got under way, and marched slowly along the bank of the Tarim towards the little lake of Tana-baghladi. At its extreme southern end we halted for a little, hewed four small holes in the ice, and for the last time let the camels drink their fill; and they seemed to understand what was expected of them, for they drank and drank, swallowing down the water in long gulping draughts, as if they never meant to stop.

After crossing over a threshold or cross-ridge of high sand, we encamped beside the last patch of thick kamish. Having made a little clearing amongst the reeds, we managed to get a certain amount of shelter against the wind, though the sky was our roof.

When I awoke in the semi-darkness of the following morning the storm was still raging; nevertheless, we continued our slow plodding march to the ting-tang of the last camel's bell. The ground was soft and the camels sank in deeply, especially the leader, which served as a "sand-plough" for the others. I came last in the procession, riding my little grey horse and keeping, of course, to the track which the camels had trampled. Even thus early the scene was one of appalling desolation. If there are sand-deserts on the moon, I am positive they cannot be more destitute of organic life than this was. There is

The Outermost Sand-dunes at Yanghi-köl. (Parpi Bai, Palta, and Islam Bai.)

nothing—absolutely nothing whatever—to show that life in any shape or form ever existed there. That evening we missed the shelter of the reed thicket, for we were completely exposed to the whirling, choking drift-sand, which swept across our little camp-fire in smothering clouds. Islam and I, having already made one dangerous journey across the Takla-makan, knew what was before us. The desert here was twice as wide as where we crossed the Takla-makan in 1895, when the whole caravan perished. The question we put to ourselves every day, though we never gave expression to it, was, would any of us issue alive from this new attempt to cross the desert?

It was very fortunate for us that the prevailing wind had built up the drift-sand into dunes in a direction so regular and so advantageous for our particular line of march. The wind in question, which blows especially in the spring and summer with unparalleled violence, though remarkable regularity, comes from the east-north-east. It heaps up the sand in waves, like the waves of the ocean, though unspeakably higher; in fact, they sometimes attain altitudes of 300 feet or more, or only 50 or 60 feet short of the top of the dome of St. Paul's. These mountains of sand stretch in endless lines from north-east to south-west, but in the troughs or valleys between them the ground is level and bare. Another system of dunes, though considerably lower, intersects the former system at right angles, thus making a gigantic network of sand-dunes. The meshes, or hollow spaces between the dunes, are in reality depressions, which the natives call *bayirs*. By following these depressions south-west, and crossing the sandy passes which separate them at each end, we were able to avoid the lofty swellings of sand which accompanied us on both sides. As an actual fact we travelled in all nearly 90 miles on the level ground of these *bayirs*, but the rest of the journey was on the sand, which, especially in the southern part of the desert, was fearfully heavy. Had the whole of the desert consisted, as I confess I previously thought it did, of a chaos of sand-dunes 300 feet high, our journey would certainly have ended in disaster. But counting on my previous experience, I thought that, even if we lost the camels and had to abandon all our belongings, we five men would nevertheless be able to make our way out on foot.

The scene that meets the eye to the east from the top of one of those high dune-accumulations can only be described as appalling, and yet it is at the same time unspeakably grand in the sublimity of its desolation. You can see nothing but the steep leeward slopes of the dunes shooting almost vertically downwards from the crest of each successive dune-accumulation. You imagine that it is a veritable ocean of sand, the gigantic waves of which have been suddenly arrested and fixed where they stand by some invisible power, and only await the utterance of some magic formula to roll on irresistibly farther, engulfing and destroying everything that lies in their path.

At the third camp we tried to dig a well. At the depth of 3¼ feet we got plenty of water, with a temperature of 40°.6 Fahr., but it was as bitter as the most concentrated salt-solution. It was evident we could not rely upon that treacherous ground; we must, therefore, exercise the greatest possible economy in using up our blocks of ice. Morning and evening we thawed only just as much as we barely needed, and confined ourselves to three logs of wood, two in the evening and one the next morning.

On the fourth day the storm blew from the north. The atmosphere was heavily charged with flying dust and sand, so that all we could see, through the thick haze which surrounded us on every side, were the objects in our immediate vicinity, and even then only indistinctly. The effect upon our minds was both strange and awe-inspiring. At noon it was no lighter than at ordinary twilight. We were penetrating into the murky realms of winter.

After crossing the twelfth depression the country ahead looked really alarming. On, on we went, climbing up the next sandy pass; but it seemed as if we were never to get to the top, for no sooner did we reach one eminence than a fresh one loomed up in our path. The tired camels kept stopping at shorter and shorter intervals to catch their breath. At length, however, we did get to the summit, and there, far down below our feet, lay outspread the thirteenth *bayir*, its floor lost in the haze. We descended by glissading down the slope, and upon reaching the bottom encamped.

During the night the storm subsided, and when at daybreak I peeped out of my furs, the moon was still shedding her pale frosty light over our silent camp. All the men were sleeping heavily, and the long-drawn breathing of the camels was the only thing that broke the brooding silence of the desert. As I looked up, I sent my greeting by the wintry moon to my home in the Far North, for it was Christmas Eve—Christmas in the desert!

After our strenuous march through the sand of the day before everybody was tired, men and animals alike, and I let them have a thorough good rest, so that by the time the camp had begun to stir, the sun had already climbed above the tops of the dunes. The camels, which always lay in a clump close together for warmth's sake, cast long shadows in strong relief across the ground.

It was now time to weed out everything that we could possibly do without, for the little supplementary caravan, under Parbi Bai, was to return to our winter quarters at Yanghi-köl. Each of the men who was appointed to go back came and begged earnestly to be allowed to accompany me across the desert; its weird fascination held them in its spell, even as it held me. But requests, even entreaties,

Descending the Steep Face of a Sand-dune.

were of no avail ; our supply of ice was limited. Very soon they disappeared like black dots on the expanse of yellow sand, and thus the last tie which linked us to civilization was severed, and we had but the silence and mystery of the desert to lean upon.

Christmas Day was a hard day for us. The level depressions seemed all at once to have come to an end, and we lost our way amongst the sand, which continued to grow higher and higher. The caravan advanced with painful slowness, step by step, with frequent and exasperating stops. Now a camel would fall, and then we had to unload him, get him on his feet, and load him up again. Another time it would be a steep and awkward crest which had to be levelled down with spades. Then, to make matters still worse, the wind from the north got up again, and enveloped the country in the hateful dust-haze, filling our minds with a sense of helplessness and strange disquietude. It was as if we were making desperate efforts to get ourselves entangled in a maze from which we should be unable to extricate ourselves.

I dismounted and led the way on foot. And when I at length reached the summit of a dune 200 feet high, the prospect which met my gaze was anything but reassuring. The leeward side of the dune was almost perpendicular, and the sixteenth *bayir* gaped like a coal-black pit at my feet, its surface wet in the middle, with a girdle of salt all round it, shut in everywhere by lofty dunes. It made me think of the entrance to the infernal regions. When the caravan overtook me we once more did a glissade to the bottom, and then encamped on the edge of the foreboding pit.

Never have I spent the evening of Christmas Day amid more gloomy or more depressing surroundings ! The only thing common to the happy memories of that festive season was the cold. After sitting shivering and shaking, with chattering teeth, and clustering like bats round our niggardly fire, above the embers of which the expiring blue blaze was feebly dancing, we rolled ourselves in our sheep-skins and went to sleep. Although we hospitably left every door open, none of the messengers of Santa Claus took a single peep into our airy domicile. A Christmas at the North Pole could not be more dreary.

## CHAPTER IX.

### IN THE HEART OF THE DESERT-OCEAN.

THE next day we travelled close upon 12 miles, the storm keeping us company all day; while the light, buoyant sand, whipped unceasingly by the wind, streamed out from the crest of every dune in the shape of gigantic plumes and camels' tails. Everything was smothered with sand; it even made an uncomfortable garment next the skin; it gritted between the teeth when we clenched them. In fact, particles of sand are dropping out of the leaves of my note-book now, as I turn them over, four years after the journey was taken. The day after Christmas Day the ground was unfavourable, heavy sand predominating. Every time that we toiled up to the top of a sandy pass we found ourselves on the upper ledge of a straight slope going down at a break-neck angle into the next *bayir*. The camels let themselves glide helplessly down without trying to guide themselves. The sand, once it started slipping under their weight, poured like a cascade down the steep slope, and carried the animals stiff-legged with it. But by this they had grown accustomed to that method of descent, and no longer lost their balance. At the same time, it was very comical to see the entire caravan sliding down in that headlong way, like schoolboys tobogganing down a steep hillside. Our fuel was running out; we had to husband it with the greatest care. Our camels, too, had sometimes to go hungry; we had nothing better to give them when we stopped than the straw stuffing of one or the other pack-saddle.

The 27th December brought me a great and glad surprise. As usual I was leading the way on foot, the caravan following in a long string behind. Upon reaching the summit of a high dune, I stopped to consider seriously the situation, and began to search the desert with a telescope. Away in the south my eye fell upon a *bayir* that presented an unexpected appearance; it was sprinkled with black dots. Down I hurried, and to my growing amazement I found that the black dots were wind-driven kamish leaves, and amongst them were signs of a small rodent no bigger than a rat. Advancing a little farther, I discovered to my great delight that there was kamish, dry it is true, but nevertheless kamish, and it was growing in thin clumps.

When at length the caravan caught me up, the men were as jubilant as if it was the gates of Paradise they beheld opening before them. The camels dilated their nostrils, sniffing food; and in truth it was a discovery as welcome as it was unexpected. Indeed, it inspired in us the hope that we should get out of that dread desert without losing our lives. Yes, grazing in the middle of the sandy desert, over 80 miles from the nearest water!

We encamped and turned the animals loose; then, gathering up the kamish by the armful, we made a rousing fire. That evening each camel was allowed 6½ gallons of water to drink. The bucket was emptied in a couple of greedy mouthfuls. This made our loads of ice very appreciably lighter; but the presence of this vegetation led us to hope that the ground water could not be very far down. We spent the whole of the afternoon melting ice for the camels. Then the storm-clouds began to separate; on the upper side they were a greyish violet, with an edge of glittering gold, but their underside was the same dirty yellow as the sand-dunes. During the night the temperature dropped to $-5°.8$ Fahr., and when we awoke in the morning the east wind was again blowing, the sky full of leaden clouds and the atmosphere thick with dust. Nor was there any lightening of the sky to show where the sun was. We were in the country of perpetual winter twilight. The sand accumulations, although in reality quite close to us, loomed faintly through the haze like mountain-ranges a great many miles off. I was chilled to the bone by the never-resting icy wind, and preferred to get off and walk and lead my horse, even where the ground was hard and level.

Upon reaching the thirty-third depression, I was led to hasten my steps by seeing a black object. It was the first tamarisk bush. It still retained a feeble glimmer of life; but round about it were scattered the branches of other bushes long since dead and shrivelled; but they made a welcome addition to our supply of fuel. A little farther on I found a kamish thicket, which afforded a certain amount of shelter against the blast; there I stopped, and, tethering my horse, set to work and made a fire.

The caravan did not turn up before dusk, and when they arrived I could only count six camels; the seventh had given up and been left behind. After supper Islam and Turdu Bai went back to fetch him, but found him dead, with his mouth open and his eyes half closed. The other six were in excellent condition, although this was our ninth day in the desert. On our Takla-makan journey, it was on the ninth day that I lost two men, most of my remaining camels, and all my baggage. But whereas we were then overwhelmed with thirst and heat, we were now chilled to the bone by an icy wind, and had any quantity of water.

Next morning, after securing the pack-saddle of the dead camel, we continued our weary march. At night when we encamped, there was an abundance of dry tamarisk and of kamish, which was in part still green, an indication that the ground-water was near the surface; in fact, we found it at a depth of 4½ feet, and it was almost perfectly fresh, so that here we had almost everything we wanted—water, fuel and fodder. We kept two huge fires blazing all the evening in the fierce blast, and they shed a lurid light upon the crests of the dunes, from which the drift-sand was raining down in showers over our devoted heads.

As we no longer required to march for dear life, and both men and animals needed rest after the strenuous toil of the preceding days, we decided to remain a day beside this most welcome well, and proceeded to make our camp as comfortable as circumstances would allow. Out of the white felt carpet, on which I usually spread my bed, we made a makeshift tent, holding it up with branches of tamarisk; it afforded at any rate some shelter against the tempest, which continued to rage all day. On the other side I had a brazier, which was kept hot; then, whilst I lay and read and became gradually smothered with drift-sand, the men watered the camels, an operation which took a good long time, for the water only trickled into the bottom of the well. Meanwhile, the camels stood round in a ring expectantly waiting. As soon as the bucket was full, it was hauled up and was emptied in one draught. The thirsty animals drank not less than nine buckets each; two of them even drank eleven, and we could literally see their sides swelling out as they sucked the water down. This put new life into them, and they were almost lively as they turned to and began to tug away at the thin kamish.

The last morning of the 19th century broke quite promising; from my sanded-in bed I saw the stars glittering over our bivouac, round which the tamarisks on their pedestals of clay appeared like dusky spectres. The camels, strengthened by the good drink they had had, accomplished an excellent day's work, and covered 13 miles. In the evening when we encamped, the wind had dropped, and the smoke and flames of our camp-fires curled straight up towards the brightly sparkling stars.

The 1st January, 1900, rose gloomily, without giving us a single glimpse of the morning sun. The day's march was very heavy, for there was no longer any level ground to march on. As far as we could see to the south, there was nothing but a chaos of more or less connected sand-dunes. Up to that point we had been like a vessel navigating the calms; now we found ourselves all at once flung into the middle of the storm-tossed ocean. The waves were as high as houses, and we made desperately slow advance, tramping up and down the heavy dunes, first one camel stumbling and falling, and then another. The vegetation once more came almost entirely to an end. A long way to the east there still appeared to be bayir depressions, but they lay too far out of our line of march. The southern horizon presented a serrated outline, like a saw-blade, the points being lofty, dominating pyramidal dunes. That day we did not cover more than 8½ miles.

Next morning an unexpected scene met our eyes. It had snowed during the night, and the dunes were clothed with a sheet of dazzling white, the effect of which was to make them appear even more desolate and naked than usual. There were no longer any friendly bayirs to help us, nothing but sand!

During the afternoon a strong gale sprang up in the south-south-west, and the snow whirled about the caravan in clouds. Twilight settled down upon the inextricable chaos of snow and sand, and for a long time we searched in vain for a suitable place to encamp in; at length, when it was as dark as pitch, we stopped beside a dead tamarisk, and it afforded us a little fuel. The small oases of kamish which we had found in the middle of the desert had now

The Interminable Desert "Ocean."

entirely ceased. The men were again seriously anxious, Ördek especially being filled with disquietude, for the desert seemed as if it would never end, and the sun never shone. He talked of the green banks of the Tarim, and its flocks of sheep, and its reed huts, and dancing canoes, and fish, as of a paradise which he should never see again.

The camels were now so exhausted that we had to grant them another day's rest. I myself was almost dead-beat with weariness, and could do nothing but lie in the sand and read, although it snowed heavily all day, while the snow-flakes, big and thick, fell hissing into the fire and staining the leaves of my note-book. At noon even it was a thick twilight; dunes, sand and sky melted together into one white, dizzy, whirling mass in a faint, diffused light without any relief whatever. The snow was still falling late at night. The sparks, flying up from the blazing fire, encountered the snow-flakes, and converted them into drops of water, making them glitter like iron spray.

It was rather a cool night to lie out in the open, the thermometer registering $-22°$ Fahr., and when I crept out of my sleeping-bag in the morning there were still 43° of frost. I was entirely covered up with snow, and the snow was falling as fast as ever. Before I could get up, Islam had to dig me out, and brush the snow-drift away with a wisp of reeds. I always used to undress as I do at home, and I can assure you that undressing under such circumstances is anything but an unmixed pleasure. I used to perform the operation in the following manner. Sitting in front of the fire, I flung off my clothes as quickly as ever I could, while Islam gathered them up one by one and stuffed them under my pillow, to keep them dry during the night. Then I wrapped myself in a woollen nightshirt, two yards long, and thick and soft, and having crept under the bed-covering, I pulled a soft fox-skin *basklik*, or "hood," over my head, and was well tucked in all round by Islam. At first I used to be perfectly stiff with cold, for there were 36° of frost inside my bed, and for some time I could do nothing but lie perfectly still; but gradually my limbs used to thaw, and after stopping up every chink and cranny at which the cold was able to penetrate, I eventually became quite warm, and the gradually thickening coverlet of snow kept me warm all night. I slept like a log till morning, and it was very seldom that the chance snow-flakes, which trickled down from my neck on to my bare shoulder, were able to waken me.

The worst of all was, however, getting up in the morning, for the night cold literally "tied me up into knots." As soon as the fire was briskly burning, I used to dress in a sitting posture in front of the blaze. The temperature in front of me would be 86° Fahr., while at my back it was −22°, and time after time I had to thrust my hands almost into the blaze before I could feel to fasten the buttons. Sometimes the snowflakes would shower down upon my neck and back in a way that was the reverse of agreeable. Islam then brought me a metal basin with warm water in it for washing, and it was simply delightful. But once I had got my wolf-skin coat over my shoulders, and sat drinking my boiling hot tea, I soon forgot all the little inconveniences of the night.

In our next day's march we were less fortunate. The wind was against us, and at the very warmest part of the day the thermometer only registered 8½° Fahr. Deeper and deeper we penetrated into the high sand, and there was not a scrap of fuel to be had. Fortunately, we had brought some with us from our last camp, but it was all too soon used up, and after that it got so cold that we could do nothing but go to bed. Next morning, the 5th January, the snow, after a very heavy fall during the night, lay so thick that it cost us a certain amount of trouble to gather our effects together. The very places where our fires had been were covered with snow. The camels looked splendid with snowdrifts on their backs, snow-powder on their heads, and long icicles hanging from their beards; and when they began to march, the snow crunched under their feet with quite a wintry sound.

During the course of the day it cleared up for awhile, and the sun peeped out, but even then the air was filled with myriads of flashing ice-crystals, and our eyes were blinded by the glittering reflection of the snow. The immense dunes resembled mountain-ranges capped with perpetual snow, and seen through the strong sunlight presented a fascinating play of colour in pale-blue shades.

Next day the sand-dunes seemed to be higher than ever, and it was hard work travelling amongst them. The men's spirits again began to sink. Would this desert never come to an end? Were they never to get out of this everlasting sand? But the next day brought a welcome change, for when, from the top of a high dune, I swept the distant horizon to the south with my telescope, I detected a number of black points and lines standing out in sharp relief against the snow. These could only mean one thing—dead forest. Full of eager expectation we quickened our steps and soon reached the place.

It was as I had expected: there had once been a forest there, but it had been overwhelmed by the sand, and nothing of it was left except a few dried-up tree-trunks. Within an hour we had piles of wood stacked up beside the camp. One tree, which was too big to be cut down, was set fire to as it stood, and for a long time it blazed out like a gigantic torch across the immense white pall of the desert. A hollow poplar, which the men flung across my fire, made quite an interesting spectacle. The flames darted along inside it as through a tube; it glowed, it crackled, it glittered like rubies; the ancient bark burst and writhed in despair, as the sharp flames bit their way into its icy wood.

Gigantic columns of smoke curled up from our camp towards the moon, which at length emerged from her jealous hiding-place. That night the Mussulmans proved themselves too clever for the cold; they dug holes in the sand, filled them

A Poplar beside the Lower Tarim.

with hot embers, covered them up again with sand, and then lay down and slept on the top.

Throughout the whole of the journey I kept a detailed map of our route, and as I was, from my former journey, well acquainted with the positions of Yanghi-köl and the river Cherchen-daria, I was able on the morning of 8th January to promise my men that the ensuing night they should all sleep on the bank of that river. Nor was I mistaken; for before long I perceived from the top of a lofty dune a dark line on the southern horizon. It was the forest-belt beside the Cherchen-daria. After threading a labyrinth of tamarisks and poplars, we at length reached the goal of our desires, the Cherchen-daria. It was then, however, thickly sheeted with ice. My men were amazed that I was able to calculate the distance so exactly. They hardly knew what to make of it; I suspect they imagined that some time or other I had tramped across that trackless region alone. At all events, they declared that they were now ready to follow me without a moment's hesitation or fear wherever I might choose to lead them.

From Cherchen I then made a reconnaissance westwards of close upon 200 miles, accompanied by four mounted men. It was a bitterly cold ride in a violent wind and whirling snowstorms, and at night we slept under the open sky. I can almost hear still the monotonous thud, thud of the horses' hoofs as they struck the frozen ground. We were unable to ride longer than half-an-hour at once, and then had to get off and run to keep from freezing. Every time we found fuel we stopped and made a little fire, and after thawing ourselves pushed on again; and in this fashion we made our way from fire to fire, as though we were gaining ground inch by inch against our enemy, the biting cold. In the saddle we sat leaning forwards, doubled up in a heap, with our arms crossed, and let the horses take their own way. The last 24 hours on the return journey were the very worst of all. During the night the thermometer dropped to 25° Fahr. below zero. We made a more than ordinarily long stage, keeping on several hours after dark, and then it once more turned bitterly cold; the wind, too, was against us, and though not very strong, it was nevertheless quite enough to make us freeze in the saddle. I tried to protect my face with a comforter, but my breath froze in my moustaches. The water that came into my eyes in consequence of the cold stuck the eyelashes together, and turned them into fringes of icicles, and I had to keep thawing them in order to see.

# CHAPTER X.

## IN THE COUNTRY OF THE WILD CAMEL.

AFTER a long and tiring journey through the forests of the Cherchen-daria and beside the deltaic arms of the Lower Tarim, we at length, on 24th February, once more safely reached our headquarters at Yanghi-köl. Six or eight miles from camp we were met by troops of villagers from the neighbourhood, besides beks, couriers, and messengers. After we had disappeared without trace into the depth of the desert, they hardly expected to see us again, and now gave expression to their joy in the frankest way. But the finest sight of all was to see my four Cossacks gallop up, amid a cloud of dust, on their snorting black horses. The two Buriat Cossacks from Trans-Baikalia had now arrived. They were dressed in full uniform of dark green, carried their sabres in a belt hanging from the shoulder, and wore high black lambskin hats and riding boots of polished leather. Notwithstanding their decided Mongolic cast of feature, they made quite a striking appearance as they managed their big horses with masterly skill. Beside them I, after the hardships of my winter campaign, looked like a veritable tatterdemalion. Pulling up in front of me they saluted in military fashion and reported themselves.

Their names were Shagdur and Cherdon; they belonged to the army of the Trans-Baikal Cossacks, and were both 24 years old. They spoke a language closely akin to

On the Bank of the Cherchen-daria.

On the Frozen Cherchen-daria.

Mongolian; but they also spoke Russian fluently, and during the time they were in my service they learned to speak Jagatai Turkic, so as to be able to speak freely with their Mohammedan comrades. They brought with them from Chita weapons, ammunition and clothing, and had received their pay for two years in advance. The Czar had commanded that they were not to cost me anything.

Reed Huts at Sheitlar.

Within a very short time they grew so devoted to me that they would have laid down their lives to serve me, and I grew as much attached to them as I already was to their Russian comrades, Sirkin and Chernoff. As for these two I felt I could not part with them, but instead despatched a courier to Kashgar, with the request that I might keep them as well.

Then, accompanied by a long cavalcade of horsemen, we made our entry into our own village in state. In the

Chernoff, Sirkin, and Shagdur.

middle of the market-place I saw, in the midst of the men and animals, a gigantic tiger, glaring ferociously at us. Upon nearer examination it turned out to be dead, and after being set up on its feet had frozen hard in a natural attitude.

We found all the animals in a satisfactory condition—the mules and horses fat and sleek; the camels and dromedary that we had left behind full of flesh, but very wild, as they always are at the beginning of Spring. The dromedary in particular was almost uncontrollable in his frenzy; he gnashed his teeth and foamed at the mouth until the froth dropped in big clots to the ground. His scream was hoarse and awe-inspiring, and he rolled his eyes wildly, and tried to bite. Woe to the man who went too near him! Nobody could do anything with him except Faisullah. For safety's sake we kept him tethered by ropes round the feet and fastened to stakes driven into the ground, so that he was unable to move from the spot.

During our absence one of the camels had run away. Although he was tracked and followed all the way to the mountains, he was not caught. He had evidently turned wild, having been frightened out of his wits by a tiger or a wild boar. We never did recover him again; he was lost completely.

One of our neighbours gave us two new-born puppies, which we christened Malenki (the Little One) and Malchik (the Boy), because they were so small and pretty, and these names they retained even after they grew up to be giants of their kind. They both proved to be excellent caravan-dogs, and were always specially good friends of mine, and outlived all their comrades.

A wild-goose which we brought with us from Lailik, and which had travelled with us all the way down the river, had by this become so much at home, that it no longer paid any attention to the other wild-geese. These were now

Dragging the Canoes Overland.

returning from their warmer winter quarters in immense flocks, following the tracks which they had followed for generations past. Their cries, their noisy chatterings, were to be heard at all times of the day and night, and in all weathers. We saw them by day, whether calm or stormy, whether the sun was hidden or peeped out through the ragged clouds. We heard them on the pitch-dark nights, when the sky was black with clouds and the earth shrouded in mist. It was amazing to me how they were able to find their way along their aerial pathways. On, on they flew in never-ending columns, without rest, without pause, always in a breathless hurry. The natives said that the same flock always returns year after year to the same breeding-places, and that they have the same laws as to the rights of possession as the Lop-men themselves have.

Every day the Cossacks used to go out hunting, and they always returned with their hands full of pheasants, wild-duck, wild-geese, or deer. The country swarmed with game, so that they were able to keep our larder well supplied.

Our camp was gradually converted into a market-place, and became an important and well-known centre for the whole of the Lop country. Thither the peasantry brought in their products, and at intervals merchants from Kutchar and Korla came bringing sugar, cube tea, Chinese porcelain, Russian tea-cups, cloth, cottons, etc. One merchant settled on the spot and built a "house," and opened a shop as good as any to be found in the bazaars of Central Asia. It became a very popular resort, where the Mussulmans and Cossacks used to sit and drink tea, and smoke, and bargain. Ali Akhun, a tailor from Kutchar, also set up an establishment, and I can assure you he found plenty to do from morning till night.

Thus, after the profound stillness of the desert I now found myself the centre of extraordinary activity and bustle. Our market-place swarmed with horsemen and travellers, and all sorts of visitors from the neighbourhood. There was a constant coming and going, and it was not until the last visitor had departed that we put out the big Chinese lantern, which was hung up in the middle of the market-place. The fire, however, was kept burning all night, during which our camp was peaceful and quiet

A Tamarisk Thicket.

except for the pacing to and fro of the night-watchmen and the barking of the dogs.

The delightful days of rest, amounting to little more than a week, were soon past, and it was time to be starting again for new adventures in the desert, if we did not want to be surprised by the excessive heat of early summer. Good-bye then to Yanghi-köl, with its pleasant rural scenes, its hospitable tents, its never-empty fleshpots!

The object of the journey, which I began on 5th March,

was to solve several geographical problems; above all, I was anxious to trace and map the river-bed of the ancient Kuruk-daria, which was abandoned by the stream more than 1,000 years ago; though before that time it used to empty itself into the Lake of Lop-nor, now likewise dried up, although well-known from older Chinese maps.

Chernoff was appointed my body-servant; the rest of my little troop consisted of Faisullah, Ördek, and Khodai Kullu, besides Abdu Rehim and his two younger brothers. The three last, who accompanied us with eight camels, were, however, to leave us when we reached the spring of Altimish-bulak; their home lay to the north, amongst the mountains of the Kuruk-tagh. I took five camels of my own, all fresh, well rested animals, and my own little grey desert horse. The only dogs that accompanied us this time were Yoldash and Mashka, one of the greyhounds.

Meanwhile, the other three Cossacks, together with Islam, Turdu Bai, and Parpi Bai, and several other servants whom I had engaged, were commissioned to take care of the winter quarters at Yanghi-köl.

After two long days' march towards the north we reached the foot of the mountains, and then kept along them towards the east. One day we accomplished as much as 26 miles, a very long day's work for the slow-stalking camels, and that evening we encamped at the spring of Bujentu-bulak. I remember the next morning as if it were only yesterday. Chernoff had been in as usual whilst I still slept, and had lighted the little stove which I had this time brought with me, but he failed to observe that the wind, which was blowing down the glen, pressed the canvas of the tent against the heated funnel. I was awakened by an uncomfortable sense of warmth, and opening my eyes I saw the canvas in flames. I shouted to the men. In a moment they had the tent down, and with Chernoff began to drag out the boxes, maps, and books

A Sand-storm in the Desert.

that lay scattered about inside it. Meanwhile, I had not been idle, but seizing a felt carpet had flung it upon the burning tent, and so stifled the fire. Upon reaching Ying-pen, an oasis beside the dry bed of the Kuruk-daria, we rested two or three days, so as to give the camels an opportunity to get a good feed before we plunged into the desert. There I dismissed several men who had accompanied us thus far on horseback. They took back with them all our superfluous winter clothing, the stove, and certain other things that we could do without.

On 13th March we continued our journey towards the east. During the night a strong gale had sprung up from the east, and had torn my tent up by the roots, so that the canvas streamed out cracking on the wind like a loosened sail. We had only got about five or six miles when the storm developed into a perfect hurricane. The surface of the desert consisted of fine, powdery dust, and it streamed out behind the caravan like a comet's tail. The men sat crouched under their *chapans*, or "overcoats," bobbing up and down between the camels' humps. By two o'clock it was dark as twilight, and we were enveloped on every side by impenetrable clouds of dust and drift-sand.

As, in Abdu Rehim's words, it was blowing "hard enough to break the camels' backs," we thought it best to stop where we were; and, indeed, it was impossible to see where we were going to. All the same we attempted to find a place in this curiously-modelled clay desert that would afford us, at anyrate, a little shelter against the wind. We were in great danger of losing one another. I myself went a little bit down the wind in search of a hollow. Went! did I say? I was literally carried by the wind; in fact, I thought I was flying. When I at length turned to go back again, I had to meet the full fury of the tempest, the thick reddish-yellow dust driving full into my face. Where were the rest? I shouted; but I scarcely heard my own voice; mouth, eyes and nose were all chock-full of sand. I had to stop to catch my breath; I felt as if I were wading through mud or water; I turned giddy; I knew nothing of my people. My position was growing critical, I thought I had lost my way in the blinding clouds of drift-sand. It is always dangerous to leave a caravan during a storm; you may perhaps never find it again. At length, however, I caught sight of a spectral figure looming through the haze. It was honest Chernoff looking for me. He had shouted himself hoarse, but I never heard his voice, not even when he was only a yard or two distant from me.

Meanwhile, the other men had freed the camels from their burdens. My tent was put up behind the shelter of a tamarisk-mound, though only the upper half of the tent-poles were used. The side-ropes were lashed round the projecting massive roots, and the superfluous folds of the side canvas were anchored with heavy pieces of timber. After that the tent stood pretty firm. But the men were unable to use their tent, because the poles could not be taken to pieces.

The men sat crouched together in a heap. The camels lay in a long line, with their backs to the wind and their necks flat on the ground, stretched out in the direction towards which the wind blew. The wind had a velocity of 60 miles an hour, and we had to exert ourselves to the utmost to stand against it. When I stooped down I was almost suffocated with the dense clouds of dust and sand that were swept along the ground. It was impossible to think of preparing any food to eat; we had to content ourselves with water and bread—and a strong seasoning of sand. The sand penetrated the canvas of the tent and whirled in from every side. Every object lying about was covered within the space of half-an-hour; the ink dried up in my pen, and the pen rasped against the tiny sand-dunes which formed on the pages of my note-book. My bed, too, was thickly strewn with sand. It was as much as ever we could do to breathe in the stifling dust-laden atmosphere.

It was an extraordinary country we passed through during the next few days. The old river-bed is very distinctly marked, being deeply sunk in the dry clay desert like a winding furrow or corridor. On each side of it are weather-worn yellowish-grey tree-trunks, all dead and dried up to tinder. They put me in mind of the gravestones of a pre-historic churchyard did those embalmed mummies of most ancient trees, a stubble-field of Brobdingnagian dimensions!

For several days we marched through a waterless region, but as we carried with us several goat-skins filled with ice we suffered no inconvenience. Traces of wild-camel were extraordinarily numerous. Chernoff, who was a mighty hunter, was burning with impatience to try his skill upon this, the shyest and noblest of big game. His wish was fulfilled at Yardang-bulak, a spring where we stopped for a day's rest. In the morning he saw a wild-camel approaching the well-known drinking-place without any suspicion of evil. After the first shot the camel turned and went slowly off towards the east, the last shot having struck her—for it was a young she-camel—full in the body. Down she fell, but got up again and ran on a little way, then fell again; and this she repeated two or three times, until she finally dropped dead. The flesh was especially welcome, as for several days neither we nor the dogs had had any meat. Several foxes and a vulture also got a good feast. We took possession of the fine wool; it was useful for twisting into cords and ropes.

Some days later we accomplished an unusually long march through the desert, eagerly searching for the next spring, Altimish-bulak, or the Sixty Springs. On and on

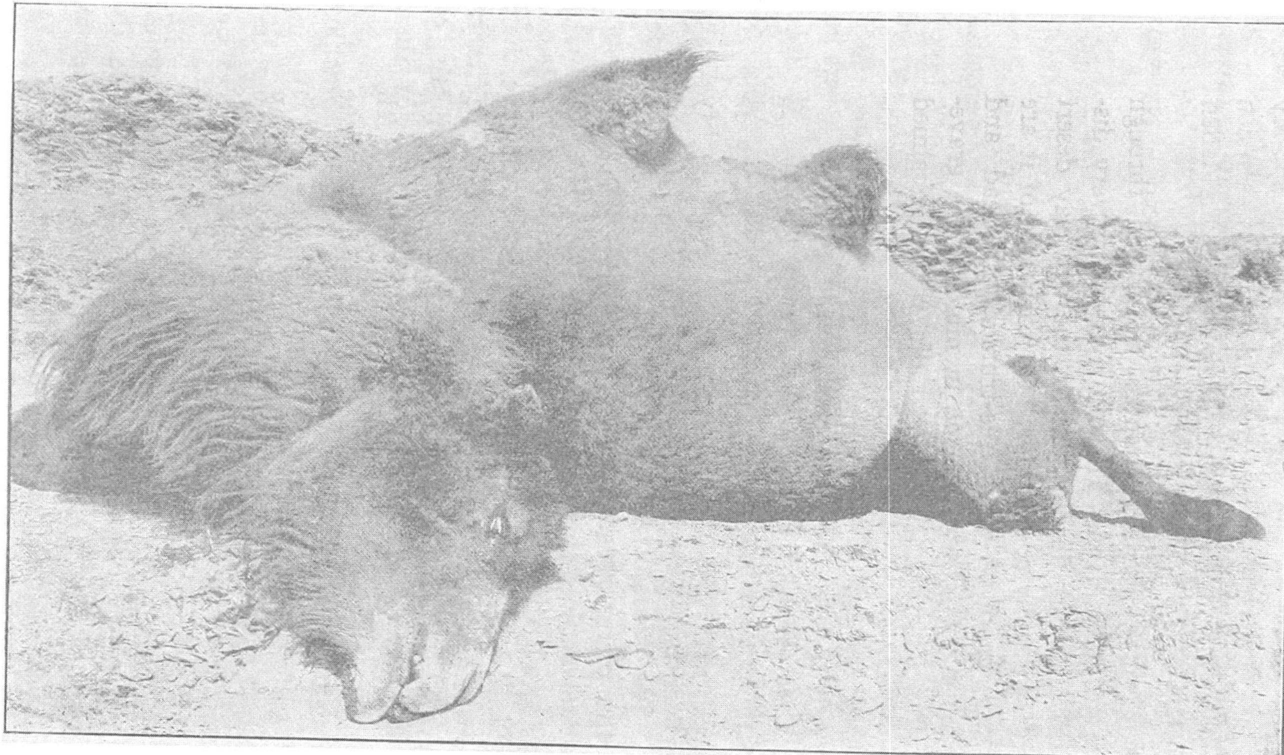

A Wild Camel Shot at Altimish-bulak.

we marched, long after it was pitch dark at night, but without finding it, and at length we were compelled to encamp where we were in the wilderness. But the next day we saw, behind a hill, a bed of yellow reeds—it was the splendid oasis of the Sixty Springs.

Abdu Rehim, whose sight was quickened by his constant life in the open air, at once detected a herd of wild-camels grazing on the farther edge of the oasis, although I, even with my field-glass to help me, could scarce distinguish the animals. The experienced camel-hunter now took the lead, and, followed by Chernoff and myself, hurried towards the belt of reeds. After crossing the rivulet from the salt spring—though it was then full of large sheets of fresh ice—we skirted round the greater part of the little oasis before Abdu Rehim stopped behind a couple of tamarisk bushes.

The herd consisted of a big dark-coloured male camel and five others of a lighter shade. The old one and one of the young ones were eagerly grazing; the others lay motionless, with their heads turned towards us; that is to say, away from the wind. As they were only 300 paces distant, I had an excellent opportunity to observe their movements when they believed themselves to be unobserved. The two that were grazing had their heads, of course, down on the ground, and when they got their mouths full they would lift their heads and grind the dry kamish (reeds) slowly and powerfully, until it crackled between their teeth, meanwhile searching the distant horizon with their glances. They showed not the slightest sign of uneasiness and had no suspicion of what was about to happen. I felt it was cowardly to steal upon these noble animals and shoot them by treachery, and I confess it was with a sigh of relief that I at length heard the report of the hunter's rifle. Meanwhile Abdu Rehim, silent and invisible as a panther, but with his eyes gleaming with the passion of the chase, disappeared amongst the bushes, his old-fashioned muzzle-loader in his hand. For a while there was the silence of the grave. I watched the herd in trembling expectation. Crack! and up leapt five of the camels and started to come at a slow trot towards our hiding-place; but suddenly they turned tail and set off at a wild gallop towards the mountains of the Kuruk-tagh. The younger of the two camels that were grazing received a bullet in his breast, and when he got up to follow the others, a second one in the neck stopped him for ever.

He lay in a kneeling posture, chewing away at what he had in his mouth. Every now and again he tried to get up, but his fore-legs refused to support him. His look was calm and resigned, and hardly showed either fear or astonishment; but when I tried to stroke him on the nose, he attempted to bite me. A swift, powerful stroke across the throat with Abdu Rehim's hunting-knife, followed by a few convulsions, and this noble son of the desert, who so lately was peacefully grazing upon the edge of the spring, was dead. The other camels had meanwhile disappeared like the wind. Abdu Rehim was immensely delighted; he was provisioned for several days to come.

## CHAPTER XI.

### ACROSS THE DESERT OF LOP.

At the oasis of the Sixty Springs we granted ourselves and the camels a few days of much-needed rest. Starting again on the 27th March, we set out to cross the Desert of Lop towards the south-west, our object being the northern shore of the Kara-koshun, the vast marsh in which the Tarim river pours its immense volumes of water. Whilst crossing the desert, I intended to examine the basin that was formerly occupied by the ancient lake of Lop-nor.

Abdu Rehim was to accompany us for two days, with some of his camels laden with ice from the springs. We filled all our sacks and goat-skins with bright, clear ice; but although we protected them all we could from the sun, two or three bucketsful dripped away during the very first day, for the temperature at noon now rose to between 62° and 64°, and when we got down into the desert itself the heat was oppressive. We did not exactly run any real danger, for I calculated that we should reach the marsh in a week, and even though our supply of ice were insufficient, we were not likely to perish of thirst.

We were the worse off for provisions, for what we brought with us from Yanghi-köl soon gave out, and although we still had some rice and old hard, dry bread, one soon grows tired of such monotonous fare. Fortunately, the Mussulmans were fond of camel-meat, though I and Chernoff

A Tame Camel, which Participated in my Journeys of 1896 and Died in Tibet 1901.

9*

were unable to touch it. However, just as we were starting, my excellent Cossack, with a masterly shot, brought down five wild-duck that were resting beside one of the springs, and with them we replenished our larder for a few days.

Next day, about three o'clock in the afternoon, when we were threading our way along the deep gullies which the wind had excavated in the clay desert, Chernoff and Ördek, who were leading the way, stopped and shouted

Chernoff amongst the Ruins.

back to us, that they had found the ruins of two or three houses. Now, the country round about was plentifully littered with mollusc-shells, showing that there had once been a lake there.

Traces of human existence, an ancient village on the northern shore of Lop-nor! This was indeed the most remarkable discovery that we made during the whole of our journey. And this I owe to my fortunate star, for had we gone but a stone's throw to the right or to the left we should never have seen these ruins, for the beams and posts, of which they principally consisted, had, when seen from the distance, an extraordinary resemblance to the dry tree-trunks that stood scattered all about the locality.

"Halt!" I cried, "and up with the tent;" and the next moment we were hard at work amongst the ruins with our only spade. I sketched them and measured them. Our excavations brought to light various articles

A Door-post still Standing *in situ*.

of value, such as Chinese money, fragments of earthenware, iron axes, small sacrificial bowls. On some of the pieces of wood were artistic carvings of human figures; one of them resembled a king with a crown on his head and a trident in his hand, probably a representation of some Buddhist divinity. These wooden sculptures must at all costs be preserved, and accordingly we laid them on one side in a heap.

Then we explored the immediate surroundings, but

found nothing further. However, we made very good use of our time, and it was quite late when we went to bed. I should have liked nothing better than to spend several days in that locality, but, unfortunately, the water was all the time drip-dripping from our ice-store, so that we durst not linger. Here Abdu Rehim and his camels turned back. At the same time, I sent with him Khodai Kullu, to carry back the finds we had made at the ruins, some way or other, to our head-quarters at Yanghi-köl. The man was extremely reluctant to leave us; but apart from other reasons for sending him away, our water supply was now reduced to a very low ebb, and every mouth less was of consequence. Upon continuing my march from the ruins, my caravan consisted of only Chernoff, Faisullah and Ördek, with four camels, one horse and two dogs.

After proceeding about 12 miles we pitched our camp in a hollow and resolved to dig a well. If only we could get down to the ground-water we should be independent of the ice, and it might melt away as much as it liked. But we found that the spade had been left behind at the ruins, and Ördek, who was responsible for leaving it behind, at once proposed to go back and fetch it.

I hesitated to let him undertake such a long journey on foot, for if a sandstorm sprang up there was great risk of the man perishing. On the other hand, it might be that our very lives would depend upon the spade, if our position became at all desperate for want of water; without it we could not get down to the ground-water. However, I lent him my saddle-horse, and strictly enjoined him to keep to our trail. I told him we should not wait for him, but should push on further, and if he lost our trail all he had to do was to keep steadily on to the south, and he would come to the shore of the Kara-koshun. Then at midnight, after two or three hours' sleep and a good meal of rice and camel-meat, he disappeared into the darkness.

About two hours after he had started there arose what I dreaded most, namely a tempest from the north-east. Clouds of drift-sand were swept with hurricane violence along the ground and the air became thick with dust. When I looked out of the tent, it was as black as pitch; I couldn't see my hand before me. "Poor Ördek," thought

The Scene of Ördek's Discovery—Photographed a Year Later.

I; "I hope he will have the good sense to turn back." Next morning there were only two men to load up the caravan, so that I had to lend a helping hand myself. Then on we went again. Gloomily and eerily rang out the camel-bells in the dark desert, and the storm whistled past our ears; but while we on the one hand welcomed it, because it kept off the burning heat and helped us on our way, we on the other hand dreaded it because it might cost Ördek his life.

However, it turned out not to be so bad as that, for just as we were putting up our tent at nightfall Ördek appeared with the spade on his shoulder, leading his horse. Both were completely exhausted. Ördek's first cry was for water! water! His throat was completely parched with all the dust he had swallowed, and he was hardly able to stand.

It was with breathless attention that I listened to Ördek's story. In the dark and stormy night he had lost our trail and gone astray. But at daybreak he had stumbled across the ruins of several houses, where there was any quantity of richly decorated timber. Knowing that I was strangely interested in such things, he carried away with him two of the best of the planks. Then he set about searching for the ruins where he had left the spade, and did not give up the search until he found them. Having recovered the spade, he at once set off to return. Two or three times he tried to fasten the planks on the horse's back, but as the animal would have none of them, Ördek was forced to drag them along himself, and he showed me the bleeding sores which the rope had made on his shoulders. Once more he made an appeal to the horse's compassion, but the ungrateful animal broke loose and galloped away. Upon this, Ördek abandoned the planks, and had no end of trouble to catch his four-legged companion. When he did at length catch him, the poor fellow was so overcome by weariness and thirst that he made all the haste he could to find us. This was not the first time that I had had occasion to wonder at the marvellous topographical knowledge displayed by the natives.

This story produced upon me the effect of an electric shock. I at once ordered Ördek to go back first thing next morning and fetch the planks which he had left behind. And when I saw them, and perceived that they came from an entirely different place from the scene of our first discoveries, I instantly resolved that I must go back. In fact, the ground literally burned under my feet, so

Some of Ördek's Discoveries—A Meter-length (3.281 feet) is Shown on the Right by Way of Scale.

impatient was I to lift the veil from the secrets which had lain for a thousand years or more hidden in the heart of the desert. But to return then was impossible. Our supply of water was very nearly exhausted and the burning hot summer was close at hand; it would have been madness to have gone back just then. This discovery completely altered all my plans. My journey was originally calculated to last two years, but in consequence of this discovery it was extended to three. For even though it should cost me my life, I *must* sooner or later return to the place in which we had been so fortunate as to discover the remains of an ancient but forgotten civilisation. For the present, however, I had to content myself as best I could. We would spend the summer and autumn amongst the cool, snow-clad mountains of Tibet, our winter in the desert of Gobi, and in the following spring, when the wild-geese were returning from India, we would pitch our tents among the ruins of the ancient town.

We therefore continued our journey towards the south-west. Soon the dead forest came to an end, and at the same time the sand-dunes began to increase steadily in altitude. I was acting as pilot to the caravan, leading the way bare-foot, but shortly after noon the sand grew so hot as to blister my feet, so that I had to go last and tread in the footsteps of the camels, who ploughed up the sand that the night had cooled. On the 1st April we gave each of our camels a whole bucket of water to drink, for they were tired and exhausted; but this reduced our supply to such an extent that we had only enough to last one day more. We must quicken our steps, for we were still more than 40 miles from the Kara-koshun.

The scene around us was heartbreaking, nothing but dreary yellow dunes without a vestige of vegetation. We had to keep stopping at ever shorter intervals. The heated air trembled and vibrated above the sand. Oh! that another storm would come and cool the atmosphere! I was again a long way ahead. Wearily I dragged my steps to the top of a high dune to take a look about me.

View from the Northern Shore of Kara-koshun.

Still the same unending labyrinth of dolphin-backed dunes.

But what in all the world is that I see? Far away to the south, beyond the last of the dunes, there is a flash of something blue, a lake! What? water in this burning, scorched-up desert? Impossible. It must be a mirage! With winged steps I hastened down the dune-side and hurried towards the blue expanse. On and on I hurried until everything grew dark before my eyes. The men behind must have thought me mad, or stricken with sunstroke. But before I heard the faint echo of the camel's bell I had reached the lake, I had drunk of its water, and was sitting beside it resting. And what joy there was in the caravan when the camels bent down their long necks and began to "sloop" up the water in long greedy mouthfuls. We were so delighted that we could not help smiling for pure joy.

The water had a slightly saltish taste, but was nevertheless quite drinkable. It was no easy matter to get across the long, narrow lake which lay between us and the Kara-koshun. Chernoff, however, refused to give in until he had discovered a suitable ford where the water was only about three feet deep. Next day we crossed over. The camels were so delighted with their bath that we could hardly get them out of it. The opposite shore was uncomfortably soft, just as though a gutta-percha sheet were spread over a gigantic bowl of porridge; we were afraid we should go through and perish in it.

South of the lake we once more plunged into a labyrinth of sand-dunes 30 to 35 feet high. The camels kept casting longing and melancholy glances behind them, wondering why we left so soon the pleasant water that had saved our lives. The heat was stifling and the sun shone straight in our faces. In the hottest part of the day we used to dawdle along at the pace of a funeral procession, and it was not until well on in the afternoon that our energies woke up again. That afternoon we at length beheld, from a hill-top, quite close to our feet the vast expanse of the marsh of the Kara-koshun, with its perfectly fresh water and girdle of thick reeds. We were saved—delivered from the ban of the desert.

No traveller crossing the desert could dream of a more delightful view than that which presented itself from the opening of my tent close at the water's edge. The evening breeze, which came across the immense open expanse of the lake, made the tent canvas flutter with a most pleasant sound. The ripple of the water against the shore was the sweetest of music to my ear, and I could not take my eyes off the flocks of wild-duck and wild-geese which rocked far out on the rippling wavelets of the lake. But just then they led our minds to other thoughts, for we were ravenously hungry, reduced to nothing but skin and bone.

The 3rd April broke with a hard tempest from the north-east. The surface of the lake was covered with foam-crested waves, which drove straight across towards my tent on the south-west shore. The sight of them inspired me with a crazy idea. My lungs were so full of sand and dust that I felt I could not withstand the temptation they offered. Cost what it would, I must out upon the bright water. But where were we to get a boat from, for we had none, and the shores of the lake were uninhabited. But where there's a will there's a way. Round the shores there was plenty of dry wood, but it was so heavily charged with drift-sand that, when I tried it, it sank. Well, never mind, here are six empty goat-skins and the wooden frames with which they were fastened on the camels' backs. Carrying these materials round to the north-east end of the lake, we inflated the goat-skins, tied them fast to two of the frames, and, behold! our vessel was ready. When

Chernoff put himself on one of the frames, the crazy affair threatened to capsize, until I took my place on the other, and so restored the equilibrium. There we sat straddlings, half-naked, with our legs dangling in the water. Our backs acted as sails, and away we went, slowly drifting before the wind, straight across the lake towards the tent. As we advanced, the wild-duck kept rising in tumultuous flocks above our heads. Every wave that passed us wetted us to the skin; but we had no time to think of such things; we had to hold on tight and keep our balance, to prevent ourselves from being washed "overboard."

The wind chilled our backs, so that by the time we reached the middle of the lake I had had more than enough of it, and wished I were well on shore. In fact, we got so cold that our teeth actually chattered. And no sooner did we land than we flung off our clothes, dried and warmed ourselves, and then went to bed to get our blood in circulation again.

At sunset the sky assumed a remarkable appearance. The whole of the eastern horizon turned a strange fiery yellow, as though it were on fire. I knew from experience what that meant, and soon the "black tempest" was sweeping like thunder across the earth, and the waves were beating with frenzied fury against the shore, so that my tent was smothered with spray and had to be moved further back. The next few days we travelled beside the Kara-koshun, searching for the fishing settlements. Once we saw a black column of smoke rising skywards; it showed that the Lop-men were out in their canoes and had set fire to the reeds. At length we reached their village of Kum-chapghan, after traversing a labyrinth of marshes and connecting strips of dry ground. At Kum-chapghan we rested, living almost entirely upon fish.

From that village I made two excursions by canoe across the marshes and lakes, penetrating as far as the reeds would allow me; but these grew at last so dense that we were easily able to walk upon them in those places where they had been beaten down by the storms. Here the natives were busy plundering the nests of the wild-ducks and wild-geese of their eggs. I was paddled from lake

A Chapghan or Reed-pass in Lake Kara-koshun.

to lake by sinewy and confident Lop-men, who forced their long canoes through the narrow passages which they cut through the reeds. On one open expanse of water we saw a solitary swan. After him went my canoe-men as hard as they could paddle. The swan tried to escape by diving. The canoes were hurriedly driven to the spot where the men expected the swan to reappear; and in this way the poor bird was driven bit by bit towards the edge of the reeds. These were at least 25 feet high and proportionately thick, and when the swan dived in amongst them, it was done for, being unable any longer to use its wings. After it went the canoe like an arrow, and one of the men, jumping into the water, seized hold of the swan and killed it. In the reeds close by we found a dead swan, which had been wounded two or three days before and had died from its wounds. It was its grieving mate that we now killed. I do not know whether it is true, but the natives of Kara-koshun told me that swans are very sensitive and feeling birds. Ördek once let fly into the middle of a flock that was flying overhead. Two of the swans tumbled into the lake, but only one of them was dead, the other came down because, he said, it was unable to desert the object of its affection.

It took me 25 days to return from Kum-chapgan to our winter quarters at Yanghi-köl. The Mussulmans took back our animals, while Chernoff and I made our way by canoe. The first day two of the camels which were now shedding their winter wool, so that they looked as bare and comical as newly-fledged crows, dragged our two splendid canoes sledge-fashion overland to a newly-formed river-arm. Then we made our way up one deltaic branch of the Tarim after another, paddling against the current, crossing the lakes and threading the labyrinthine ways of the stifling forests of reeds until one evening we at length landed at our peaceful bay, where our brave old ferry-boat lay rocking at her cables.

There we found everything well, except that Parpi Bai had died during our absence. I missed him greatly, for he had been with me in Tibet in 1896.

In my capacity as chief of the expedition, I now granted myself ten days' leave of absence, but spent them nevertheless in arduous work. Meanwhile, the commissariat department had their hands more than full. In addition to buying some 30 horses, they laid in a stock of provisions to last for several weeks. The market-place in our little village was transformed into a shipyard ; we had to repair the big ferry-boat, which we were about to use again. In place of the tent on the fore-deck we constructed a very

Poplars Growing Beside the Ilek, a Branch of the Tarim.

comfortable hut, which we covered with white felt carpets and furnished in the usual way, except that there was no mat on the floor, for I should now want all the air I could get, including that which came up through the chinks of the floor. My writing-table was shaded by an awning, while at night the hut could be entirely closed so as to keep out the gnats and mosquitoes. From one of the beams of the roof was suspended by wires our best candelabra, constructed out of a sardine-box. The Cossacks made for themselves a similar hut on the afterdeck.

No sooner was all this finished than I set the Cossacks a fresh problem to solve. The fact is my little canvas skiff always excited the greatest possible amazement in the honest Lop-men, but when I went on to tell them that we had at home a boat that was able, with the help of a sail, to advance against the wind they shook their heads and cried: "No, sir, it's impossible to ad-

Among the Reeds in a Tarim Lake.

vance against the wind without paddles." I therefore bought a suitable canoe, decked her over and provided her with an iron keel—namely, two of our iron bars—a rudder, mast and sail. At the end of a couple of days the Cossacks had the little "cutter" ready, and I tried her on the river, where it was broad and open. It was blowing hard, and the little craft cut like a knife against the wind. Great was the amazement of the natives who had gathered from far and near to witness the spectacle. But I did well not to mind about water, for the little craft

The Ferry-boat after its Re-construction.

lay over to such an extent that I had to sit astride the windward gunwale.

The happy days of my holiday were soon past, and once more the caravan was loaded up and ready to start. This time the Cossacks Chernoff and Cherdon were the leaders of the caravan, and they had orders to make their way to the fertile valley of Mandarlik in Northern Tibet, where I was to join them two months later. Accordingly we said good-bye to our peaceful village by the Tarim, to which the natives had given the name of Tura-salghan-uy, meaning "the house which the great man built." As we turned our backs upon it, we saw a flock of conceited crows marching about inspecting it, though for the future the chief inhabitants of our deserted huts would be scorpions and spiders. It was very fortunate that we were not settled there a year later, for when the spring freshets swept down the river early in 1901, they carried away the whole of the left bank, and our huts and stable and the solitary poplar that adorned our market-place all disappeared in a moment and were never seen again.

## CHAPTER XII.

### BOAT EXCURSIONS ON THE STORMY LAKES.

No sooner had the echo of the caravan-bells died away in the forest than I, with Sirkin, Ördek and some men to paddle, set off from the ferry-boat in two canoes, to map and sound the lake of Gölme-ketti on the right bank of the Tarim. This lake, which is barely six miles long, lies embedded amongst gigantic dunes. Current and paddles helping them, our light craft danced merrily down the river, and shot into the narrow canal which connects the stream with the lake. The bright green, white-crested waters of the Gölme-ketti stretched a long way to the south. But it was a rather dangerous journey, for the wind increased to half a gale. Even whilst on the river we had had to stop two or three times to bale. Now, however, we had the broad deep lake before us, and its waves were running high. Deep did I say? indeed no. For a long way out the water was so shallow that, when our canoes dipped down into the troughs of the waves, they were in danger of grounding on the sandy bottom. The real danger lay in a wave striking us broadside on. For your Lop canoe is a mere cockle-shell of a thing, hewn out of a single poplar-stem, and round underneath, so that one who is unaccustomed to it has the greatest possible difficulty in keeping his balance. At the least movement over turns the canoe, and its occupant is spilled into the water.

But this tendency the Lop-men parry with their paddles, which nearly always lie flat on the water; besides which they balance themselves with as much unconscious ease and certainty as we do on a bicycle.

In order to avoid the shallow water we had to keep a good bit out from land; but the lake now ran so high that the crest of every wave swept right over the low gunwale of the canoe, and I was soon sitting in a sitz-bath. The situation was critical; we could not hold out much longer, and the canoes were already half full of water. All at once down went Sirkin's canoe, and its occupants lay scrambling in the surge. The men reached shore partly by wading, partly by swimming, and after a while we saw them calmly wringing the water out of their clothes.

Meanwhile my canoe was being tossed about like a nutshell. I was kept busy bailing, while the canoe-men plied their paddles with all their might, making straight for shore. Every wave drenched us as with a shower-bath; so that the felts upon which I was sitting were soon saturated through and through. Involuntarily we shrank from every fresh wave that approached. Ha! down we go! Out jumps every man, and fortunately the water is shallow, only reaching to our waists. I only just managed to save my instruments and papers.

It was pitch dark when we began our return journey. Indeed, it quite puzzles me how the canoe-men were able to find their way amongst the sand-banks in the river, yet they never once ran aground. A fire was burning on the shore, and the "saloon" of our ferry-boat was brilliantly lighted up when we arrived alongside.

The next day we started with the ferry-boat, which travelled down stream at a good smart pace. The crew consisted now of Sirkin and Shagdur, Ördek, and four men at the punting-poles, besides two fine old fellows, namely, Pavan Aksakal (the white-bearded hunter) and

Kirgui Pavan, an old man who rendered me very important service in 1896, for he knew all that country most intimately. Our dogs consisted on this occasion of Mashka, Yoldash, and the two pups that had just been given to me. These last were very comical little creatures, especially when, in spite of their vigorous protests, they were dipped in the Tarim.

The current ran strong, and it was grand to see the banks disappearing so rapidly behind us. An entire flotilla of

Children on the Bank of the Tarim.

native canoes manœuvred around us. All was life and movement on board; and the Cossacks, when they were not sitting talking outside their cabin, spent their time on shore duck-shooting.

But after a few days the river became irregular, being broken up into a number of small shallow lakes, entirely overgrown with reeds, through which it was not easy to force the ferry-boat. It is true there were a number of canals, in which the Lop-men were accustomed to place their nets, but these were generally too narrow for our vessel. In one of these canals we very nearly got stuck helplessly fast. It was five feet too narrow, and shut in on both sides by hedges of reeds 12 to 14 feet high and of amazing

Women and Children Looking on with Curiosity.

density; while, to make matters worse, the passage was so shallow that the ferry-boat would not float. We were obliged to call in people with spades from all the adjacent fishing villages. At the end of a couple of hours the native canoes came streaming up from every direction. The canal was deepened, and the reeds chopped away on both sides, and we were then able to force the ferry-boat along, though only foot by foot. All this took, it is true, a good deal of time; but it was delightful, although close, in the watery avenue. The gadflies, however, were an intolerable nuisance, filling the air in perfect crowds, and swarming all over the sheet of the map I was at work upon.

When the reeds grew so thick that spades and axes were no longer any use we set fire to them. And even though the sun was shining brightly, this marsh fire made a magnificent spectacle. The flames spread with alarming rapidity. The dry kamish stalks crackled and exploded, and when the flames came in contact with the water they made it hiss and boil and steam. The fire spread through the reed-brakes like flowing lava, while clouds of pitch-black smoke hung like a pall above the marsh. Two or three times the fire began to run in the direction of the ferry-boat, and I feared that she too would fall a victim to its rapacity. It was like adventuring upon a burning lake. The device proved, however, successful, and we eventually encamped at the village of Jekkenlik-ui, or the House of Sedges, situated on an island.

On 25th May, accompanied by Shagdur and two or three trusty canoe-men in two canoes, I made an excursion to the large lake of Begelik-köl situated in the sandy desert. Old Kirgui Pavan also went with us. After crossing over the Yäkänlik-köl, we dragged the canoes over a tongue of land and launched them upon the long narrow canal-arm which leads into the lake we were bound for.

The air was perfectly still, not a leaf of the reeds moved, and not a sound was heard except the occasional quacking of a duck. The immense lake was as bright and as motionless as glass; it was a shame to disturb its limpid purity. The reflection of the chain of dunes on the water was as clear and sharp-cut as the original; in fact it was confusing, for we had one scene above us, another below us, and both alike presented the same features of yellow desolation and sterility. The lake, however, was a lovely sheet of water, one wide expanse of glittering crystal blue. We were paddling due south and the sun shone in our faces, making the lake like a heated oven. It was only by dint of continually sprinkling my thin white clothes with water that I was able to keep myself in any degree cool.

The day was spent in strenuous and successful labour, in sounding and measuring the lake. When I climbed to the top of a high dune to study the country around, the sand was so intensely hot that it burnt through my shoe-soles. And after returning to the canoes it was delightful to sit for awhile with my feet dangling in the water. But we were soon awakened out of our *dolce far niente* by Kirgui Pavan, who pointed to the top of the steep dunes on the opposite or eastern side of the lake, and cried in a questioning undertone, "Kara-buran" (Black Tempest)? A dark column was rapidly lifting itself above the horizon, bearing on its shoulders a wreath of lighter-coloured clouds. Then several others mounted up on both sides of it, and gradually they all fused together, making one vast cloud with a serrated upper edge. Everybody knew what that meant.

For one moment we paused to consider what we should do. The Lop-men voted unanimously for waiting where we were. Kirgui Pavan, whilst not at all afraid, said that it would be difficult to paddle across the biggest and deepest basin of the lake, which separated us from the entrance to the canal, before the storm burst. Had we been able to keep along the shore, it would not have been so dangerous; but the western shore where we were was penetrated by a broad deep fjord, so that whether or no we had to cross the open part of the lake.

Nevertheless, I decided to risk it. In a moment every man was in his place and the paddles in the water, and in the course of two or three minutes we were well out from

On the Begelik-köl in a Sandstorm.

shore, with the whole of the broad lake spread out before us. We raced across the peaceful water, making the spray dash high from the prows. The paddles were bent like bows, and every moment I expected to see them snap. According to the log, we travelled at the rate of $2\frac{1}{2}$ yards a second, or about $5\frac{1}{3}$ miles an hour, which may be considered pretty good for paddling. The Mussulmans were, however, uneasy in their minds, and kept ejaculating in hollow, earnest tones, "Ya Allah! Ya Allah!" (Oh God). All this while the atmosphere was perfectly motionless; but one could not help feeling that something appalling was about to happen, and the rapid changes of colour in the sky betokened how swiftly the storm was gaining ground.

"There it comes!" cried Kirgui Pavan, "over the top of the dunes!" and at the same moment the sharply defined outline of the yellow ridge disappeared and the whole of the eastern shore of the lake was swallowed up in a thick greyish-yellow haze. "Row, children, row!" he added encouragingly. "Khodaim var!" (there is indeed a God).

For one minute more all was peaceful and still, and the next the glittering mirror of the lake vanished as though it were eaten away in an instant of time by a powerful acid. The wind came with an eerie sough. Then the black tempest swooped down upon the lake, and then the first gusts struck us, and were instantly followed by several others in quick succession. Darkly the waves came rolling broadside on towards the starboard of the canoes, while broader and broader grew their hissing crests. The Lop-men plied their paddles with desperate energy; I am sure we must have travelled at the rate of six miles in the hour. "We sha'n't win through!" they cried. "We sha'n't win through! Ya Allah!" Hurriedly I divested myself of half my clothing, and made haste to secure the instruments and papers which I could not afford to lose.

"Here it comes!" screamed the canoe-men, falling on their knees, bending their bodies forward, and paddling with desperation. The strokes of their paddles followed one after the other as quickly as the blades of a paddle steamer. The canoes cleft the water like sword-fish, the spray dashing high into the air in front of them.

These first gusts were but the advance guard of the black tempest itself; that, however, very soon followed upon their heels, and struck us with such terrific force that our frail canoe would infallibly have been swamped had not the experienced Lop-men suddenly flung themselves over to windward. A moment ago, and the northern shore had hovered before us in the distance like a thin yellow line; now every feature of the shore had disappeared and we were swallowed up in the dust-haze. The gravity of the situation impressed itself upon every one of us, when we saw nothing but the seething, ravenous waves hissing all around us, and felt our canoes dancing upon them like straws.

"Hold fast to the canoe if she fills," I cried to Shagdur, who was unable to swim. Now comes the pinch! The waves rolled upon us with a hollow rumbling roar, and their plumes of foam were scattered to powder by the maddened gale. My canoe-men met the danger with marvellous skill, guiding their canoes diagonally up the waves to breaches in their crest. So far we had not taken in any very great quantity of water, and I kept bailing away with all my might; but we were all drenched to the skin by the spray which mingled with the drops of sweat that trickled down the men's foreheads.

This desperate struggle lasted for what seemed an eternity. The waves began to strike in over the bulwarks with ever-increasing frequency, and we were deluged at shorter intervals by the clouds of spray. While with one hand I bailed away without pause, with the other I endeavoured to parry, at all events to some extent, the worst onset of the waves; but in spite of all our efforts our canoe gradually filled, and became a heavier and heavier dead-weight to row. We were getting completely exhausted. We could hardly hold out another minute. Although the sun had not yet set, it was as dark as midnight.

What now? What has happened? As if by magic the tumultuous water grew smooth. We could see nothing,

Sand-dunes on the Right Bank of the Tarim.

and yet the waves had almost entirely subsided, and their crests were no longer whipped into foam. It was just as though tons of oil had suddenly been poured upon the lake. "Two feet of water!" shouted Kirgui Pavan in a tone of mingled triumph and relief. "Khodaim var!" It turned out that there was a long, narrow sandy headland jutting out from the northern shore, and, without knowing it, we had had the good fortune to land on the leeward side of this, and it now acted as a breakwater, sheltering us from the storm. A little while afterwards we caught sight of two dark objects looming through the haze; they were tamarisks, and we soon drove the noses of our canoes deep into the soft sand of the shallow beach.

Our canoe-men were quite overcome, but more by their emotions than by their exertions, and we had to let them rest a while. In the meantime Shagdur and I looked after our own belongings and bailed out the canoe. It

The Ferry-boat Fast in the Reeds.

was quite late when we started to return. After such a storm you may imagine how dark it was, in fact it could not be darker in an underground windowless vault. Even to this very day it is a perfect puzzle to me how they managed to find their way. They could not speak or take counsel with one another, they could not warn or advise one another; they might shout at the full pitch of their lungs, yet they could not be heard. The howling of the storm drowned all other sounds, as it whistled, whined, and shrilled through the kamish, the long sharp leaves of which threatened to cut our faces had we not kept them off with our arms. Thanks to them, however, we had a smooth passage through the Jekkenlik-köl. For my own part I snoozed, for I was unable to see anything at all, and could hear nothing for the deafening roar of the tempest. It was only the measured clicking of the paddles which told me that we were moving at all.

At length the reeds began to thin. A single spot in the wall of darkness ahead gleamed out a murky yellow, then grew quickly brighter—it was fire. Two seconds later we reached our ferry-boat. The air was so heavily charged with dust that we were unable to see the fire more than a score of paces away, and yet it was burning at white-heat in the fierce blast.

This was one of the very worst storms I have ever experienced. Our old ferry-boat was threatening every moment to break loose and drift across the lake, until we doubled all her cables. In the evening I packed away all smaller objects into my boxes; and it was fortunate I did so, for in the middle of the night the hut was blown over, and had to be hurriedly fastened down with ropes. But I must now cut short the story of our drift down the river, loath though I am to part from it, for it counts amongst the happiest recollections of my life.

Leaving the lakes behind us, we once more pushed out upon the Tarim. Late one night we were encamped in a quiet, peaceful recess by the river side. The men had already gone to bed, and I was sitting up alone writing. All at once the dogs began to bark furiously. I heard the splashing of paddles, and a canoe shot to the side of the ferry-boat. After a quick conversation I heard hurried steps approach, the curtain of my hut was lifted, and an unknown stranger presented himself. He was a courier from Kashgar, bringing with him a heavy post-bag of

Natives of Abdal.

letters and packets from home. After ordering Shagdur to give the man a good supper, I set to work to devour the good news he brought me, and it was three o'clock in the morning before I extinguished my light.

On the whole, however, our days passed quietly and uneventfully. When we were prevented from advancing by the storms the Cossacks used to amuse themselves with fishing. When the weather was fine we continued far on into the night, our course being illuminated by Chinese lanterns and oil lamps, which the canoes carried ahead of the ferry-boat. At such times the Cossacks used to sit in front of my work-table and chat with Kirgui Pavan and Pavan Aksakal, and at the same time the musical-box was kept going at full swing. How delightful the cool nights were after the oppressive heat of the day!

Our further course down the Tarim was through veritable clouds of gadflies, gnats and mosquitoes. But the river was now rapidly nearing its termination in the Kara-koshun, the lake, or rather marsh, in which it finally succumbs after struggling for 1,200 miles against the desert. At the fishing-station of Chighelik we said good-bye to our brave old ferry-boat, giving her as a present to the inhabitants of the place, who were beyond measure delighted with such a magnificent present. Then on a sort of make-shift craft we made our way to Abdal, where the river comes to an end. During the last few days of the journey I heard news I did not like. A fresh courier arrived, with the information that Sirkin and Chernoff were ordered to return to Kashgar in consequence of the Boxer troubles in China. There was nothing for it, but I had to send a special messenger to our head-quarters in Northern Tibet, bidding Chernoff hurry back to Abdal.

At Abdal my arrival was awaited by a caravan of camels and horses, led by Turdu Bai. There I was detained several days, first by one thing, then by another. In the first place, I had to wait for Chernoff's arrival, and then we were kept waiting several days for a good storm before we durst start. The fact is the lowlands around the marsh of Kara-koshun were rendered uninhabitable by gadflies, so that it was impossible, indeed positively dangerous, for both men and animals to venture out. Our camels had just shed their winter wool, and were perfectly bare. Both they and the horses were kept hidden in a large kamish hut, well packed all round with reeds, and it was only at night that we dared take them out to water. But it only needed a good storm from the east, and the gadflies would at once vanish like smoke.

I and the Cossacks also had to live in kamish huts. At length Chernoff turned up, but considerably cast down at having to leave us, just when we were about to begin our longed-for life amongst the mountains. Whilst waiting for the storm that would not come, I amused myself with studying the poetry of the Lop-men. I need not say it was very simple and artless, turning, as poetry does all the world over, upon love. The ideas of these people extend but a little way beyond their canoes, their fishing-nets and their excursions on the lakes. An under-current of melancholy runs through all their songs, but the dominant note is love for home and the domestic circle, sentiments which in all their touching naïvety never fail to move. Unpretentious, monotonous, and poverty-stricken though the lives of these people are, they nevertheless cherish a warm affection for their native land and its reed-grown lakes.

## CHAPTER XIII.

### UP INTO DESOLATE TIBET.

At last I grew tired of waiting, and on 30th June I issued orders that the caravan should appear at nightfall, ready to start, outside our hut. No sooner were the camels led out of their stable than the gadflies began to buzz about them in clouds. As fast as each was loaded up, four men were told off to drive away the insects from it with wisps of kamish. As soon as the sound of the caravan-bells had died away, I turned to say good-bye to Sirkin and Chernoff; and after thanking them for all they had done for me, I shook hands with them and watched them disappear, amid a cloud of dust, along the road leading to Charkhlik and Kashgar.

As soon as it was night, I took my place with two canoe-men in a light and comfortable canoe, and was speedily flying along the very last section of the course of the Tarim. The moon was just setting, but the air was clear and the stars glittered brightly above the wandering lakes, upon which we soon glided out, whilst a gentle breeze breathed softly through the reeds. But we were soon in the midst of the dense reed thickets, where no summer night breezes were able to penetrate. There it was oppressively warm, and miasmatic and other evil vapours arose from the heated water. I had already mapped this region, so that I was able to let myself drop off into an occasional doze.

Towards morning my canoe-men fell to singing to keep themselves awake; but we were then not very far from the rendezvous, and just as day was breaking, up came the caravan, marching to the sound of their own bells.

Here we quitted the canoe for the saddle, and turning our backs upon the southern shore of the lake, we proceeded to cross the perfectly level, but monotonous and dreary, salt desert that stretches to the foot of the mountains. The sun rose in majestic splendour, flooding the desert with light and warmth. His rays, breaking against the fine flosky clouds which hung like a veil before him, lit them up from behind, making them look like chaplets of melting gold. The sky was as pure and as spotless as turquoise. In the brilliant illumination of the oblique, almost horizontal, rays of the rising sun the panorama of the mountains stood out in sharp, distinct outlines—an intensely fascinating picture! The mountain ranges, changing from pink to purple shades, both alike toned down by the distance, made a harmonious but charming background to the dry desert.

But no sooner did the sun shine out in the plenitude of his power than the heat became oppressive, and the air again swarmed with myriads of gadflies, which we in vain attempted to keep off with our riding-whips. We halted at an early hour of the morning beside a salt well, and for the rest of the day it was an awful business to defend the camels against their sworn enemies.

Next morning I was called at three o'clock, and breakfast, consisting of tea, eggs, and bread, was served by candle-light. An hour after that we were off, for we had a long road, about 40 miles, before us. We took water with us in two or three copper utensils. The surface, which was hard and strewn with gravel, with not a blade of grass to be seen, ascended gently towards the foot of the mountains. At varying and capricious distances small heaps of stones were built up for the purpose of guiding travellers in a storm. Asiatics manifest a certain amount of respect for their roads and tracks, and gratefully consider it their duty, when passing, to add a stone or two to each of these wayside mounds.

Our two little pups soon grew tired, and were then packed away in a basket and covered over with felts. Yoldash and Mashka were unable to endure the heat, and although we gave them a drink of water occasionally, they kept dropping behind incessantly. At length we neither heard nor saw anything of them. Thereupon Shagdur rode back and found them lying amongst the sand, which they had scratched to one side, in the shade of a little clay terrace. Yoldash at once rose and followed when Shagdur called him, but Mashka refused to move. Shagdur thereupon put him on the saddle in front of him; but before he had got very far the dog turned queer, and his head drooped limply against the horse's shoulder. The Cossack poured down his throat the last few drops of water he had, but it was no use; the poor beast was already dead, and he left him lying by the roadside. With the view of saving Yoldash, we tied him, notwithstanding his desperate protests, on the back of a camel and covered him over with a felt, and there he lay and growled, and felt "awfully sea-sick." The big caravan which preceded us to Mandarlik had suffered greater losses amongst their dogs than we did, for no less than eight either died on the way up or ran away back to the lakes.

Yes, it was a bad bit, this strip of desert that separated us from the mountains! But by the time the sun had got over to the west we had reached our goal, after a tramp of 14½ hours. We rested for a while in the first little glen we came to, where there was a brook rippling amongst the luxuriant grass. And you should just have seen Yoldash, when he heard the water singing amongst the stones!

He pricked his ears, barked, and bit at everything he could reach in his frantic efforts to get at liberty; and no sooner were he and his two younger playmates—the latter somewhat stiff and "groggy" on their feet—set down than they plunged into the brook and began to lap up the water with feverish haste. I confess it was a real pleasure to see them. When they had drunk their fill, they stretched themselves at full length in the water, and then went

The Dogs Malenki and Malchik.

and had a good roll in the grass, and then back again to drink. If only Mashka had been there to share it with them!

We now made our way slowly up over the double range of the Astyn-tagh, which forms a boundary wall between the Central Asian desert and Tibet. Fresh air, bright nights, an occasional light and welcome rain, no gadflies—how delightful it all was! Upon reaching Temirlik, in the broad valley of Chimen, we were already 13,000 feet above the sea. There we were met by two messengers from our head-quarters camp, announcing that all was well. Both messengers were strangers to us. One of them was called Khodai Värdi, a stupid fellow, who afterwards tried to play me a nasty trick. The other was a young Afghan from Cherchen, called Aldat. He had spent the winter amongst the mountains shooting yaks, the skins of which he used to sell to merchants in Keriya. Young and handsome, he roamed those high mountainous tracts all the year through, leading the life of a hunter. The only things he carried with him were his rifle, sheepskin coat, knife and steel for striking fire. He supported himself upon the flesh of the yaks he shot and the spring water from the melting snows. Aldat was a likeable, though singular, person. He never laughed, never spoke, except it was necessary; answered questions curtly and to the point, and almost always kept to himself, with his rifle on his shoulder. His countenance was melancholy, his glance questioning and full of wonder. His gait was like that of a king; he seemed to skim over the ground as lightly as the antelopes, and the thin mountain air never made him tired, though it caused all the rest of us violent heart-beating. Without a moment's hesitation Aldat accepted the invitation to accompany me in my first Tibetan expedition. What a strange, and yet, at the same time, what a delightful life was his!

"What do you do," I asked, "if you fail to shoot a yak and have nothing to eat?"

"I go hungry," he answered.

"Where do you sleep of nights?"

"In a crevice of the rocks or in a ravine, sometimes in a cave."

"Are you not afraid of being disturbed by wolves?"

"I have tinder and flint, and every night I make a fire. Besides, I have my rifle."

The Head-quarters Camp at Mandarlik—Looking Down the Glen.

"But don't you sometimes lose your way amongst these tangled mountains ?"

"I *cannot* lose my way. I have crossed over the passes scores of times."

"And do you never grow tired of being alone ?"

"No, but I always look forward to the spring, when my brothers come to fetch the yak-skins."

What a restless wandering spirit in human guise! I can hardly imagine a more dreary region to be alone in than Northern Tibet. In the daytime it would perhaps not be so bad; but what about the nights, when the cold freezes you to the marrow, and the dark mountain-ranges loom up weird and threatening in the moonshine? I confess the man was a puzzle to me. I had everything I wanted—servants, a bodyguard of Cossacks, sentinels and dogs to keep watch at night; nevertheless, when the snowstorms whirled and whined around my *yurt* (Mongolian tent) in the mountains, I confess I felt it decidedly eerie.

Two or three days later we arrived at our head-quarters in the valley of Mandarlik, and found everybody, men and animals included, in first-rate condition. The fresh caravan which I here organized embraced the following: Cherdon, my right-hand man, tent man, valet and cook; Turdu Bai, leader of the seven camels; Mollah Shah, chief of the eleven horses and one mule; Kutchuk, boatman for the lake trips I contemplated; Niaz, a gold-hunter, whom we came across in the mountains, was to look after 16 sheep which we took with us to kill; while Aldat acted as guide as far as his local knowledge extended. Yoldash, Malchik, and a big yellow Mongol dog, which we had obtained from our nearest Mongol neighbours, were also of the party.

Shagdur was appointed chief of the head-quarters camp, with instructions to remove it after a few days to Temirlik.

Clearly and distinctly the echoes gave back the sound of the caravan-bells, when, on 20th July, we started up

The Start from Mandarlik.

between the granite cliffs of Mandarlik to explore regions that were then absolutely unknown. Even at the first camp we made the scenery had assumed a more typically Alpine character, the altitude being 13,070 feet above the sea. There was a brook in the valley, which made a merry tinkling as it flowed, and beside it were pretty little flowers embedded in luxuriant moss. The only fuel to be obtained was the dry dung (*argol*) of yaks and *kulans* (wild asses). The shrill whistling of the marmots outside their earthen burrows, and the chattering of partridges, echoed on the mountain sides. Cherdon shot some of the latter for our larder.

Next morning, July though it was, we were in the midst of winter, the country being buried under a thick fall of snow. If the weather was like that in the middle of summer, what must it be in the depth of winter? When we continued on the 22nd, making for a glen with scanty grazing, it was still snowing, and during the following night the snow came down thick and fast, and we had 8½ degrees of frost.

At daybreak I was awakened by a fearful tumult in the camp, and hurrying out saw plainly that something strange had happened. The ground between our two tents was trampled by wolves. All the sheep had disappeared, with the exception of the four which were tied up, and Niaz had vanished too. All the men went off to look for them, and managed to find nine sheep scattered amongst the hills, but all torn to pieces by the wolves; they only saved one, while one was missing altogether.

Niaz, who was so excited that he was trembling from head to foot, described the night's adventures as follows. He had lain down to sleep as usual under a felt carpet near to the sheep, and had been awakened in the middle of the night, which was pitch dark, by hearing the bleatings of his charges, though their cries were but faint, owing to the roar of the storm. Jumping up, he detected three wolves amongst them, which had stolen up against the wind and were in the act of cutting them out and driving them away from camp. It never occurred to stupid Niaz to awaken any of the rest of us, but away he rushed impetuously on foot after the sheep, and had spent the whole of the night running up and down like a madman, without saving more than a single animal. The attack had been cunningly carried out. The dogs even had noticed nothing ; but then our Mongol beast had run away. Yoldash was sleeping in my yurt, while the inexperienced Malchik lay curled up like a hedgehog behind the men's tent. Next day we had only just started when we saw the lost sheep come galloping down the mountain-side. It was welcomed with shouts of joy, for it was but natural that we should rejoice more over the one sheep that was found than over the nine that were lost.

Upon reaching the crest of the gigantic range of the Chimen-tagh we attained the respectable altitude of 14,000 feet, and during the course of the 24th July we crossed over two ranges even higher. I was always a long way behind the rest of the caravan, for I had my map to make, photographs to take, and so forth. My companions on this occasion were Cherdon and Tokta Akhun, one of our special friends from Abdal, who was accompanying us the first few days of our journey. The day sped on ; we kept closely in the track of the caravan, and began to look eagerly for the column of smoke that should show where our camp-fire was. We had already crossed one of the ranges, and were riding up a narrow glen, which led to the summit of the second. The vegetation began to die away, and we were reaching more inclement altitudes. It grew dusk, and soon it grew dark. Evidently the caravan had pushed on over the next pass. It would, of course, have been an easy enough matter simply to have ridden on after it until we overtook it. But then I was tied down by my map, which I could not continue in the dark. There was therefore nothing to be done but we must stop where we were. I sent on Tokta Akhun, with orders to return as quickly as possible with my yurt and my boxes.

The beat of the horses' hoofs on the gravel in the bottom of the valley soon died away, and I and my Cossack were left alone in the darkness and bitter cold, at an altitude of 15,240 feet above the sea. We crept deeper into our skin overcoats, and sat and talked. Cherdon told me about his adventures during their military manœuvres in Trans-Baikalia, and I described the melancholy nights I had spent in the Desert of Takla-makan. The frost began to nip, and the wind came cutting like a knife down the glen. We sought shelter behind two big blocks of stone, but it was too cold to sleep. We were tired after being eleven hours in the saddle, and a cup of hot tea would have gone down amazingly. It would not have been so bad if we could have made a fire, but there was no fuel to be had, and even if there had been any we could not have found it in the dark. Then we dozed off a little, but were soon wakened up by the long-drawn howl of a wolf; evidently there were more than we that were going supperless that night. Finally, we had to get up and stamp our feet, and swing our arms about to keep our blood in circulation. At length, at three o'clock in the morning, after a wait of five hours, the relief caravan turned up, and I need not say how good supper tasted after our seventeen hours' fast.

After that we crossed the mountain-range of the Kalta-alagan, and directed our steps westwards along a broad flat valley, in which a great number of kulans were grazing. Upon reaching Camp No. XV. I was astonished to find at the entrance to my yurt a couple of fresh acquaintances, namely, two small kulan foals, only a few days old; they were trotting about at liberty and showing not the slightest

Two Views of the Wild Ass Foals.

sign of fear. The men had ridden them down after their mothers had taken to flight. They were pretty, charming creatures, were these young wild asses, and I wanted to try and rear them on porridge and take them along with us. But Tokta Akhun, who was an experienced kulan hunter, declared that they could not live five days without their mothers' milk. When he told me that, I ordered the little things to be taken back to the locality where they had been captured, so that their mothers might find them again. But even of this Tokta Akhun would hear nothing. He had learned by experience that the wild she-ass shuns her offspring like the plague once it has been touched by human hands. The only service I could therefore render to these helpless creatures of the wilderness was to have them killed, to save them from being cruelly torn to pieces by the wolves which abounded in that region.

Our route still lay towards the west, down the valley to the lake of Kum-köl. Immediately on the left of our route was a continuous belt of gigantic sand-dunes. The open valley was infested by a species of gadfly, which terribly tormented our horses and the wild game by fastening themselves in their nostrils. When the kulans are attacked by these enemies, they protect themselves by keeping their noses close to the ground and grazing. The yaks, on the other hand, quit the scene, taking refuge at sunrise up amongst the sand-dunes, where there were no gadflies, and towards evening they used to come down to the steppes again. That afternoon, however, about four o'clock, there sprang up a violent storm of intermingled hail and rain, and the yaks understood that their tormentors would then retire from the scene, so that they might safely go down and begin to graze. The first to show itself was a cow with her calf, which came sliding down the steep sandy slope; but as soon as she caught sight of us, she at once turned back. Then appeared a herd of over thirty indivi-

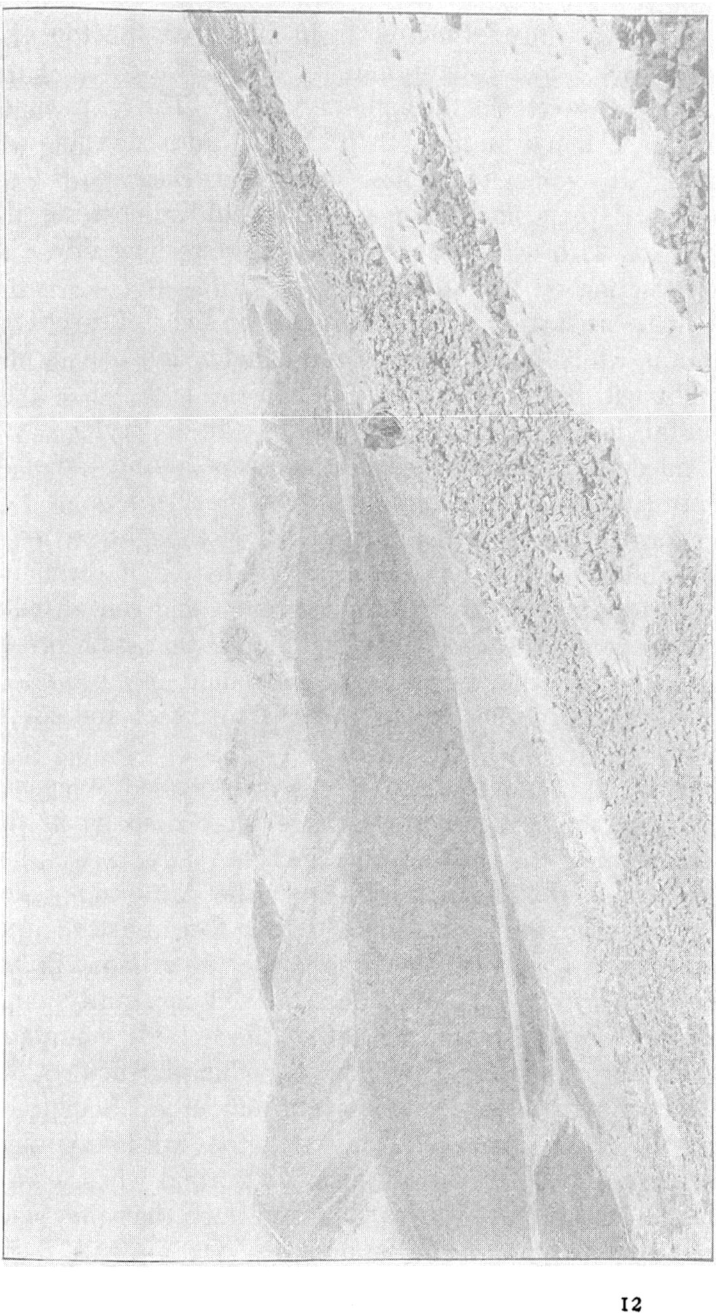

View from the Pass, over the Arka-tagh.

duals, who arranged themselves in a line on the top of a lofty dune. I had to stop and for a time watch the truly magnificent spectacle through my glass. The yaks made an extraordinary picture, their black hides standing out sharply cut against the yellow sand, while their heads were lifted as if they smelt danger. We could almost see the enjoyment with which they sniffed the refreshing rain that was pattering on the hillsides.

A little bit farther on Cherdon caught sight of a solitary wolf-cub, which he rode down, and caught, and bound, and brought with him to our camp beside the lake. The little brute bit fiercely, and made no end of a to-do, trying every art and device it was master of to escape. And although the Mussulmans, who could not forget the sheep which had been torn to pieces, tied him up as they thought securely, the cunning beast managed to get the better of them, for during the night he bit the rope through and ran off with the noose round his neck. My men hoped that, as he grew, the rope would choke him; but I thought it more likely that the cub's mother would gnaw it to pieces and so set him free.

During the next two weeks we crossed over the biggest and highest mountain range, that is so far as the general level of the crest is concerned, not only of Asia, but of the whole world—that is to say, the Arka-tagh. The main pass reached an altitude of 17,000 feet above the sea, or more than 1,200 feet higher than the top of Mont Blanc. Then for nearly two months we remained constantly at an altitude considerably above that of the highest mountain-peak in Europe. Need I say that travelling in such regions is attended with a certain amount of difficulty. Sometimes we would travel for several days together without finding a blade or a twig for the animals to eat, and when we did at length find any, it was so thin and hard that they were unable to satisfy their hunger upon it. Our animals, there-

The Pass over the Arka-tagh, Looking North.

fore, began to grow thin and weak. Cherdon's horse, of which he was especially fond, and which would come when he called it, was the first to succumb. The nature of the ground, too, was trying in the extreme. We were incessantly going up passes and down glens and gorges, threading a perfect labyrinth of mountains. Almost every day I had to send one or two men southwards to find out a path by which the caravan could advance. Day by day we penetrated some twelve or fifteen miles further towards the heart of unknown Tibet. But in proportion as the animals' strength gave out so did our store of provisions shrink, though this helped them by making their loads gradually lighter. We had not the heart to slaughter our four remaining sheep, which now followed us of their own accord like dogs, and fortunately we had no need to do so, for in the entrance to a glen Aldat managed to surprise and bring down two orongo antelopes, creatures which have elegant, lyre-shaped horns. Cherdon's cartridges were now all finished, and the only ammunition we had was that which Aldat used for his old-fashioned musket.

Nevertheless, I enjoyed the journey, and rejoiced in the knowledge that I was the first European who had ever travelled amongst those mountains, where tracks there are none save those made by the wild animals, and footprints there are none except those impressed by yaks, kulans and antelopes. It was a No Man's Land; rivers, lakes and mountains were without names. For the space of some six or eight weeks I felt as if it were my kingdom—a land of stupendous earth-waves suddenly converted into stone!

On the night of 6th August, when, after a hard day's work, I went out of my tent, the sky was clouded; but far away in the south there was a massive glacier, the broad *firn* expanses of which shone pale and cold under the midnight moon. My men were all fast asleep, the caravan animals all secured, the camp-fires burning low, and not a

On the Summit of the Arka-tagh.

sound was to be heard save the pensive, murmurous song of the brook rippling amongst stones. The night was brooding silently and serenely above the untrodden wilderness. Far away in the south I pictured to myself the mighty buttress of the Himalayas, with India and its sultry jungles at their feet. Far away in the west our Tibetan mountains merged into the Pamir highlands, while in the opposite direction when the sun rises upon us it is already noon-tide in the Celestial Kingdom. In vain did I look for a fire or any trace of a human being. I was in an uninhabited and uninhabitable part of the earth. I felt like a grain of dust in the midst of the boundless universe, and almost fancied I could hear the "swish" of the planets as they rolled on their never-ending orbits through the immensities of space.

## CHAPTER XIV.

### EXPLORING THE LAKES OF TIBET.

CAMP XXIV. was made on the shore of a salt lake, with not the slightest suspicion of vegetation anywhere visible. But to make amends, we had on the south only a low chain of rounded hills, a mere bagatelle in comparison with the ranges we had recently crossed. I rode on in advance towards the summit of the range; but the surface, which consisted of wet mud, grew softer and softer, and splashed and squelched with every step the horse took. At last I had to get off and lead him, until, finally, I nearly lost one of my own boots, sucked off my foot by the mire. After that I decided to wait for the caravan. When it came up, the men were panting, and the patient and submissive camels toiled after them, sinking in foot-deep at every step, and yet they were better supported by their broad, padded feet than were the horses with their hard hoofs.

Our hearts beat violently until we feared they would burst. The ground rocked and heaved, making us all giddy. There were several slabs of stone lying scattered about, but even they sank into the ooze when we trod on them, leaving a hole that rapidly filled with water. You would think that the entire range of soft, jelly-like mud would flatten itself out more and more, until it ran into the lake. The causes of the ground turning to this abominable consistency were the rain and the entire absence of vegetation.

At length it grew so bad that we had to turn back, and then we made our way down a broad valley, in which we found a small flat expanse, with miserable grazing. Our animals were completely exhausted, so that we had to give them two days of rest. On the first of these we were visited by a tremendous storm. It thundered and lightened several times in the minute, and the tempest swept right over our heads quite close to the earth. The thunder crashed as though the mountains were being rent in twain, and the broken fragments were careering headlong down the mountain-sides. We were blinded by the forked lightning, and distinctly felt the earth tremble when it thundered. It is a solemn and awful thing to be at the very centre of such a tempest as that, exposed to the full brunt of its fury. The dogs howled dismally. The men's tent threatened to blow away and had to be anchored afresh. The hail clattered on the mountain-sides, and was succeeded by a copious fall of snow. At dusk all the camels were made to lie in a close ring, and were covered up with all the felt carpets we could spare, for they were literally shaking with the cold.

On 12th August we set off again, determined at all costs to get over the southern range. This time we proceeded up a broad open valley; but there, too, the ground was just as horrible, nothing but a quagmire of yellow mud, as full of water as a wet sponge, fearfully treacherous, killing! Every time an animal lifted up its foot the tenacious mire sucked audibly. The surface was now so excessively soft that footsteps, which showed at first as dark holes, were soon closed up again by the ooze. Truly, an accursed country! That grazing and fuel should be wanting at an altitude of 16,000 feet is easy to understand; but why on earth should the ground not bear us? Why should it

A General Drying. The Men, going from Left to Right, are—Aldat, Niaz, Kutchuk, Mollah Shah, Turdu Bai, and Cherdon.

threaten to engulf the entire caravan, and why was the ground as thin as the atmosphere—the last alone was almost enough to make our hearts burst when we got down and walked ?

I again mounted, but it was as much as I could do to keep my horse from pitching over on his own head at every step. It was just as though his feet were entangled with cords, from which he had to free himself before he could take a fresh step. I rode on first, seeking out a path. The caravan crawled behind like snails, and the beasts of burden, being afraid of the deepest holes, refused to step into them, but swerved to one side, though in nine cases out of ten it was like jumping out of the frying-pan into the fire. Hour after hour passed as we struggled on and on, slowly and painfully, up towards that low pass.

In the pass we met a solitary wolf. What was he doing there ? Although it was only four o'clock, it turned as dark as an autumn evening, when the usual storm came crashing like the bombardment of a fortress. The horses walked sideways, to screen themselves from the hail. "Stop ! " I at length cried, for we could see nothing. We encamped, therefore, on the miry slope, making ditches round the tents to drain off the water. There we remained an entire day, for one of our camels had lagged behind and had to be fetched in. It was as much as the men could do to make him rise, and after he did so, he soon fell again, and had to be slaughtered. It rained cats and dogs all day, and on each side of my bed there was a pool of water, which had to be conducted away by grips. The rain dripped in everywhere, through the felt coverings of the yurts, and everything was wet and uncomfortable. We all longed for a change ; we could not very well change for the worse.

On 14th August the sun once more showed himself, and we had the good fortune to find a patch of tolerable grass.

Turdu Bai and Kutchuk, with the Skiff Folded up, the Sounding-line and Lifebuoys (from a Photograph taken at Temirlik).

There we encamped and thoroughly dried our wet belongings. A week later our progress was stopped by a large lake. Encamping on its northern shore, I set off on 22nd August, with Kutchuk for my boatman, to row diagonally across the lake towards a mountain-peak near its south-east corner. Meanwhile, the caravan was to skirt round the western end of the lake and along its southern shore, until they came to the same mountain, where, at nightfall, they were instructed to light a fire, which might serve as a beacon for us in case we should still be out on the lake.

A more peculiar lake I have never seen: on the north it was so shallow that we had to walk fully a mile and partly carry, partly drag, the canvas skiff, before the water was deep enough for her to float in. The bottom of the lake was everywhere covered with a layer of salt as hard as stone, the crystals of which stuck to our boot-soles. I had brought with me a sounding-line some hundreds of fathoms long, thinking that the new lake might be as deep as the Kara-kul on the Pamirs; but the greatest depth only amounted to a paltry 7½ feet, so that our graduated seven-foot oar sufficed almost everywhere.

After passing a little bread-loaf-shaped island, we steered straight for the mountain appointed for the rendezvous. The weather was magnificent, not a cloud in the sky, which was reflected with the greatest sharpness and clearness on the surface of the lake. The tops of the encircling mountains were, however, wreathed with numerous white fleecy veils. The sun, a rare visitor in those regions, was quite warm, and we rejoiced to see this seldom glimpse of summer. Here there was not the buzz of a fly to be heard, nor the gleam of a fin to be seen in the lake; the water was as lifeless as a chemical solution. Viewed through the pure and rarefied atmosphere, the landscape presented itself as something exceptionally light and evanescent. I can only compare it to a bride in an "empire" robe of white and

A Tibetan Salt Lake.

sky-blue silk. It was the airiest *aquarell* in diluted colours, everything ethereal, transparent, like a *fata morgana*, or a half-remembered dream. The water of the lake was a lovely ultramarine blue, except close to the boat, where it was emerald green.

The lake appeared to extend east and west to an infinite distance, and it was more than six miles broad, so that from its surface we had a splendid panoramic view of the surrounding mountains. Kutchuk was rowing with steady, powerful strokes, yet we seemed to get no nearer to the object we were making for. The gurgling of the water round the oar was the only sound that broke the all-pervading silence of this Tibetan Dead Sea, the surface of which lies at an altitude of 15,635 feet above the level of the sea.

The water was so salt that the drops which trickled into the boat set like stearine, and when the moisture had evaporated it left a thin, chalky-white bee-hive shaped mass, which speedily collapsed. The oar-blades were as white as if they had been painted; our hands were white and rough, our clothes splashed all over with white spray, and the interior of the boat looked as if she had been employed for transporting flour.

In the morning we had seen the caravan skirting the western shore, but as the distance increased we lost sight of them. Upon approaching the southern shore, I began to keep a sharp lookout for them with the glass, but failed to find any sign of them anywhere.

Towards evening the hills before us began to stand out more distinctly, but the lake became as it were clouded over, and we heard a distant roaring, which we at first took for a river entering the lake. It was, however, a gale of wind setting in, and soon the lake began to run pretty high. Thereupon we hoisted sail, and very soon covered the rest of the distance.

Before twilight gave place to darkness we hurried up to the top of the nearest hill to look for the caravan. But no trace of either men or animals was to be discovered; the entire scene was lifeless, soundless, and wild, almost unearthly. I felt as if I were setting foot in a monastic ruin which had not been trodden for a thousand years. Whilst Kutchuk gathered together the scrubby *yapkak* bushes, which grew there pretty plentifully, I took a ramble on foot amongst the hills. On a slope I found a bleached kulan's skull and the footprint of a bear in the soft ground. I shouted, I listened; but I could hear nothing of the caravan, nor could I see any fire to show where it had encamped.

It was dark when I returned to our landing-place, and found that Kutchuk had gathered together a big heap of fuel. We took counsel together what was to be done. It was evident the caravan had met with some unexpected hindrance, or else a couple of the men at least would have come to the rendezvous to tell us what was amiss, and—most important of all—to bring us food, water and warm clothing. How would it be if we took advantage of the favourable wind, and sailed westwards? No, that wouldn't do; it was too dark, and the lake was too stormy for our fragile boat.

There was nothing for it but we must spend the night where we were. After carrying all our belongings up to our camping-ground, we took the boat to pieces and hauled her up too. Raising the two halves on end, we contrived behind them to get a certain amount of shelter against the wind. We had just finished our preparations when the rain came; but by tilting each half-boat at an angle and supporting it on an oar, we obtained a roof which kept us dry. I took one of the life-belts and Kutchuk the other, and with them for our pillows we succeeded in sleeping awhile before the night got too cold.

At nine o'clock we kindled a fire, and then sat over it and chatted for a couple of hours. If only we had had a little warm tea and some bread to eat, or even a glass of water, it would not have been so bad. When all our fuel was done we turned in and went to bed. After spreading the sail on the gravel, though it made it very little softer than it was before, and sinking the cork life-belt half in the ground, I lay down, drawing my limbs up into a suitable attitude, and Kutchuk placed one-half of the boat over me. My head was only an inch from the bottom of the boat, and I was packed in as tightly as if I were in my coffin, an illusion that was still further strengthened when Kutchuk, using an oar-blade as a spade, began to pack the sand and gravel all round me to keep out the draughts. My night-quarters were actually as confined and as dark as a grave. When he had done, Kutchuk packed himself away in the other half of the boat in a similar manner. Then we lay and talked for an hour or so, but my boatman's voice sounded like a voice from the dead, and my own echoed hollow and sepulchral. About midnight the rain began to pelt down, rattling like drum-sticks against the taut canvas of the boat-bottom. But what did it matter to us, we were under cover, and warm and dry. Although we were as hungry as wolves, natural weariness eventually asserted its right, and we dropped off to sleep, oblivious of the wild beasts of the wilderness and everything else.

As the night went on it turned very much colder; indeed, the cold woke me up more than once. At length daylight crept in under one of the bulwarks, and I called to Kutchuk to come and let me out. We were stiff with cold, and our first concern was to gather fuel for a fire. The next thing was to go in search of our lost caravan.

Having screwed the boat together again, we fitted her up, launched her, and stepped on board, and then hoisted the sail, one of the oars serving as a boom, the other as a rudder, and away we went westwards at a spanking pace, keeping pretty close to the shore. The wind was strong and the lake rough, so that our little craft rolled a good deal, making Kutchuk, who sat in the fore part, pale and sea-sick. Ere long I perceived at the end of the lake two white dots—our tents—and a number of black ones round about them—our animals and men.

It turned out that the caravan had been stopped by a broad stream, which issued from a large fresh-water lake farther west, and emptied itself into the salt-water lake we had just crossed. The stream was so deep that, when Turdu Bai tried to ford it on horseback, he very nearly got drowned. They had, therefore, encamped, and made up a huge fire, which, however, we had failed to see because of the great distance. Aldat fortunately shot a kulan, the flesh of which was very welcome. The men caught another little wolf-cub, which, however, took it so much to heart, that it lay down and died at once.

Here we were, then, in a nice fix! The river stopped our path on the south, while east and west were the large lakes, which it would take us several days to go round. But we could turn back? What! and cross again that abominable slough of despond, which had threatened to swallow us all up? No, thank you; we should take precious good care not to return there until after the ground froze in the autumn and was hard enough to bear us.

Forward then! I undertook to get the entire company safely across the stream, a proposal which was received by the men with a certain amount of incredulity. The river at its narrowest was 190 feet across and the current ran strong. Marching the caravan to that spot, we unloaded, collected everything in the nature of a rope that was fastened round packages and sacks, and tied them all together into one long strong cable, one end of which was secured on the side of the stream where we were. Then, after the cable had been stretched along the bank, I and Kutchuk stepped into the boat, and whilst I paddled with all my might diagonally across the stream, Kutchuk stood with the other end of the cable in his hand, ready to jump ashore and make it fast the moment we reached the right bank. The rope, however, proved too short; we failed to make the opposite bank and were carried down by the current, but eventually managed to haul ourselves back to the starting-point. Then, after adding another length of rope, we repeated our former manœuvre, and this time with better fortune. Having made our cable fast, we drew it tight from both sides, until it no longer touched the surface of the water.

Our next proceeding was to drive the horses together in a bunch, and we induced them after some hesitation to swim across the river; but to get the camels across was a far more difficult task. Nothing we could do would induce them to swim; indeed, I never have seen a camel swim. The only thing, therefore, was to haul them across one by one. After having by main force pushed and shoved the first camel into the water, we flung a rope round his neck, by means of which Turdu Bai, kneeling in the stern of the boat, kept the beast's head above water. Meanwhile, I pulled the boat across the river by hauling at the outstretched cable. But as the camel did nothing to help himself, only lay on the water and complacently floated, I had his entire weight as well as the force of the current hanging upon my hands and arms, and had to exert myself to the utmost to keep my hold, for if I had once let go we should all have drifted out into the salt lake, and the camel would have been lost. However, I got him safely across, and it was a sight to see him sprawling about until he felt firm ground under his feet, and condescended to stand upright. As he stood on the bank alone, looking wonderingly

Towing a Camel Across the River.

Firm Ground under Foot.

back after his comrades, the water ran in streams off his woolly flanks.

By the time I got the third camel hauled across my hands were quite blistered, and I had to get Cherdon to take my place. The last camel was accompanied by our last surviving sheep, for the creature always stuck close to the camels. After that we carried across all our baggage in fourteen journeys, and then re-arranged our camp on the right bank of the stream. Although that stage we only travelled between 60 and 70 yards, nevertheless we were hard at work all day from morning to night.

During the next few days we travelled across broken ground, past two or three other salt lakes. Beside the first of these Aldat shot a yak, bringing him down at the first attempt, thus enhancing his reputation as a skilful and brave hunter, for when wounded the yak is a dangerous animal.

On 28th August we found a fresh hindrance to our advance in yet another river. Whilst we were waiting for Mollah Shah, who had gone to look for a suitable spot for fording the stream, the thunder began to growl and the sky in the west grew black. Dense masses of cloud as heavy as lead rolled over the country like an invading army; but whilst the clouds of the left wing were dark, with red-coloured edges, those of the right wing were black as ink. Meanwhile, the scouts—that is to say, the advance battalion, torn to pieces by the frenzied storm—were racing along in the strangest shapes possible. In the east the country was still bathed in bright sunshine, but in the west the enemy was gathering closer and closer about us. "Off with the loads and up with the tent!" I shouted. We had only just got up the outer framework of the yurt, and flung two or three felts over the top spars, when the storm burst, assailing us with its heaviest artillery of hail. Every hailstone came as if discharged by a shot-gun, making our hands and faces smart. We literally ran helter-skelter for the nearest shelter.

We spent the next day in reconnoitring by boat. This large stream also emptied itself into a salt lake; and the salt lake was joined by yet another broad, but short, stream, which likewise came from a fresh-water lake. During the course of the trip we surprised two or three score wild-geese. As soon as they perceived us, they all took wing except one. Kutchuk lay to his oars and we soon got near to the laggard. Having no other weapon except an oar, I flung it like a spear at the bird, and managed to hit it, and a welcome change it made for supper. I may say that, our cartridges being now at an end, we made ourselves bows and arrows, and lived like Robinson Crusoe.

The last discovered lake whetted my appetite, and I resolved to ride round it, taking with me a small lightly-equipped caravan, consisting of Cherdon, Mollah Shah and Kutchuk, together with a few horses and my faithful foot-warmer-at-night—Yoldash. The rest of the men I ordered to remain where they were, with all the camels and four tired horses, for there happened to be good grazing just there.

It was not altogether an easy matter to reach the north side of the lake. Twice we had to have recourse to the skiff to ferry us across, first the river and then the broad sound. But after that all was easy. Alongside the northern shore of the lake ran a secondary mountain-range. Yaks were grazing on its hollow flanks, and inquisitive kulans advanced quite close to us to look at our horses. Moreover, foxes, hares and antelopes abounded, while the grass was better than it had been anywhere before, so that I was almost tempted to stay there awhile. A long way off in the south we could see some magnificent mountains, covered with glittering white snow-fields and crowned with vaporous clouds. The air was milder than it had hitherto been; but

The Fish Mountain.

The Fish Mountain Seen from the Middle of the Lake.

View Down the Lake—The Storm Disappearing in the Distance.

The Sun Setting on the Lake.

then we were lower than we had been for a long time, and yet for all that we were still considerably above the top of Mont Blanc. After our recent experiences this Tibetan lake-land seemed to us like an El Dorado.

Climbing to the top of a hill at the east end of a lake, I spied out the country ahead. Before me lay outspread yet another large lake, separated from the one behind me by a narrow neck of land. Very well, then, let us ride round it also. Forward! March! But the mountains grew more difficult, and we had to keep to the crest. And what a wonderful view it offered us—to the north the salt lake we had last left, and to the south the new fresh-water lakes. Tibet appeared in that part to be richer in water than in land. At one point, where the lake was broadest, the brick-red sandstone cliffs shot vertically downwards into the water. It was there that we encamped. Here, again, I went in for a similar adventure to that on the great salt lake. Next morning, whilst Cherdon and Mollah Shah continued on round the lake, Kutchuk and I set off to row across it to its southern shore.

We were in no hurry, for under the mountains were big shoals of fine fat *asmans* (fish). Our fishing-tackle was of a very makeshift description. Our fishing-rods consisted of a couple of tent-spars; our hooks were made out of Yoldash's collar; our floats were empty match-boxes, and for bait we used small pieces of yak-flesh. We anchored the skiff under the mountain precipice, although its rocks appeared to hang by only a hair, as if ready to plump down into our frail craft.

Having lit my pipe and assumed a comfortable position, I flung out my line, and then gave myself up to a delicious *dolce far niente*, while my match-box float bobbed up and down, until a good-sized *asman* succeeded in overcoming its repugnance to a "collar" hook. We were not fishing for amusement, we were fishing for food. It is true, our

A Struggle for Life.

catch was not very great, and barely sufficed for one meal all round; nevertheless, I enjoyed the rest, and found pleasure in listening to the nor'-wester, which came tumbling like a roaring cascade over the top of the mountain behind which we were sheltered. And even the imperturbable Kutchuk, whom nothing hardly could ruffle, was quite excited at finding that the fish he caught here were of precisely the same kind as those he had been accustomed to catch from his boyhood in the lakes beside the Tarim.

In this pleasant occupation the hours slipped rapidly past, and it was long after midday when I at last tore myself away from that charming spot. Just as we turned to go, it darkened in the west, and the sky filled with black clouds. Another storm was brewing. Should we wait until it had gone past, or should we risk it across the broad expanse of the open lake? I chose the latter alternative. Kutchuk had little need to row, for we very soon began to feel the nor'-wester behind us, and it helped us along splendidly. The leaden-grey hail-clouds were already trailing their long fringing draperies across the mountain-sides on the south, gradually hiding them from sight, and behind us on the north a similar act of scene-shifting was taking place. Nearer and nearer came the storm, higher and higher ran the lake, and all around us the waves were tipped with white.

"Here we are in the middle of the hail!" And down came the big hailstones, splashing the water on every side. Within a minute the inside of our boat was white. It grew as dark as twilight when we shot into a hanging cloud of hail. Not a glimpse of shore or mountain to be seen, nothing but a small patch of the tossing and tumultuous lake. "Now for it, Kutchuk! Look alive, man, we've got to fight for our lives!" The chief thing was to keep an eye on the waves, which, under the impulse of the constantly increasing wind, were being lifted to an unusual height. Fortunately they were several times longer than the boat, so that she curved gently and obediently up and down their long rolling swell. Immediately south of the cliffs where we fished I had sounded a depth of 157½ feet, but after that the lake rapidly shallowed. The further we advanced from the cliffs on the northern shore the more we became exposed to the brunt of the tempest. What would happen in this dense haze supposing the southern shore were flat and shallow, and our little boat were flung like a nutshell amongst the breakers. Fortunately, before we had travelled half the distance, the hail-storm passed over, so that we were, at all events, able to see where we were going. But, at the same time, the velocity of the wind increased, and the waves ran so high that, when we dipped down into the troughs between them, the shore became entirely lost to sight. Every now and then the sun shone through the ragged storm-clouds, weirdly lighting up the crests of the waves, which, bright as the backs of dolphins, glistened and glinted in emerald green and deep blue, whilst at the same time they were tipped with sparkling snow-white tossing spray, which flashed like jewels in the sunshine.

This time, too, everything ended happily; the storm passed on farther across Holy Tibet, the wind dropped, the features of the shore came out in sharp relief, and a column of smoke showed us where to find the welcome camp. From the lake we witnessed a glorious sunset: the sun himself was hidden behind a cloud, but his rays broke from beneath it and flooded the lake, making it glitter and vibrate like quicksilver.

## CHAPTER XV.

### SEVENTEEN THOUSAND FEET ABOVE THE SEA.

AFTER various adventures, which I have not space to relate, and after yet another dangerous boat-excursion across one of the more westerly lakes, we arrived, tired and stiff with cold, late one night, in a violent storm and blinding snow, at Turdu Bai's camp. Aldat brought me as a surprise four fat orongo antelopes, which provided us with meat for the immediate future. This camp, No. XLIV., counting from the start, was the turning-point of the journey. We could not venture to go farther south, for we had only brought provisions to last 2½ months, and it was already 50 days since we started. But before leaving this part of Tibet there was one other excursion I wanted to make. To the south was a mountain-mass covered with snow. It looked inviting, so I made up my mind I would try to get to the south of it, and chose Cherdon and Aldat to accompany me. Meanwhile, the caravan was to travel, on leveller ground, by the north side of the mountain, and it was arranged that we should meet at its western extremity at the end of four days. Whichever party arrived first was to wait for the other. As for us, it was hardly possible that we could miss the caravan's trail, but for safety's sake, in case we should miss the caravan, we took with us all the ammunition that Aldat had left. Followed by the two men, I rode up towards the mountain through winding glens. Two big white wolves followed us for a long way, and Yoldash, who was in a perfect fume at their impudence, had to be kept tied up, for he would certainly have been torn to pieces had we let him have his own way. The next evening we encamped, stiff with cold and half asleep, on a mountain-slope where a last few wretched blades of grass were growing.

As soon as the camp was ready—on these excursions we always slept under a make-shift shelter of felts—Aldat came to tell me that there was a big yak grazing high up on the mountain-side, and to request permission to stalk it. I watched him crawling like a panther along the hollows, so as to get sufficiently near to his unsuspecting victim. Thanks to the strong counter-wind, he was able to creep within thirty paces of the yak and get his weapon raised upon its fork without being perceived. Aldat fired. The yak leaped into the air, sending the earth flying all round him; then he advanced a few paces, stopped, reeled, tried to keep his balance, but fell. Raising himself, however, he repeated these movements several times, before he finally tumbled head-foremost and remained motionless. Aldat lay behind his weapon without moving a muscle, lest he should attract the dying animal's attention and draw its vengeance upon himself.

It was a fifteen-year old bull, well-grown and very fat. Our night-quarters were at an altitude of 16,875 feet above the sea, and it was trying work to climb up to the yak. After every few paces we had to stop, our hearts beat so violently that they were like to burst, and we were nearly suffocated for want of breath. It was dark before we had finished our work of cutting out the fat; but next morning Aldat went off to the yak at day-break. After that, however, we heard nothing more of him, so I sent Cherdon up to see what was become of him. Cherdon found him lying beside his victim; he had turned suddenly ill and came staggering down the mountain-side, bleeding at the nose and with a violent headache—unmistakable symptoms of mountain-sickness, a thing we were quite accustomed to, and, as a rule, it soon passed away. Cherdon and I gathered our belongings together, and loaded up our two pack-horses, and having helped Aldat up into his saddle, we began our march towards the pass which we saw like a low saddle in the west. On our right we had the massive mountain with its glacier arms; the ground was soft and the horses sank into the mire. After struggling on for several hours, we at length reached the pass, but beyond it there appeared a second, yet higher pass, and after that a third. Higher and higher we climbed in the thin murderous atmosphere, with a storm driving straight in our faces, chilling us to the very marrow. Sometimes we actually had to stop behind the nearest big block of granite for shelter. At last we did reach the very highest pass, 17,800 feet above the sea. Imagine two Eiffel Towers standing one on the top of the other, and both planted on the top of Mont Blanc! It is a giddy height, half-way through the atmospheric envelope of the earth!

Our next camp was made in an absolutely sterile region. The next day we saw in the distance some black dots down on the lowlands. They turned out to be Turdu Bai and Kutchuk; they were busy building up a pile of stones to serve as a guide to us. We now began to feel the cold keenly, and every morning I had a pot-lid filled with hot embers brought into my tent, otherwise the ink kept freezing in my pen. On the 14th September, the ground being favourable, we covered over eighteen miles. At night we were visited by an exceptionally bad snow-storm. When I stepped out as usual at nine o'clock to read my thermometers, it was pitch dark, and I could not see the men's tent, although it was only a few yards distant, but I heard the tent-canvas flapping in the wind, and the heavy and tired breathing of the camels. It continued to snow wildly all night, as I could hear by the snow being blown over my yurt.

Owing to the large quantity which fell and then melted, the country we travelled across during the succeeding days was made even more miry than it was before. The ground, however, remained frozen till noon, when it was like walking on thin ice; but in the afternoon it thawed. In one place, which the first five camels passed over without anything happening, the last, the sixth camel, went through with both fore-feet. The mire held him fast, and he began to sink in deeper and deeper. The other camels, led by Turdu Bai, continued to march on, tightening the rope which went round the nose of the sixth and connected him with those in front of him. This made the poor beast scream with pain. All the men hurried up, and began to unloosen his load and take it off. Whilst they were doing this, the camel fell over on his side, softening the ground still more. The animal refused to help himself, as he had done in the water, and there we were, floundering and stumbling about in the quagmire. I feared the camel was lost. His pack-saddle was sucked into the mud and had to be cut off where it was. It went immensely against the grain to lose this fine animal in this stupid way. Hurriedly unfastening some of the tent-felts, we brought them to where the camel was every moment sinking deeper into the slough, and putting a rope round each leg in turn, we hauled them up, first one, and then the other, and as we did so, placed each on a roll of felt. In this way we gave him firm supports to stand upon; then, after allowing him a couple of minutes to recover, we forced him, by shouting, whipping and hauling at his nose-rope, to make a desperate effort to rise. The device was successful, and the camel staggered on to firm ground, the mud and mire dripping in lumps from his legs and sides. Whilst he stood trembling, breathless and bewildered, we took our knives and scraped off his body the thick coating of clay with which it was covered.

In this way we crept across the dreary wilderness of Tibet, longing eagerly for contact with our fellow-creatures; but we had still over 240 miles to go to reach our head-quarters camp. Our animals were getting rapidly exhausted, and were only able to do short stages; accordingly, I now made it a rule that we should march three days and rest every fourth.

Meanwhile, poor Aldat was growing steadily worse. He had lost complete control of himself, both bodily and mentally, was as limp as a rag, and had a fixed vacant look in his eyes. At nights he used to ramble, talking about his mother who was dead and his old father in Cherchen. His former hunting exploits kept haunting his mind, and he continually called upon me, begging permission to go out and shoot wild yak, although he was unable to move hand or foot. At first he was able to sit upon horse-back when well tied on, but latterly we had to make a sort of bed for him on the back of a camel, in which we packed him as comfortably as we could. His feet were cold and hard as ice, and of a blue-black colour. I tried rubbing them with snow and giving him warm foot-baths; but the ominous dark colour gradually crept upwards towards his knees. He had no feeling whatever in his feet, but suffered a good deal of pain in the heart. One evening he asked to be put on the ground between two camels, for the Mussulmans believe that the warmth which is radiated from the bodies of these creatures supplies health and strength to an invalid whose own powers are waning. Once, when he was ill before, down in Cherchen, he was given small scraps of paper to swallow, written over with holy texts from the Koran; but we had no Mollah (priest) with us learned in the Mohammedan scriptures, so we could not give him that remedy. One day, when Cherdon shot an orongo antelope, we tried another Mussulman cure. Stripping the invalid completely naked, we wrapped him in the soft, still warm skin of the antelope, with the hair outwards, and pressed it close to his body till it adhered. It was indeed heartbreaking not being able to help him.

Making a Sick-bed for Aldat.

Animal life again began to be more plentiful. One morning I was awakened by a tremendous hubbub in the camp. Dogs were barking themselves frantic, the men shouting themselves hoarse. Hurrying out, I saw a big bear calmly and leisurely trotting away from the camp, which, during the night, he had subjected to a minute examination; but when the dogs attacked him, he thought it prudent to beat a retreat. Another day, Cherdon, having found one or two stray cartridges, managed to place one of them in a fatal spot in the head of a gigantic yak, whose portrait I herewith reproduce. On another occasion an inquisitive wolf met with the same fate.

This part of Tibet was literally honeycombed with the burrows of marmots. They are very comical creatures, those big, stoutly-built rodents, when, either alone or in couples, they sit sunning themselves on the heap of soil at the entrance to their holes. When we approached, they greeted us with shrill whistlings from every hillside, and tumbled into their burrows like billiard-balls. In fact, we were literally hissed off the stage by these over-critical spectators. One old patriarch, who had wandered farther than was prudent from his home, lay on his back sunning himself on the hillside with his fore-paws crossed over his stomach in an excruciatingly funny attitude. Yoldash dashed down upon him and disturbed his siesta, and whilst the old gentleman was defending himself, the men seized him and bound him, and packed him away uninjured on the back of a camel. We kept him two months and tried to tame him; but it was no use. No sooner did anybody approach him, than he sat up on his hind legs and showed his sharp teeth. The bite of this animal is said to be very difficult to heal. When we gave him a stick, he bit it to splinters. In camp we kept him fastened to a short iron rod, the other end of which was tied with a rope to a stake driven in the ground. He was thus able to range in a circle all round the stake, and every evening he began to make a hole in the ground. If he served no other purpose, he at any rate amused the men by his comical antics whenever we encamped. He manifested a deadly antipathy to our dogs, which, however, never molested him.

Kulans were now numerous, and I never grew tired of watching the perfection of their slender forms and their elegant movements. Six individuals came one day quite

The Wild Yak Shot by Cherdon, with Mollah Shah, Turdu Bai (Standing), and Kutchuk Beside it.

close to us and followed us for some distance, as if they wanted to show their sympathy for our tired horses. Round and round they would gallop in a half circle, inclining at an angle of 45° to the ground, then all at once would wheel sharply about and pull up suddenly, facing us in a line. Their manœuvres could not have been more regular and decisive had they been ridden by invisible Cossacks.

My men were now dying to get out of this inhospitable region, and kept counting the days and the miles we still had to go to reach the head-quarters camp; nor were they at all pleased when, on the 22nd September, I proposed, because of Aldat's condition, to take an extra day's rest on the shore of a moderate-sized salt lake. But next morning after the animals were all loaded, and Aldat had been placed on his camel, with a rolled-up fur under his head and his feet wrapped in felts, just as I gave the order to march, the poor fellow breathed his last. Thus ended the strange life of this Afghan yak-hunter.

The Mussulmans gathered silently and solemnly around the dead man's bed, now his bier. At length Turdu Bai broke the silence by asking me what we were to do with the dead man. One or two of the others proposed burying him at once; but I could not have the poor fellow disposed of with such indecent haste, and therefore commanded "March."

Our caravan was now converted into a funeral procession through the dreary valleys of Tibet. A feeling of depression and solemnity pervaded the caravan; nobody spoke, and kulans and yaks were alike unmolested that day. The black crows followed our march at a distance. Upon reaching the west end of the lake we halted for the day, and while the other men attended to their ordinary duties, Mollah Shah and Niaz dug a grave for Aldat. Mollah Shah had a strange and wild appearance, and scarcely

View Looking South from the Camp where Aldat Died.

ever spoke. He might very easily have passed for a convict, but if he ever had been a rogue he successfully concealed the fact. At all events, during the time he was with me, his conduct was irreproachable. On the present occasion, he, like the other men, was too tired to wash the corpse as Mohammedan custom requires. The burial was the simplest I have ever been present at. One of Aldat's skin-coats was placed under him, the other above him, and he was buried with his clothes on, and his cap and his boots. There were no ceremonies, no tears, no prayers, save those I silently breathed for the eternal peace of the dead man. After the grave was filled in an oblong mound was made above it, and at the head end we fixed a tent spar, fastening to the top of it one of Aldat's own hunting trophies, namely, a yak's tail, according to a custom common amongst the Mussulmans. Then on a flat piece of wood I engraved, in Arabic and Latin letters, the dead man's name, together with the date and my own name, in case destiny should lead any wanderer there before all traces of the grave have disappeared.

Next morning the caravan was ready earlier than usual, but just before we started the Mussulmans gathered at the grave side and murmured a silent *dua* or "farewell prayer," and so Aldat was left to his fate in the dreary solitudes of Tibet.

The nearer we approached the Arka-tagh the more desolate grew the highlands. One day Cherdon and I, riding on in advance, crossed over a range that was 17,070 feet high, and when we stopped at dusk to wait for the others, it was in a region where there was not a blade of grass of any description. The caravan straggled up in small detachments, utterly wearied out. A white horse, which we had brought from Yanghi-köl, had been left behind in a hopeless condition, while two camels and another horse had something the matter with their eyes,

Camp 16,770 feet Above Sea-level.

for they slept as they walked, just as though they were suffering from sleeplessness.

At critical times I always make it a practice to go round the camp, and inspect it and the animals after supper. On this occasion the camels lay side by side, thin and worn, the horses were all tied up, and the men asleep, wearied by the fatigues of the day. That night we had another snow-storm, and next morning the country was draped with white. Before we started, Kutchuk went back to fetch the white horse, for it was still living when it was left behind. However, the poor beast had not strength enough even to reach the camp, but fell down dead soon after Kutchuk started with him.

From these high regions we were now to make our way down into a broad open valley, in the middle of which was a large salt lake, though when we first looked down upon it, it and the whole valley were shrouded in thick white mist. As we went down we were assailed by a hurricane from the west, blowing at the rate of 56 miles an hour. We had to sit tight to prevent ourselves from being blown out of the saddle. Tails, manes and cloak-ends streamed out to leeward; while the entire caravan leaned over in the opposite direction, the camels almost seeming actually to lie upon the wind as they staggered along. Upon reaching camp, our little she-mule was taken seriously ill. She must have eaten some noxious herbs, for she swelled up to an enormous size and lay writhing on the ground. Cherdon treated her in Buriat fashion, that is to say, he drove a gimlet into her side right up to the head. This let out the gases, but not a drop of blood came. Next she was forced to get up on her feet, and a rope was slung round her hind-quarters, one man holding it at each end. Then, while a third man pulled at her bridle, a fourth whacked her with a thick stick. Every time the mule kicked out behind, the two men with the rope hauled her along, making her reel from left to right and from right to left. Whatever you may think of this method of cure, it at any rate proved efficacious in this particular case, for the mule completely recovered, accompanied me in my dash towards Lhasa (Lassa), was with me in my journey across the whole of Tibet as far as Ladak, went with me over the Karakorum Pass and down to Kashgar, and was in first-rate condition when I finally parted from her in May, 1902.

And now we had to storm once more the fortifications of the Arka-tagh. Accompanied by Cherdon and Mollah Shah, I led the way up the pass. The ascent was not dangerous, but before we reached the summit the sky clouded, and we became wrapped in darkness, a thing that was anything but pleasant amidst that world of mountains. On the summit of the pass we were exposed to the full fury of the storm, and amid the blinding frenzy of the snow we felt almost helpless. My hands were frozen and without feeling, and it was only with the utmost difficulty that I was able to read the altitude, which amounted to 1,300 feet higher than the top of Mont Blanc (15,780). The caravan lingered, and the two men who were with me went back to help them up. And there was I left alone on that sharp mountain crest, which jutted out like a spring-board at a giddy height into the vast immensity of space. I crept as far as I could into my skin-coat and turned my back to the storm, while the snow whirled about my ears in big, smothering flakes.

At length I heard the caravan-bells close at hand. The animals glided past like spectres, I heard not a footstep. At the head marched Turdu Bai, leaning far forward, with one arm raised to protect his face and walking with effort, as if he were working his way through the underwoods. A moment's rest to catch their breath! At their feet yawned the abyss like a bottomless pit, full of seething snow-clouds. The wind howled, and roared, and moaned, and whistled as it came pouring like a cataract over the steep summit of the pass.

The descent on the north was precipitous. Kutchuk, who piloted the way, disappeared at once into the welter of the snow, just as though he had lost his footing and tumbled headlong into the seething abyss. The rest of us followed after him, each in turn treading blindly in his footsteps. Our guide took the descent in endless zigzags; at every ten paces or so we had to stop and turn round to prevent our faces from freezing. Everybody was on foot, so as to lend a helping hand to support the camels. One of them stumbled and fell, and half rolled over, causing a delay. And we were little better, for we slipped and slid down, down through the snow into the depths beneath. Everything danced and spun round before our eyes, and we literally gasped for breath. Before we reached the bottom of the valley it was pitch dark, and we were forced to encamp on the first passably level spot we came to, all amongst the snow—in fact, there was nothing else but stones and snow all around us.

We still had hard days before us. It is true we were descending; but the storms came at regular intervals, generally just after we had started the day's march. At length we caught a distant glimpse of the salt lake of Kum-köl, but somehow it seemed to fly before us. We marched all day, hoping to reach it; it grew dusk, it grew dark; then the moon came out and shed her pale autumnal light over the chilly solitudes. Niaz dropped behind with a failing horse, Kutchuk lingered with another. Water, water! we must have water somehow that evening. Where we were then (14,000 feet) there was no snow, and all the rivulets were dry. At length, however, Turdu Bai came to a running brook, and there we stopped.

Before us rose a fresh mountain-range. This, after a

day's much-needed rest, we set ourselves to climb over. Up in the saddle then, and let us scale the heights, scramble up the ravines, and surmount the pass. Very soon after we started a man came to tell us that one of the horses was unable to go any further. And no sooner had the poor beast been killed than a second lay down, never to get up again. Once this pass were crossed, however, we ought not to have very much further to go to reach grass. A third horse, which was running loose without any load, gave up and fell, and was killed at once. And, upon reaching the top of the pass, a fourth was missing, namely, my faithful little grey, the same which I had ridden on both desert journeys and which had refused to carry Ördek's sculptured planks.

At the spot where we encamped there was not a blade of grass. Turdu Bai and I went together through what remained of our supply of rice, and we divided as much as we could possibly spare amongst our remaining horses. They, poor brutes, stood tied in a row, covered over with felt rugs, and in the morning one of them lay dead in the string, his head stretched out, his eyes staring, frozen hard. Nobody had observed when or how his sufferings ended. The camels, with marvellous resignation, lay as usual motionless, in the same positions in which they had lain down the evening before. They were white with frost and appeared to be casting longing glances down towards the valley where we hoped to find the means of saving the last of our veterans. How long would they continue to hold out? This was the crucial question. Our marches grew every day shorter, and the cold more nipping. On the 8th October the thermometer fell 1° below zero. We were making our way down through a narrow gorge, with lofty perpendicular walls of rock on each side, and harshly though loudly they flung back the echoes of our funeral caravan-bells, for our animals were dying as they struggled down amongst the thousands upon thousands of granite blocks with which the bottom of the gorge was strewn, while the snow came whistling round the corners of the rocks. We were here about level with the top of Mont Blanc. After a while a camel stumbled and rolled down a steep terrace; fortunately no damage was done, though his load was scattered all over the gravel. This mishap caused a long delay, for we had to make a pathway with our spades for the animal to climb back by. Soon after that, another camel gave up and was unable to go any further, so we left him, intending to fetch him in next morning. It was midnight before the camels' bells ceased to tinkle amongst the rocks, and by that time the moon had again emerged from behind the snow-clouds. Next morning, when Turdu Bai went back for the camel, he found him cold and hard as ice.

It was 84 days since we had seen a human being except ourselves, when, on the 10th October, upon reaching a heap of stones covered with religious inscriptions, and built up by Mongol pilgrims to Lassa, we caught sight of two solitary horsemen in the distance. Mollah Shah, who had good lungs, set off after them like a madman, and caught them up and brought them back with him. That evening there was great rejoicing amongst our little band. The first thing we did was to buy from the strangers, two hunters, all their provisions, consisting of a small bag of wheat flour. Thereupon Cherdon at once set about making and baking bread, a delicacy we had not tasted for many a long day. Then I bought their horses, and commissioned Togdasin, one of them, to ride night and day to our head-quarters at Temirlik, with orders to Islam Bai to hasten to meet us at the springs of Yusup-alik with a relief caravan. Togdasin took with him two empty preserved food tins, to prove that he really was my courier. I confess I did not envy him his night's ride, for the thermometer was now down to 4° below zero Fahr.; but I promised to reward him handsomely if he carried my message well. He rode the horse I had just bought from him, and had the price in his pocket, so that he might easily have gone off, had he been so disposed. But I had confidence in the man and he had confidence in me.

Three days later we started again; for that evening we were to reach the springs of Yusup-alik, so at least swore

A Young Kulan (Wild Ass).

Mollah Shah and Niaz, and they knew the region well. We marched on till twilight, and from twilight to nightfall; in fact it got pitch dark, and as yet we had never seen a single glimpse of any spring. "Oh, it's not very far now"! Mollah Shah assured me time after time, and on he tramped again. The path we had followed so long as daylight lasted became lost in the darkness.

We were almost dead beat with fatigue and want of sleep, when our two guides suddenly stopped and shouted,

"A fire! A fire in the distance"! These words acted upon us all like an electric shock. Involuntarily we quickened our steps; everybody began to talk at once, though up till then the silence of the grave had reigned amongst our little company. All eyes were bent, fascinated, upon the tiny speck of light. If it were a big fire, it was so far off that we could not possibly reach it that night; and if it were a little one, we should reach it—indeed we must reach it, even though we dropped. A final push and our troubles would all be over. One hour more and we should be sitting, amongst friends, around the warm fire, telling them of our adventures, our mishaps, and our troubles, whilst the *ash*, or "rice-pudding," with its appetising ingredients, would be spluttering merrily over the flames. In my own mind, I began to heap encomiums upon Togdasin, and I promised myself that I would give him a handsome pile of Chinese silver for his honesty.

On we went through the dark night straight towards the fire, which kept alternately disappearing and flaming up again. Our guides maintained a sharp lookout for ravines and deep watercourses. For my own part, I saw nothing, and had to hold on to the edge of the boat, first with one hand and then with the other, according as they stiffened with the cold. During the last few days I too had been obliged to walk, for our surviving horses were scarcely able to drag themselves along without encumbrance.

Then the beacon-fire died down, and it no longer flared up again; and with it died our hopes, and weariness once more laid hold upon us. Upon reaching a locality where scrubby bushes were growing, we stopped awhile and set fire to two or three of them. Then by the light they made we gathered several other armfuls and flung them on the fire. Greedily the flames leapt up into the air, flinging a reddish yellow flickering reflection across the barren steppe. But no answering signal was made—at least, we saw none.

Well, if we could do nothing else, we could at any rate thoroughly warm ourselves. Then we fired off a couple of revolver shots, but they died away in the dark void, without eliciting so much as an echo by way of answer. We shouted, we listened, holding our breath. Silence, a silence as of the grave! not a single gleam of the distant fire! Perhaps the people—our people—were tired after a forced march, and were sleeping heavily.

When we turned our backs upon our own fire, the darkness of the night was blacker and more impenetrable than ever. In fact, I involuntarily glanced up at the stars, to convince myself whether or no I had actually lost my eyesight. Hour after hour we dragged ourselves along towards the east, still seeking that faithless beacon; our animals, however, plodded pertinaciously along, as though they smelt grass.

All at once up shot the distant fire again. Soon afterwards we passed the first belt of bushes, a sure sign that water was not very far off; consequently, we must be quite close to the springs. The men shouted repeatedly at the full pitch of their lungs, but their voices died away unheard in the night. Down, down sank once more the treacherous fire, and then disappeared. Surely there must be witchery at work, or was it a will-o'-the-wisp that was deceiving us, flitting on before us whenever we approached?

The men's conversation died away and with it our lately-revived hopes. Our pace became fearfully slow; in fact, we were no longer marching—we were only crawling at a snail's pace. When at last I literally could not take another step, I gave the order to stop, to everybody's intense satisfaction. We had been marching for twelve hours continuously and had had more than enough of it.

Cherdon hastened to make up a fire. The caravan cut a sorry figure in the faint illumination. The men dropped on the ground in the very places where they halted.

The camels stood quiet, but dispirited under their loads, their breath curling up in so many columns of steam through the night air.

One reward at least we did, however, reap for our extra exertions; we found that we were in the midst of grass and fuel such as we had not seen for many a month. We had just one canful of water left, and our late dinner consisted of a small cup of tea and a small piece of kulan-meat per man. We made a makeshift sort of camp, and kept the fire burning a long time, as a sort of signal to the relief caravan—that is, if it really was their fire that we had seen. The place where we had turned in for the night, under the brilliant stars, was only about 11,400 feet above the sea.

Next morning, the 15th October, everybody slept on till a late hour. The neighbourhood was desolate and silent, not a human being to be seen. The discovery of a spring close by fortunately enabled us to remain where we were. Cherdon, who had procured bullets and powder from Togdasin, went out to try his luck, but came back empty-handed, about two o'clock. He told me, however, that he had seen something black, a long way to the west, which he had at first taken for a troop of kulans, but he now thought they were horsemen, and that they were approaching the camp.

I hurried out with telescope, and sure enough it was a troop of mounted men advancing in a cloud of dust. In a state of the greatest excitement, we all ran to a hill close by, and breathlessly watched the advancing cavalcade. They were still a very long way off, and appeared to be riding just above the belt of vegetation, which, however, they had not yet reached. From their bobbing movements we saw that they were riding hard. Then they disappeared among the dark bushes, while the cloud of dust moved on over them. It must be our men, who, not having seen our signal fire, had pushed on again at daybreak

Our Headquarters at Temirlik. In the Background my Yurt and a Terrace with Caves, and in the Far Distance the Akato-tagh.

until they came across the tracks of our camels, and then seen that we had gone past one another in the dark.

The excitement grew intense when two horsemen emerged from the bushes; then appeared two more, driving a whole troop of horses before them. They were riding at full gallop. Yes, it was they; I recognised Islam by his skin *bashlik* (hood). He was riding first on a white horse, and when he caught sight of us he dug in his spurs, raced on ahead of the rest, dismounted, saluted, and reported that all was well in the camp. The others were Musa from Osh in West Turkestan, Khodai Värdi, and Tokta Akhun from Abdal.

There is no need for me to describe our mutual delight, or the joyous spirit which reigned in the camp, or the mighty banquet of *ash*, or "rice-pudding," with which we celebrated the reunion. It took us only a couple of days to reach Temirlik, and our arrival there brought to an end this toilsome journey. Valuable indeed were the results it had yielded in the way of geographical discoveries, but it had been at a great cost of toil, suffering, and even life. Of the twelve horses we started with, only two were left alive, and of the camels only four. And one of these last, although it succeeded in reaching Temirlik, stood for two days amongst the yellowing grass as if it were a piece of bronze statuary, and then on the third day lay down and died, without having once attempted to pluck a mouthful of grass. But the most sorrowful feature of all was the loss of Aldat, a man whom we had all learned to value very highly.

# CHAPTER XVI.

## ADVENTURES IN NORTHERN TIBET.

On the 11th November we were again ready to start. The object of this new excursion, which I estimated would last about a month, was to cross over and map three of the parallel ranges of Tibet, as well as to sound the large salt lake of Kum-köl, which lies immediately west of the lake of the same name that we had visited on the journey last described. I was accompanied by a small, but carefully selected, caravan, consisting of Cherdon, Islam, Tokta Akhuñ, Togdasin, and several others, together with thirteen fresh horses, four mules and two dogs, namely, Yoldash and Malenki.

It was not exactly a pleasure trip to penetrate those high regions in the middle of winter; but the geographical problems I had set myself to solve would brook no delay. After a weary ride over those wretched mountains, we reached the lake without mishap, and dug a well for drinking water, which we found at a depth of about five feet. There we rested a day. Cherdon and Togdasin begged permission to go hunting; but evening came and they had not returned, nor was anything heard of them during the night. But in the middle of the following morning they turned up, and Cherdon had the following story to tell. They had ridden up various wild glens after a flock of *arkhari* (wild sheep), leaving their horses when the ascent grew too steep, and after that scrambling on foot over the broken rocks which had tumbled down the mountain-sides. Higher and higher they were led by the wild sheep, until all at once Togdasin collapsed, complaining of terrible pain in his heart and in his head. Cherdon then went down for the horses; but as the sick man was unable to sit upright in his saddle, they were compelled to spend the night where they

The Cossacks Cherdon and Shagdur.

were. Togdasin begged his comrade to leave him. He would certainly die anyway, and it made little difference where it happened. Several times during the night Cherdon shook the sick man, lest he should freeze to death. When daylight came they dragged themselves down to the camp. Togdasin's condition was very pitiable; his mind wandered. This was another man whom I had met up in the mountains, and it seemed not unlikely that his fate would be the same as Aldat's. However, this time the case was

The Author on the Kum-köl with Tokta Akhun.

not so fatal. I may add here that we dragged Togdasin all the way with us till we got back to head-quarters, tending him as best we could; but his illness was very stubborn. We managed to get him down to the lowlands alive, to the little town of Charkhlik, where he recovered, but he was a cripple for the rest of his life. His feet turned black like Aldat's, and they literally rotted away piece by piece, first the toes, and then the muscles of the feet. But the last time I saw him in April, 1901, he was in the very best of good humour, and never uttered one single word of complaint. I gave him a present of a horse, clothes, and a sum of money, and he did not know how to thank me enough.

To return to our expedition. The boat was got ready early on the morning of the 18th November, and Tokta Akhun then rowed me across the smooth bright lake. But this time we were prudent, and in addition to sail, oars, life-belts, sounding apparatus, and other instruments, we carried with us sufficient provisions to last two days, as well as a copper vessel full of water, a small bag filled with ice, and skins and felts. The little skiff was so packed that we had scarcely room to move.

It was lovely weather. The eastern part of the lake was thickly dotted over with thin sheets of ice, which flashed so dazzlingly in the sunshine that we had to put on snow-glasses. The very slightest disturbance made by our boat caused them to rock and grind together. This ice came out of the river which emptied into the lake, for the lake itself was excessively salt, too salt to freeze.

Whilst we were busy sounding, the time flew rapidly away. Towards sunset we saw whirlwinds of dust careering along the southern shore; then we heard the usual roar that precedes a storm, and very soon we were caught in the teeth of the wind. We kept, however, to our own course, until our heavily-laden boat began to pitch and toss to such an extent as to force us to row towards the south-east, the direction in which wind and waves were running. It was already dusk, and as it would be dangerous to land on an unknown shore with a heavy sea behind us, we grew rather anxious; our fragile nutshell of a boat might be torn to tatters. Fortunately, the waves had broken up the ice along the shore, otherwise it would have cut our boat to pieces. All at once a white line gleamed out of the darkness ahead; it was the line of the foam-crested breakers, and before we knew what had happened we were in the middle of them. A big wave caught our boat and flung her on the beach, which fortunately consisted of sand; but the next moment she was sucked down again by the backwash, and then once more flung on the beach, so that her timbers creaked. However, Tokta Akhun jumped out at the right moment, and we managed to get our little craft safely landed, though not before a couple of jealous waves had flung themselves over her and drenched a portion of our baggage. Then we proceeded to make ourselves comfortable for the night on the sheltered side of a hill. There were plenty of hard *köuruk* bushes, which made excellent fuel, and dark though it was, with the help of little supplementary fires here and there we managed to gather a big heap. After a bowl of tasty soup and some tea, which Tokta Akhun prepared, we sat and smoked our "baccy," and discussed grand plans for the proposed winter journey through the Desert of Gobi, to the old Lop-nor and the marsh of Kara-koshun, which Tokta Akhun knew as well as the interior of his own hut. As early as nine o'clock the thermometer was down to 6.8° Fahr., and when our fuel was at an end we pulled our skin-coats about our ears and crept under the halves of the boat. I will admit, however, that I slept but little that night. It is true, I had on only four pairs of woollen stockings and a pair of big fur-lined top-boots, besides felts, skin-coats, and a *bashlik*; but then when you go to bed dressed, and the thermometer drops to $7\frac{1}{2}$° Fahr. below zero, it is literally impossible to keep yourself warm.

When we awoke and crept out of our dens before daybreak, we were half frozen and made haste to get the kettle boiled. I had to take some of my clothing off, and massage my limbs well to make the blood circulate ; but after such a night you remain chilled to the marrow all day, and don't get warm until you return to your usual comfortable quarters. The thermometer was down to $2\frac{1}{4}$° below zero when we pushed off to recross the lake, this time towards the north-west ; for I had ordered the caravan to proceed farther in that direction and wait for us, building up a huge fire to serve as a beacon for our guidance. Whilst still a very long way from our goal, we thought we could make out the tent, the yurt, and the caravan animals, but when we got near enough to see them distinctly through the glass, the former turned out to be a couple of hills and the latter a troop of kulans. However, we landed to make sure that the caravan had gone past. But the only signs we saw were the footprints of two bears, which had lately lumbered past in the opposite direction, bent on disturbing the marmots in their deep winter sleep.

We had no choice but to row along the shore in search of the caravan. Once more we were deceived by a cloud of smoke under the sinking sun, for it turned out to be nothing more than dust raised by a crowd of galloping kulans. I was stiff with cold ; but Tokta Akhun kept himself warm with rowing, singing as he rowed a mournful ditty of the huts of Abdal.

At length a gleam of fire pierced through the darkness. For three hours we held steadily on towards the light, and then it disappeared. Nevertheless we still pushed on, and finally our shouts were answered by the barking of dogs. Thereupon the fire leapt up again ; we were quite close to

Our Baggage Horses beside the Kum-köl.

it, and were met on the water's edge by a man with a torch.

After various hardships and difficulties we at length reached Temirlik, where the cold was intense, the thermometer sinking to 16½° below zero. Before starting again I decided to take six days' holiday, but spent them in making preparations for my next long excursion across the desert. An Andijan merchant, who of his own accord had come to my camp to do business, was seized with the usual mountain sickness, and died and was buried with appropriate solemnities. One day Togdasin was carried out into the open air, and all the Mussulmans gathered round him, and endeavoured by every sort of prayer and exorcism they could think of to banish the evil spirits which had taken possession of his body. They also offered a he-goat to Allah, thinking to soften his heart.

On the 12th December I left Temirlik for the last time, leaving orders to Cherdon, Islam, Turdu Bai, and six other men to move the head-quarters camp down to Charkhlik, and there await my return four months hence. Amongst the men I took with me were Shagdur, my right-hand man, Faisullah, Tokta Akhun, Mollah from Abdal, Khodai Kullu, Khodai Värdi, Ahmed, and Li Loyeh, the second of the two hunters we found on the mountains. The last named spoke, in addition to Turki, his mother tongue, also Chinese and Mongolian; he had stolen horses at Bokalik and was a little bit "dotty." Our baggage was carried by eleven camels, while eleven horses were used for riding. The canine escort consisted of Yoldash, Malenki, and Malchik, the last two now big shaggy caravan dogs.

All the animals were thoroughly rested; some of the camels, indeed, had done no work for an entire year. For the first two days, therefore, they were skittish and playful, and had to be carefully led to prevent them from flinging off their burdens. I selected two of the quietest of them to carry my boxes of instruments. Our baggage consisted principally of flour, rice, maize, and *talkan* (roasted flour), with tents, clothes, cooking utensils, spades, axes, buckets, etc., etc. However, we had no mishap, and the two or three extra men we took with us were soon able to return.

Our one dromedary was an untameable beast. The

Glen Leading up to the Pass of the Akato-tagh.

froth hung round his lips like soapsuds, and kept dropping in big clots to the ground. One of his fore-legs was tied fast to his pack-saddle in such a way that, while it was no hindrance whatever to his walking, it effectually prevented him from running. He was fastened to his immediate predecessor in the string by a chain, so that he was unable to attack his neighbours, which it was his one constant aim and desire to do. Besides this, he was muzzled, to prevent him from biting. All the same, he was a magnificent animal, this veteran of Kashgar, with his wild glistening coal-black eyes, the whites of which used to show prominently whenever he was in a bad temper.

We rested a day at the Lake of Ghaz-nor, and from there I sent on Tokta Akhun on horseback to find out a suitable pass by which we might cross the Akato-tagh. None of my men had ever been there before, but they knew

Making a Road over the First Pass.

that that range is considered to be excessively difficult to cross. My scout returned late in the evening, and reported that he had found a pass which we could use, after levelling the extreme summit with spades.

On the 17th December, after over 53° of frost during the preceding night, we once more entered the mountains by a narrow winding ravine. These mountains are extremely fantastic and peculiar in their formation. They consist entirely of soft argillaceous matter, seamed by an endless number of deep dry ravines. However, we had sufficient water with us to last four days, and that night we encamped in a perfectly sterile locality not far from the pass. Early the next morning some of the men went towards the top of the pass and made a zigzag path up the steepest part of the slope. After that the camels were led up one by one, the men pushing behind and steadying the loads. Two or three of the animals fell and had to be unloaded and led without their loads, which were carried up by the men on foot. Down on the other side we made our descent by a zigzag equally steep. Tokta Akhun declared that there was only one difficult place, and it turned out to be a spot so narrow that a man on foot was scarcely able to squeeze himself through. However, we managed to get the camels past in safety.

A little bit farther on our string of animals came to a stop, and the men hurried to the front. The ravine was again so narrow that the camels' loads scraped against both sides. There was no possibility of scrambling on further by climbing up the sides or by turning round; we could do nothing but push forward, and this we did after widening the passage by chopping the earth away with axes. Meanwhile I went on ahead, until I came to a place that was still worse. The ravine had contracted to a mere strip of a torrent, which had eaten its way in under the soft wall on the left, making a dangerous overhanging roof, cracked and crumbling in places. In fact, an avalanche had taken place just there quite recently and the passage was blocked by gigantic lumps of *débris*. Some of them we were able by united effort to roll in under the overhanging eave, while those that were too big for us we chopped to pieces with spades and axes. Then after widening the passageway, the horses went on first and made a path for the camels, which were led forward one by one with the utmost caution. If a fresh fall of earth took place the caravan would be caught as in a rat-trap. The beast that was most difficult to get through was the camel that carried the fuel. He literally stuck fast in the middle of the gap, and in making a desperate effort to force his way through, his load of wood fell off with a crash, bringing down with it two or three big slices of clay. I can tell you it made me feel decidedly queer when I saw the entire caravan disappear in a thick cloud of rising dust.

However, we pushed on further, stopping incessantly, now to chop away projecting corners, now to break down masses of clay that impeded our advance. Again the caravan stopped. Downcast and ashamed Tokta Akhun came to tell me that the glen was blocked and we could advance no farther. He had always hitherto distinguished himself by his safe and reliable reports, but this time he had led us into a veritable rat-trap. Gigantic masses of earth had fallen down from the mountains, a thousand feet or more high, and choked the gorge. Underneath the material of this landslip some torrent had tunnelled a path after rain, and over this hollow crust we might advance if we liked, provided it did not fall in under the weight of our camels.

Before venturing to take such a risky step, I went on farther and reconnoitred myself. Before I had gone very far, the gorge contracted to a mere rift not more than two feet broad, though it was between 40 and 50 feet deep. It descended, moreover, at a precipitous angle and terminated in a dark subterranean tunnel, the outlet of some ancient river. It was a place a cat could hardly see to find its way through, let alone a camel.

There was no longer any room for doubt : we must return by the same intricate and difficult path by which we had come, and try to cross the range in another place. And at the next attempt we did succeed ; then, after travelling for some days through an absolutely sterile and waterless

The Cul-de-Sac in the Akato-tagh where we Turned Back.

region, we fortunately discovered a spring, surrounded by sheets of ice and good grass.

At length another Christmas Eve came round, for me a long and gloomy day, solitary and alone as I was in the wilds of Asia. That evening we encamped in the entrance to a glen of the Astyn-tagh, a terribly desolate spot. Fortunately there was plenty of fuel, and a lively crackling fire was soon blazing, the only thing to remind me of the happy gatherings at home. In order to banish to some extent the depressing thoughts that naturally crowded in upon my mind, I called Shagdur, who was the beau ideal of a good and faithful servant, and invited him to come and sit down beside me. It was now I unfolded to him my plan for trying to reach Lhasa. He literally beamed at the idea; the prospect of such a wild adventure filled him with joy. From my childhood I had heard speak of that holy place of pilgrimage of the Lamaists, and I believed it would be possible to reach it in the disguise of Mongol pilgrims. It was nearly midnight when I dismissed Shagdur, and I am sure that night he must have dreamed of great things. After that we frequently talked of the venturesome plan, but we always conversed in Russian, so that the Mussulmans should not understand what it was we were discussing.

Our steps were still directed towards the east through the mountainous regions, desolate and uninhabited, of the Astyn-tagh. On the night of 31st December we were visited by a terrific storm. The spars were torn from the roof of the yurt, although they were tied together with ropes. For safety's sake we had to let the fire go out, and it was not until I had undressed entirely and crept amongst my furs and felts that I thawed; after that the storm might thunder and rage as much as it liked. Next morning it was dark, although the sky was clear, and the wind whistled and howled as it cut round the shoulders of the mountains. Thus the close of the century was celebrated in those

Our Camp in the Glen of Jong-duntsa.

regions with a bacchanal of the elements. To ride under such circumstances is torture. It is useless to fight against the cold; you can hardly keep your vital powers awake, but grow benumbed and drowsy, your limbs stiffen in the positions they have assumed in the saddle, and it requires a deliberate effort to dismount and put your feet to the ground.

The last night of the year set in stinging cold, but bright, the moon glittering with electric brilliance in the frosty sky. I read the Bible texts and Psalms which are sung on the last night of the year in every church in Sweden. And though there were no church bells to ring out the old and ring in the new, the tempestuous wind, which knows nothing of the waxing and waning of the centuries, lent the torrent of its organ notes to celebrate appropriately the dawn of a new era.

On the 1st January, 1901, the inexhaustible cascades of air still continued to pour with undiminished strength down the glens and gorges of the Astyn-tagh. Upon reaching the top of a low pass, we saw before us the gigantic snow-clad mountain mass of the Anambaruin-ula. The circuit round this mountain-knot, for the purpose of visiting the Särtäng Mongols on the other side of it, meant a *détour* of nearly 190 miles. I will pass over the details of the journey. It must suffice to say that the cold was intense, the thermometer dropping to 26½° below zero; that we had a friendly reception from the Mongols; that we rode right round the mountain, admiring its magnificent scenery, and especially its stupendous valley portals, of which Jong-duntsa is the finest; and that we returned safely to the point from which we had started, namely, the brook of Anambaruin-gol.

Now, however, I had to make an important decision. It was my intention from that point to cross the Desert of Gobi or Sha-mo northwards; and as we might reasonably

Stone huts near the Anambaruin-ula.

One of our Mongol Guides.

expect to have to make long stages through an unknown and waterless country, it was not advisable to take so many horses with us. Picking out, therefore, the three best, I sent all the rest, together with a part of our disused and unnecessary belongings, to Charkhlik, putting them in charge of Tokta Akhun and Ahmed. At the same time I gave them a letter to Cherdon and Islam Bai, containing an enumeration of such supplies as we should require, together with other instructions. Tokta Akhun was then to take the supplies and three fresh unloaded horses, as also the post-bag, which would in the meantime have arrived from Kashgar, and go to Kum-chapghan, the point where the Tarim empties into the Kara-koshun. From there he was to continue for three days along the northern side of the marsh, and then establish a permanent camp, build a hut, and have ready at hand fishermen, who were well acquainted with that part of the country, with their canoes, and finally to lay in a stock of wild-duck and fish, so that when we emerged from the heart of the desert, we might find, not only shelter, but the wherewithal to recuperate our energies. Besides all this he was to select a hill that was visible a long way towards the north, and every day, first at noon, and again immediately after dark, he was to kindle a big fire, so that its smoke column and its flames might serve us as a beacon. He was instructed to be at the rendezvous at the latest on the forty-fifth day after the 27th January, and was then to begin the signal fires at once, and to continue them every day until he heard from us. My plans were framed in blind dependence upon this arrangement, for, unless I was deceived, our position might be rather critical.

## CHAPTER XVII.

### WATER! WATER!

WE began our journey through the desert on the 27th January. For the first few days the ground was favourable—steppe diversified by low gentle hills. There was, however, not a drop of water; but against that we had provided by loading two or three of the camels with ice. After crossing over the last low ridge at the foot of the mountains, we saw spread out before us the old familiar picture—the ocean of sand, literally an ocean of gigantic dunes. As usual, I went on first, partly to prevent myself from getting frozen in the never-ceasing wind, and partly that I might pilot the caravan.

On the 9th February we dug a well on the northern edge of the sandy desert, which yielded us saltish water. When we started again on the following day, we carried with us sufficient ice to last men and horses, though not the camels, for ten days. We now had before us the mountainous and stony desert, where there was little prospect of finding water; I was well aware, therefore, that it was a venturesome journey.

The country we now marched through was one of almost incredible desolation and sterility; it was the greatest rarity to find even the footprint of a wild camel. Nevertheless, it afforded me the keenest gratification to traverse it, for no European had ever before set his foot there, and on our maps of Asia that part of the continent is nothing but a big white blank. Our course for several days was towards the north-east. At intervals we would cross a low ridge, behind which the stony desert extended for miles, until we at length reached another slight swelling of the surface. But not a drop of water anywhere, and to dig for it in those everlasting gravel-beds would have been labour wasted. But as the country still continued to main-

Watering the Camels on the Edge of the Desert of Gobi.

tain its aspect of dreary desolation, I saw that something would have to be done, for for several days the camels had not had a drop of water.

Here we were, then, in the middle of an arid and hopeless region, where not one blade of grass ever grows. Should we go back all the way to the Desert of Gobi, where by digging we might get at least brackish water? No; it was much too far, and the result altogether too uncertain, for we might perhaps strike a locality in which there were no water-bearing strata. To continue on towards the north would be sheer madness. What was to be done then? The best thing appeared to be to trust to the map I made the year before, and to the route which I had just plotted across the desert, and try and reach the spring of Altimish-bulak, the position of which I did know. Thither, then, we now directed our steps, making long stages every day. I led the way on foot, and seldom took refuge in the saddle; for when matters are serious, I am too uneasy to ride. All the men, too, travelled on foot, for we had only three horses, and they were all pretty well exhausted.

On the 16th February we came across a regular wild camels' highway, for we counted no less than 87 tracks, some of them quite fresh. Now it was quite certain that all these camels were bound for some spring; the question was, how far away was it? Perhaps several days. But no; we must not let ourselves be turned aside from the course we had once decided upon. I entered on my map every camel-track we came across; after a while their positions might possibly point to some conclusion that would serve as a useful guide. For as far as ever we could see, the country was silent and deserted, and yet only a few hours before probably a whole troop of wild camels had passed that way.

Things now began to look serious. For ten days our camels had not had a drop of water. It was no use expecting them to do impossible things; we must make haste if we wanted to save them. On the 17th February we were on foot all day, and all day I heard behind me the melancholy tingle-tingle of the caravan-bells—an insistent *memento mori* from which it was impossible to escape. That day I turned in as tired as a dog, building all my hopes upon the morrow. On the morrow, when Shagdur came and called me, I was far from rested. At daybreak there was half a gale blowing from the north; but it soon in-

Our Camp in the Middle of the Sandy Desert.

creased to a buran of the first magnitude, and raged without a moment's cessation. Running, stamping, all were no use; we were chilled to the bone by the icy blast, and our hands grew swollen and devoid of feeling. Difficulties of all sorts began to increase upon our devoted heads. The surface was now difficult, for we had to cross at right angles an endless number of low transverse ranges of hills. Our supply of fuel was long ago exhausted; we had not a scrap of wood left as big as a match. All round us there was nothing but stone and sand. The range towards which I was leading, and at the foot of which I was hoping to find a spring, seemed to recede from us the farther we advanced, until it disappeared entirely in the dust-haze raised by the storm. That evening, therefore, our goal appeared more unattainable than ever. Notwithstanding the forced march, our camels carried themselves with royal dignity; and although we had not a blade of grass to give them to eat, or a drop of water to give them to drink, they marched along with the same solemn stride, the same lofty poise of the head, the same philosophic calm as ever. The wild camels' tracks were now for the most part directed towards the north-east; no doubt they led to the mysterious spring which, as we had reason to believe, we passed some days before.

As soon as it grew dark we encamped in an open hollow, or natural trench, without any protection whatever against the tempest. And although we managed to get the yurt up and covered with triple felts, we were unable to use the stove for want of fuel. The trifling amount of warmth diffused by my own body, the body of my faithful dog, and the flaring candle, was dissipated by every gust of wind. And although the men built a wall of sand round the lower part of the yurt, its interior was as cold as a cellar in winter. Our water, too, was nearly at an end; all we had left were a few splinters of ice.

When I rose on the morning of the 19th February, it was raw and chilly without my usual brazier. After a very simple breakfast I hurried on ahead on foot. Water! water! was the sole dominating thought, or, rather, desire, uppermost in the mind of every one of us. We must at all costs find a spring somewhere, for this was the twelfth day since we left the last well, and as its water was saltish the camels had drunk but little of it. If we did not find water within the next day or two the camels would assuredly perish, and what would then become of us? I estimated that we had still four or five days to go to reach Altimish-bulak. The question was, could we hold out until we got there?

Abdu Rehim, the camel-hunter of Singher, who had so cleverly led us to Altimish-bulak the year before, had told me that there were three other salt springs to the east of Altimish-bulak; it was upon them I largely built my hopes. Yet how easily we might pass them without seeing them, hidden as they no doubt were in some gully or hollow of the ground. Once before I had walked, or rather crawled, for my life—namely, in the Takla-makan. But on that occasion I knew for certain that if I could only continue far enough to the east, I was bound to come to the Khotan-daria; that is to say, it was a *line* I was making for. On the present occasion, however, the objective was a single small *point*, Altimish-bulak, unless fortune so far favoured us as to guide us to one of Abdu Rehim's more easterly springs. Perhaps you will think it was a stupid and senseless thing to risk my valuable caravan, and the results I had already obtained, in this way. Yes, that was precisely the thought of every traveller who had explored this part of Asia before me, for each had carefully avoided crossing this particular belt of country. Both east and west of my present route the desert had been traversed by a few explorers; but just here, in the very centre of the stony wilderness of the Kuruk-tagh, or the Dry Mountains, nobody had ever ventured.

I was now desperate, and determined I would keep on until I did find water. I tramped doggedly, doggedly on, and kept at it without stopping. Soon I left the echo of the caravan-bells far behind me. The new boots with which I had started at Temirlik would now hardly hold together after the 180 miles tramp, and my feet were sore and blistered. The day, the 19th of February, has more than once played an important part in my life. It was on the 19th February, 1896, that I found water after struggling across the perilous desert of the Takla-makan. The 19th February was also my birthday; and somehow I had got it into my head that I should meet with a happy surprise before the day was done.

The farther I advanced to the west the greater grew the number of camel-tracks; I came across them every two minutes, or less. This quickened my hopes. At last I reached a low spur of the mountains, which turned me to the south-west along a dry water-course, and in it I found the tracks of 30 camels. Shortly afterwards I came upon a tamarisk, and observed the footprints of hares and antelopes. I stopped. These animals are not able to live very far away from water. Whilst I was reflecting up came Shagdur. We discussed the situation together. A little way to the south we perceived several tamarisks; we walked towards them. The ground round about them was very moist, but coated with a thick layer of salt. We waited until the caravan came up, and then dug a well. The water was intensely, bitterly salt! On, therefore, again towards the south-west. But as the tempest was now behind us, marching was easier work.

Taking Shagdur with me, I once more hurried on, leaving my white horse to follow me, which it did of its own accord like a dog, while Yoldash was running about hunting and sniffing, here, there and everywhere. We were following closely the trail of a troop of 20 wild camels. It brought us to the entrance of a glen, opening out between low hills on the right. It was upon that point that all the camel-tracks in the neighhourhood converged, and then united into one common track, leading straight up the glen. Now it is repugnant to the instincts of that shy creature the wild camel ever to enter glens or similar confined places, where it may readily fall into an ambush; it loves rather the open country, where it can see a long way about it. Evidently, then, there must be some special reason why all these wild, shy creatures should have made their way into this narrow passage; and the only thing that could have brought them there must be a spring. I turned, therefore, and followed the trail up the glen, and before I had gone very far I saw Yoldash drinking beside a bright sheet of ice.

We were saved! The first thing was to let our animals have a couple of days' rest. It is true, we had no fodder to give them beyond one small sack of corn, left over from the supply which we bought from the Särtäng Mongols. I spent the greater part of the first evening feeding the camels with pieces of ice out of my own hand; for, though the water that trickled out of the spring was salt, the ice it engendered was fresh.

The animals stood in a ring, patiently waiting their turns, their eyes glistening like those of a child when it sees a lump of sugar-candy, and a very pleasant thing it was to hear them crunching the pieces of ice between their strong teeth, just as a child crunches candy.

Upon leaving this spring, we carried with us sufficient ice to last for several days. As it turned out, however, there was no need to have done so, for after only a few hours we passed a second spring, the ground round which was greatly trampled by camels and antelopes. Whilst Shagdur dropped behind in the hope of shooting a wild camel, I proceeded farther by myself, and upon turning up a little valley between some low hills I saw immediately before me a big and handsome wild camel, which was quite unaware of my presence, owing to the wind being contrary. The dogs, however, came and warned him of his danger; and after that we kept them tied up, for not only were we greatly in need of fresh meat, but I was anxious to take home with me the skin and skeleton of a wild camel.

After proceeding for some hours we saw something yellow looming through the haze in the south, evidently another attractive oasis. On the far side of it I saw 18 wild camels grazing. I therefore stopped and sent back Li Loyeh to fetch Shagdur. The wild camels watched the long black line of their tame congeners with steady attention. At length, up came the Cossack breathless, but he was impatient, and fired too soon. The animals disappeared westwards with the speed of the wind, and it looked as if I were not to get my skeleton. Altimish-bulak was now my only hope, for upon leaving it we should pass out of the domain of the wild camel.

In this yellow oasis we found Abdu Rehim's third spring, so that his statement turned out to be perfectly correct.

According to my topographical determinations, we had now only 17 miles to go to the west-south-west to reach Altimish-bulak. Had the weather been clear, we could have seen the oasis from a great distance; but owing to the incessant wind the atmosphere was now thick, and we were unable to see far. Without knowing it, we might easily go past the oasis, and in that case we should be launched once more in the desert, and unable to find water before we reached the Tarim, a trial which the caravan could scarcely have endured.

My lucky star, however, guided our footsteps aright, and we eventually saw the yellow reeds looming through the haze, and above them detected the silhouettes of five wild camels. Here was an opportunity for Shagdur to retrieve his reputation as a hunter; accordingly, flinging off his cloak and cap, he crept stealthily in amongst the bushes. I watched his proceedings through the glass. At the first shot the animals moved off, first slowly, then more quickly, hovering above the kamish like black spectres, and then they disappeared beyond the confines of the oasis. There were 14 of them. After a second shot Shagdur came back,

Altimish-bulak or Sixty Springs.

and triumphantly reported that he had brought down a magnificent male and wounded a young female. The skeleton of the former is now in Stockholm; the flesh of the latter went to fill our long-disused flesh-pots.

The Mussulmans were greatly astonished that I had succeeded in finding the well. We had, however, to go 19 miles, instead of 17, to reach Altimish-bulak; that is to say, I was two miles out in my reckoning, which is not so very bad in a journey of over 1,200 miles.

I must now tell a little story about Khodai Kullu. The

honest fellow possessed an old muzzle-loading musket, fired from a forked support, and on the strength of it he was ambitious to be taken for a great hunter; but during the 14 months he had been with us nobody had ever seen him injure so much as a hare. Everybody believed, therefore, that he did not know how to shoot, and, consequently, it occasioned no surprise, when one fine day he sold the weapon for an old song to Li Loyeh, in whose hands it was

Khodai Kullu and his Wild Camel.

equally harmless. The year before, when Khodai Kullu returned to headquarters at Yanghi-köl, he boasted to the other men that he had shot a wild camel at Altimish-bulak. He was now cornered by his comrades, who mockingly begged him to be so kind as to show them the victim's bones. Khodai Kullu was evidently in a quandary, and excused himself by saying that it was not at Altimish-bulak, but at another spring in the neighbourhood that he had shot the camel. Yet nobody would believe him, and the other

An Ice-Sheet below Khodai Kullu's Spring.

men only made fun of him. Now Khodai Kullu was a peaceful and phlegmatic man, both clownish and jovial, the expression of his countenance being very comical; but as a servant he was faithful, and worth his weight in gold.

One morning before sunrise he disappeared silently from camp, and as nothing was heard of him all day, we wondered where he had gone to; and it did strike one or two of us as suspicious that his former weapon had disappeared also. At dusk he came waddling back, and even at a distance his proud and self-satisfied bearing at once attracted attention. Anybody that liked might, he said, go with him to the spring and see the skeleton of the camel he had shot the year before. That year the spring had indeed dried up, but the skeleton remained. Moreover, he had discovered a second spring, where he had surprised four magnificent camels, and had shot one of them. Khodai Kullu now assumed great airs of *bonhomie* and condescension, and he rose very considerably in the eyes of the other men, who were somewhat ashamed of the suspicion they had shown. I must confess that I, too, had shared their opinion; but I encouraged the injured innocent with a small silver gratuity over and above his usual monthly wages. When on the 1st March we proceeded to Khodai Kullu's spring, the great discoverer himself marched at our head, very conscious of his importance, whistling and singing, and carrying himself as though he were the sole monarch of all those deserts and oases, and of all the wild camels that roam to and fro in them, while the rest of us followed meekly and silently at his heels.

The discovery of this spring was so far important, that it lay nearer to the ruins in the desert, and was, therefore, more convenient as a base. Accordingly I left behind there three tired camels and the three horses, with Khodai Värdi to look after them, bidding him content himself there until he received further orders. The only stores we gave him out of our own scanty supplies consisted of a matchbox

The Clay Tower seen from the South.

and a pinch of tea! This would enable him to kindle a fire and make tea for himself, and he was at liberty to carve as many steaks as he chose out of the dead camel which lay under his nose.

Taking the rest of the caravan and nine sacks crammed with ice, I, on the 2nd March, went down into the desert, and discovered, not the ruins of the year before, nor yet the ruins that Ördek stumbled upon when he went to look for the forgotten spade, but a third place, an ancient town. We counted 19 houses still standing in part, and I was easily able to measure them. At the northern end of the place was a clay tower, nearly 30 feet high, commanding the entire neighbourhood, and standing on a wind-sculptured mound, likewise nearly 30 feet high. At its foot, on the morning of the 4th March, we put up my yurt and the men's tent, and stacked our ice in the shade, covering it over with a roof of clay.

As soon as the seven camels had rested a little, I ordered Li Loyeh to lead them back to the spring. There he was to remain two days, and then during the next two days he was to come back to the ruins, bringing with him Khodai Värdi and the horses and all the camels, and he was to pack upon them as much ice as they were able to carry, for we were going to make yet another march across the desert, all the way to the marsh of Kara-koshun. On the 9th March, therefore, he had to be back at the ruins, and I promised to light a big fire on the mound as a beacon to guide him.

Then we went to work with crowbars, and axes, and spades, and dug and poked about amongst the ruins of the 19 houses, and managed to bring to light various domestic utensils, money, pieces of pottery, a lamp, and so forth. Perhaps the tower, like an Indian *stupa*, contained some secret in its interior? We excavated a hole from the top; but the tower proved to be solid right through, though before we satisfied ourselves of that, we had to pull down a large portion of the upper part.

The Ruined House Nearest to our Camp.

During the following days we made exploring excursions in the neighbourhood, and re-discovered Ördek's ruins, amongst which we excavated the remains of an especially elegant little temple, bringing to light several planks carved with pictures of Buddha and various smaller objects. But the most important of all was a small wooden tablet, bearing lettering which none of us knew. Shagdur was the finder, and thus earned the reward of 10 *liang* (33s. 4d.) which I had promised to the man who brought me the first word of writing. And after I promised to give the same reward for a similar find, all the men worked with redoubled zeal and energy, scarcely giving themselves time to eat or sleep. Their efforts were crowned with greater success than I had dared to hope for. First came Mollah with a small scrap of paper, having Chinese writing on it, and after that we found several hundred others all written upon. This was a stroke of rare good fortune. I should be able to prove in black and white how old these antiquities were, and what the place was called; nor was I deceived in this expectation. Mr. Himly, of Wiesbaden, a well-known and learned Chinese scholar, has interpreted the documents for me, and he tells me that most of them date from years 264 to 270 A.D., that is, from the time of the Chinese Emperors Yüan Ti and Wu Ti. We also learned that the town was called Lôu-lan; that the inhabitants carried on agriculture, and were in communication with several other Chinese towns named in the documents; we are also told about an army which was to be quartered in the country, about high officers of state, about trivial events that happened in Lôu-lan, about hunting, and about tribute of seed-corn. In a word, this collection of documents which I found throws unexpected light upon the political and physical geography of Central Asia during the first centuries after Christ. How enormous the changes which have taken place during the 1630 years that have elapsed since then! Then

Carved Pieces of Wood from the Ruins.

there existed fertile fields, green woods, canals of running water, prosperous towns, Buddhist temples, and highways thronged with traffic alongside the former large Lake of Lop-nor. And what is it now? It would scarcely be possible to imagine a more dreary or more desolate prospect than that which unfolded itself from the top of the tower. Not a trace of organic life of any description whatsoever!

The Ruined Building in which the MSS. were Discovered.

The entire expanse, right away to the very verge of the horizon, silent and gloomy as a burial-place! And why has this great change come about? Simply because the Tarim river, which formerly flowed to the east, and emptied itself into Lop-nor, has changed its course to the south-east and south, and formed the lake of Kara-koshun. Meanwhile, Lop-nor dried up, and after the water disappeared the vegetation died out, and the inhabitants abandoned their dwellings.

# CHAPTER XVIII.

## A CRITICAL SITUATION.

On the 9th March a gigantic fire blazed on the tower hill, and at the appointed time Khodai Värdi and Li Loyeh arrived with all the camels, which were in excellent condition after their rest, and with the three horses. I now divided the caravan into two sections: first, I ordered Faisullah, who had been with me the year before, to take with him Mollah and Li Loyeh, six camels, the three horses, and all the heavier baggage, as well as provisions for four days (we had not any more to give them), and follow our former route across the desert to Kum-chapghan, and there wait for us. It was, I know, a risky thing to entrust the greater part of the caravan to the hands of three Mussulmans; but Faisullah assured me that he could get through all right, and, as an extra precaution, I gave him a thorough lesson in the use of the compass, and showed him how he was to follow it towards the south-west. I had greater confidence, however, in my own good fortune, and therefore kept in my own hands all the drawings I had made and the note-books I had filled during the past four months, as well as the MSS. I had discovered at Lôu-lan. When I left Temirlik, I brought away with me all the sheets of the map I had drawn throughout the whole of the journey, amounting to over 800 in all, that I might copy them over again in my spare hours. It was my intention to send them from Charkhlik by special courier to Kashgar, so that they might be in safety should the original material by any chance become lost in the adventures which in all probability awaited us in Tibet ; and lest any misfortune should overtake one of the sections of the caravan in the desert, I gave Faisullah the copies, retaining in my own hands the original maps, and all the other papers which I would not for any price have parted with.

As for my own section of the caravan, we were to march due south to the rendezvous, three days north-east of Kum-chapghan, where Tokta Akhun was instructed to wait for us. On the way I proposed to take a levelling right across the desert, with surveying staff and telescope, my object being to prove the correctness or otherwise of Baron von Richthofen's and my own views with regard to the position of the ancient Lake of Lop-nor, views which were energetically disputed by nearly all the Russian geographers, and by some others besides.

I chose Shagdur, Kutchuk, Khodai Kullu, and Khodai Värdi to accompany me. Whilst I and the three first named were carrying out the levelling, Khodai Värdi was to lead after us the four camels, one of them bearing our few belongings, and the other three ice. My tent consisted of a small felt rug, held up by a few spars, while the men were to sleep in the open air, for it was now beginning to be warmer. Our food-supply, consisting of rice and bread, was divided into rations, and with a little economy might last us eight days.

Whilst the two sections of the caravan were being loaded up, I set off with my three assistants for the south. We soon passed the shore-line of the former lake ; the dead trees, bushes and reeds which dried up 1,500 years ago came to an end, and we were out on the hard, yellow clay desert, furrowed by countless gullies and channels, excavated by the wind. Here and there the ground was

Excavating a House in Lôu-lan. In the Foreground a Big Earthenware Jar.

white with mollusc shells. We were in the bottom of the ancient lake. So engrossed were we with our work that none of us gave a thought to Khodai Värdi and the camels; we, of course, concluded that, according to orders, they were following closely in our footsteps. Ninety times staff and telescope were alternately moved and we had measured a distance of 9,950 yards, when it began to grow dusk, and suggested it was time to think of breaking off. We therefore stopped, but where was Khodai Värdi? We went to the top of one or two small hills on which in the dim distant past tamarisks had grown, and looked about us. The desert was as silent and deserted as the grave, not a glimpse of the caravan to be seen. Had the man gone astray or was he turned crazy? I was really very anxious about him. Finding some dry timber near by, we built up a big pile on the top of one of the hills and set fire to it, making a signal blaze which might be seen from a great distance. Meanwhile, Shagdur set off in the darkness to look for the truants.

If the man had gone astray and failed to see our fire, he would be infallibly lost, for he had no idea even of the existence of the marsh of Kara-koshun. To look for any one—even to look for the ruins of a whole town—in an unbounded desert is a more hopeless business than looking for a needle in a bundle of hay. If the man failed to find us then, our situation also would be critical; for without water and food we should scarce be able to reach the lake, and any oases there might be between us and it would be able to afford us nothing but water. But what worried me most of all was the thought of losing the fruits of four months' hard work through the crass stupidity of a blockhead.

High and wildly blazed the fire against the gaping void of the darkness. The country was as silent and as desolate as though it were on an uninhabited planet. We listened, but there was not the faintest sound to be heard. With feverish energy and almost in despair we set to work to gather up all the wood we could find, and flung it on the signal-fire. But at last weariness got the upper hand, and we dozed off round the crackling logs.

About midnight Kutchuk crept silently towards me and begged me to listen. There was a sound of footsteps

The Caravan for the Levelling Expedition.

in the darkness. Motionless as statues we all three listened with bated breath. "It's the camels!" whispered Kutchuk. We hurried down, and there came Khodai Värdi, with the four veterans all safe and sound. I was as happy as if I had inherited all the riches of India, and quite forgot to give the blundering camel-leader the drubbing he deserved; besides, I have a rooted objection to administering corporal punishment. Khodai Värdi told me that he had kept too far to the right and lost sight of us, but had continued towards the south-west until in the twilight he caught sight of a fire and observed the track of camels. These, he knew, belonged to Faisullah's section of the caravan, and, greatly alarmed, he turned about and plodded on until he perceived our fire, and then made straight for it. It was a wonder that none of the camels broke their legs crossing in the dark the endless trenches, gullies, and pits with which the desert is seamed. For twelve mortal hours he had been wandering about the desert, whilst we had travelled in a straight line less than six miles. He would have done better to have remained at the ruins of Lôu-lan, the old tower of which was distinctly visible from the spot where we halted.

Our first care was to get the tea-kettle on, and then we fixed up my felt tent. After that I sent off Khodai Kullu in the direction in which Shagdur had disappeared when he went to look for the camels. I instructed him to keep firing off his rifle as a signal to the Cossack; and we knew he went a pretty long way, for the shots grew fainter and fainter, and at last died away altogether. But he failed to find the man he sought. I was not, however, even for a single moment uneasy with regard to Shagdur; he was capable of finding his way anywhere, and moreover, he was perfectly acquainted with the topography of the region, for he took the keenest interest in my mapping, and knew exactly how many *versts* it was to the Kara-koshun. He always marched by the compass, and counted his steps, and knew exactly how long they were. But when I woke on the following morning and found a fierce sand-storm blowing, so that we were unable to see fifty paces ahead, I thought that Shagdur's position was anything but an enviable one, and assumed, as a matter of course, that he would give up looking for us and make the best of his way due south to the Kara-koshun. Surveying was quite out of the question in such weather; there was nothing to be done, therefore, but to stand still and wait. I spent a good deal of my time patting and caressing the camels, and so sorry did I feel for them at having been led zig-zag backwards and forwards for 20 miles across the desert unnecessarily that, be the result what it might, I gave them the whole of the sack of *kamish* (reeds) we had brought with us from the spring, and a sack of ice in addition.

A Gully in the Shor (Salt) Desert.

Imagine, therefore, my amazement and my delight when about noon Shagdur, with light and elastic step, emerged from out of the all-engulfing haze! He had been on foot no less than 19 hours, had been all the way to Faisullah's camp, and then, begging a few pieces of ice and a handful of rice, had turned round, and in the night, and in the middle of the sand-storm, found his way back to my camp, for he was afraid we should go on without him.

His success in finding us in the darkness and in the midst of the sand-storm was in every way a remarkable feat. Nobody, except a Buriat, who had spent his whole life in the open air, and was at the same time a Cossack, could have done anything like it. Shagdur was the best servant I have ever had in my life, and after the proofs of fidelity, intelligence, and ability which he so frequently exhibited, I did not hesitate to trust him fully, even on occasions of the utmost importance, as you will see subsequently.

The first thing Shagdur did after he had made his report was to give Khodai Värdi a good "jacketing," and this he did of his own accord. Evidently he considered I had been too lenient for not doing it myself.

On the 12th March we were able to continue our survey work, and by the evening of the 13th my levelling had proved the correctness of my theory; for we had crossed a depression, the basin of the former Lop-nor, and the milliards of white mollusc shells showed unmistakably that it was a former lake-basin we had crossed. Exactly at 7 o'clock that evening we heard roaring and hissing sounds approaching from the north-east, and a couple of minutes later a black tempest was careering in all its unmitigated fury across the flat, level expanse. We hurriedly made the necessary preparations, being careful not only to mark the last station of our levelling line, but also to tie down the yurt, and put out the fires, and after the camels had been placed with their heads to leeward, we were all ready to face the worst that might happen. The night was pitch-dark, not a star being visible; nobody was inclined for conversation; the storm howled and whined unchallenged. I was lying writing by the light of a flickering candle, when at nine o'clock Shagdur crept in to take the reading of the boiling-point thermometers, and to help me with the perpetually recurring

The Author Testing his Levelling Instruments at Altimish-bulak.

routine of the meteorological observations. Then he said good-night and disappeared, intending to return to the place where he was sleeping, beside the box that served as our kitchen, scarce fifteen paces to the leeward. Half-an-hour later I heard faint shouts coming from quite another direction. I shouted in reply at the full pitch of my voice, and soon afterwards Shagdur popped his head in. He had lost his way, and, indeed, totally lost touch of our camp, for this tempest was a great deal more violent than its predecessor. I now held open a chink of the covering of the yurt, and Shagdur, by creeping backwards with his eyes fixed upon the gleam of light, managed to pilot himself successfully to his sleeping-place. Only those who have themselves experienced a tempest such as this can form any conception what it is like; it makes you giddy, your sense of locality is paralysed. You imagine that you are going straight forward, and are in reality all the time going round in a circle. Nothing but a compass can lead you right, and even a compass is no use in the dark. Had Khodai Värdi been overtaken by a sand-storm such as that, he would most certainly have been lost; and as he was alone, although he might have unloaded the camels, he would have been quite unable to load them up again, because each camel's load, which is lashed on both sides of its pack-saddle, requires at least two men to lift it up. I shuddered as I thought of what would have happened had the first storm set in a few hours earlier.

On the evening of the 15th March the camels began to eat up the straw stuffings of their pack-saddles; but of these we had now less need, for our supply of ice had shrunk very considerably. We had, indeed, plenty of drinking-water, but it had assumed a repulsive and disagreeable flavour of goat-skin. There were, however, a few pieces of ice still left swimming amongst it, and this was all we had that we could drink.

We now began to look out through the glass for Tokta Akhun's signal-fire. The surface of the desert was there as flat as the ocean. When we started on the 16th, we had only about twelve miles to go to reach the lake, but our measurements took up a good deal of time. All the same, we began to note the first indications of the proximity of "land"; I mean we began to observe that we were approaching the "shore" of the desert "ocean." First came two or three dead or dying tamarisks; then small, low sand-dunes, which had formed behind the bushes—most welcome to our tender feet. Then the sight of flocks of wild-duck put fresh life into us. The ground inclined, although extremely slowly, towards the south—an indication that we were nearing the Kara-koshun.

The 17th March was a sultry day. We were all hungry and tired. The desert, again absolutely barren, burnt under our feet, for we crawled along so slowly owing to the measurements we were making. When putting in the 17th staff on the top of a dune, two of the men cried, "Water! Water! in every direction!" and in fact we were so near to the Kara-koshun that the 19th staff was actually placed in the water. Here we were then, at the end of our tiring and irksome, but none the less important, task.

The lake extended over an immense area—shallow, bare, and devoid of vegetation. The water was slightly salt, but it was at any rate better than the tepid jolted stuff we had in our goat-skins. The camels regarded the watery expanse with a calm and critical eye; evidently they thought, as we did, that this place, in comparison with the desert we had left behind us, was a perfect paradise. Along the shore was a sprinkling of steppe plants, and whilst we formed our camp amongst them, we turned our animals loose to graze. Everybody was now in the highest good spirits.

But what had become of Tokta Akhun? There were no indications that human beings had been anywhere in the locality. The shore-line appeared to extend westwards all the way to Kum-chápghan. Somewhere along that line, probably quite close to us, the relief caravan must be waiting. It could not, of course, have advanced as far as the spot where we then were, because it would be dependent upon grazing and fresh water, and there was neither of these there. I now ordered Khodai Kullu to go in search of Tokta Akhun's party, and not to rest day or night until he found them. We would wait where we were until he came back with them; it would not be more than a day at the outside. We did not give our scout anything to eat, for the simple reason that we had not anything to give him; but, whatever happened, he would not perish of thirst.

After Khodai Kullu had disappeared in the mist, we once more began to live the life of Robinson Crusoe. Our first thought was to get hold of something to eat. Shagdur therefore took his sporting rifle, and went out and brought back two fat ducks, which we shared equally amongst us; but we were so ravenously hungry that we hardly gave them time to get warmed through over the embers before we devoured them.

It was a blessing we had finished our measuring when we did, for early that evening we were assailed by the fourth sand-storm of the spring, and it continued to rage uninterruptedly for two days and three nights on end. I was sorry then that I had sent off honest Khodai Kullu; but I hoped he would find shelter somewhere during the night. He had a box of matches with him, so that he could make a signal-fire in case of need; but in such weather, with the air as thick as muddy water, no fire would have been seen more than 200 paces away.

When the second evening came, and brought no tidings

or signs of our messenger, we grew quite anxious about him. It was evident something was amiss. In vain did we keep going and looking along the shore; the only objects we saw loom up out of the haze were our own camels. This would never do; we must take action, we must do something. Nor was the situation made any the more comfortable by the never-ending clouds of drift-

A Copper Lamp from Lôu-lan.

sand which went driving past, pattering on the yurt-coverings like fine rain on a canvas-covered wagon. Fortunately, Shagdur shot five other wild-ducks, which went down first-rate, notwithstanding that they were well-seasoned with salt drift-sand.

On the morning of the 20th it was clear to us that we could no longer count on Khodai Kullu. It was evident he had failed to find the relief caravan; indeed, he would be lucky if he succeeded in making his way to an inhabited region before he perished of hunger. Our position was beginning to be desperate. I had never been in such straits since the terrible days of the Takla-makan in 1895. All we now had to live upon were the wild-ducks that Shagdur shot.

All of a sudden I made up my mind that we would push on. Accordingly we hastened to turn our backs upon that inhospitable shore which we had first beheld with such feelings of confident hope. The sky was grey and heavy after the storm ; the diffused light cast no shadows. Whilst following the shore, we found that all at once it swung away quite unexpectedly towards the north. Khodai Kullu's footsteps were perceptible every now and again. Then we came to an old, old kamish hut, buried up to the eaves in drift-sand. Upon a closer examination we detected a canoe leaning against the wall. In a moment it flashed upon me that this boat might prove our salvation. With it Kutchuk and I could in the course of a few hours paddle to those parts of the Kara-koshun in which the water is fresh and the kamish plentiful, and fish abound. At it we went, then, shovelling the sand away with desperate energy. We got down three feet, we got down six feet, then we found—a big gaping hole in the bottom of the canoe, while the whole of the forepart, which penetrated to the ground-water, was rotten. On then again! At length the shore of the lake turned once more to the west, and we still followed it. Soon after that we came to a second hut, standing solitary and deserted quite close to the edge of the water. Shagdur took advantage of it, and, creeping stealthily along the ground like a fox, let fly in the middle of a flock of wild-duck, which were chattering at the lake-side. When he returned, carrying seven birds in his hands, he was received with quite a cheer. This would keep us going for two days more.

As the lake shore now inclined to the south, we turned

away from it and directed our steps towards the south-west. Khodai Kullu's footsteps continued on to the north-west. "What in the world was he going to do in the desert?" we wondered. Well, the man clearly had a screw loose, and we decided it would be folly to keep to his wandering footsteps. Upon reaching some pools of salt water where there was both good grazing and plenty of fuel, we pulled up and encamped.

The Stag. On the Left a Chinaman, Chernoff, and Turdu Bai, and on the Right Islam Bai.

Late that night, after the air had cleared a little, we made up two immense fires of dry tamarisks; but they flared up, crackled, glowed and died down again without eliciting any answer. The night was still and silent. No suspicious sound was heard, no horseman arrived with glad tidings. I grew impatient, and my uneasiness deepened. We looked upon Khodai Kullu as already lost. Faisullah must have arrived at Kum-chapghan fully a week earlier.

Why had he not the sense to send us relief? He knew that on the 10th March we had started, provisioned for only eight days, and this was now the twelfth day since we parted. And why did we hear nothing of Tokta Akhun? When we separated at Anambaruin-gol I had distinctly ordered him to meet us here betimes. Had some misfortune happened to him, and prevented him from ever reaching Charkhlik? Or had he been confused by those wandering lakes which change their position and appearance every year? When should we get an answer to all these questions, and when would this intricate tangle be unravelled? The night, stretching dark and voiceless all around us, had no answer to give; nor were the thin columns of smoke, that curled lazily upwards from the dying embers, able to give us any answer either.

Next day we reached the shore of another lake where the reeds were growing thick. Here another couple of wild-duck fell to Shagdur's gun. I was riding my old desert camel so as to be able to see as far as possible. Next we were stopped by a narrow stream, and the rest of the day was spent in wandering fruitlessly backwards and forwards in search of a way out of the watery labyrinth which hemmed us in on all sides. Why did we not simply march straight on across the shallow canals and marshes? Simply because it was impossible. Their bottoms were so many oozy morasses, into which we should have sunk as readily as we should in water. We encamped that night in a rat-trap. The only direction in which there was firm ground was to the north-east, the way we had come.

During the evening and night fresh currents flowed in behind us, and next morning we had to make haste and start early to prevent ourselves from being entirely surrounded by the water. We could easily have got out ourselves, but not so the camels. That strange saliferous sedimentary soil is as hard as brick when dry, but no sooner does the water flow over it than it turns as soft as porridge. We had no choice, therefore, but were obliged to turn back. Beside a broad water-arm we again saw Khodai Kullu's footsteps; he had evidently swum across, for his trail disappeared at the very edge of the water. He had now been absent five days; perhaps he was lying in a swoon beside one of these water-courses vainly longing for help?

On the 23rd March we continued our course towards the north-east, for it was in that direction that these treacherous, newly-formed lakes still continued to extend. The locality was again absolutely sterile. I was a long way on ahead; and from what I saw I was no longer astonished that my servants had failed to find their way. The reality differed *in toto* from the description I had given them. These new lakes had drawn a fatal stroke through our reckoning. All the same I was immensely interested in them; they proved that the Kara-koshun is endeavouring to return to the old bed of the Lop-nor.

Upon reaching a point where the arm contracted to a breadth of 20–25 feet immediately before entering a small lake, I stopped, tired, and stood still waiting for the others to come up. The bottom of the channel consisted of blue clay, and ought, therefore, to bear the camels. But I was unwilling to take them across until Shagdur had proceeded north to reconnoitre, and ascertain whether there were any sheets of water within sight likely to stop our progress. After a good hour's absence he turned up on the eastern side of the little lake, making the most excited gestures to us to go and join him. I preferred, however, to hear what he had to say first. Shagdur therefore started running, and as soon as he came near enough to make himself heard, he pointed to the south-west, and shouted breathlessly, "Horsemen! Horsemen!"

Turning, we saw two mounted men approaching at full gallop amid a cloud of dust. At the spot where he had beckoned to us, Shagdur had observed the quite fresh footprints of five horses, and a couple of minutes later he caught sight of the two horsemen. A prey to the keenest anxiety, I steadily kept the mysterious riders within the range of my glass. What news would they bring us? A few minutes passed, and then I recognised them: they were Tokta Akhun and—what?——Is it possible?—Chernoff!

Never have I greeted a faithful servant with greater delight and with a warmer welcome than I now extended to these men. My good Cossack was also so overjoyed that he actually trembled, and his cheeks burned with eagerness, he was so anxious to tell me of all that had happened to him since we parted.

The first question I put to him was, "How is it possible that you are here, Chernoff?" He then told me that he and Sirkin had been scarcely two months in Kashgar when a telegram arrived, commanding both of them in the name of the Czar to return to my camp wherever I might be, and to stay with me as long as I might desire to keep them. I had, indeed, written to His Imperial Majesty the Czar, begging him to grant me this favour, and he had graciously accorded it.

When Tokta Akhun arrived at Charkhlik, the Cossacks were already there, and had been for some time. Chernoff therefore accompanied him to the rendezvous on the northern shore of the Kara-koshun. Upon being stopped by the newly-formed lakes, they decided to await us there, fully believing that I should be able to find them. I ascertained they had carried out my instructions to the letter, building a hut and lighting a big fire on a hill every noon and every evening; and even when a sand-storm was raging, making it impossible to see 100 yards

A Corner of the Stable-Yard in our Serai. Sirkin seated on the Rice-Sacks, Turdu Bai standing in Front of the Dromedary.

away, they never failed to carry out my orders all the same.

Several fishers from Kum-chapghan came to visit them, and a new settlement, with flocks of sheep and horses and canoes, grew up beside the new lake. For twelve days past they had been leading an idyllic life, hunting, fishing, and making long excursions in quest of us. One fine day, however, brave Khodai Kullu turned up at their camp, and all at once the situation was changed. In the course of a few minutes they had seven horses ready and loaded up, and with Khodai Kullu as their guide, they set off to look for us. They had gone straight to our first camp beside the lake, where we finished the measuring; but when they saw that we had left they followed the trail of our camels, going through all the same zig-zag wanderings that we had done.

We now set off together to look for a suitable place to encamp in, for we desert wayfarers were tremendously hungry and the rescue party had all sorts of nice things, including eggs and fish, in their saddle-bags. On the way we fell in with Khodai Kullu and the pack-horses. He was sitting on a heap of bushwood, weeping bitterly, so overpowered was he by the recollection of all the adventures and hardships he had undergone during his five days' hunting after the relief expedition. On and on he had trudged, until at last, in sheer desperation, he had swum across more than one lake. On the third day he was sitting, tired and dispirited, beside one of these when a flock of wild-duck swept over his head. As if by a miracle one of the birds dropped straight down at his feet, its wing either broken or injured. Wolfish with hunger, poor Khodai Kullu flung himself upon it and devoured it, feathers and all, just as it was. This gave him strength to continue two days longer, and within that time he at length found those he was in search of.

I gave Khodai Kullu a handsome reward in silver for the courage and resolution he had shown. He assured me, quite simply, that during the whole of the time he was firmly decided not to turn back before he had executed my order, even though it should cost him his life. Ever since he had killed the wild camel, Khodai Kullu's reputation had been rising amongst the men; but from this time onwards he was never called anything else but *Batir*, meaning "The Hero." These are the fellows you want to have about you!

Meanwhile, in the course of his wanderings he had come across Faisullah's trail, and perceived that Faisullah was going in the wrong direction, namely, right back into the desert again. As soon as Tokta Akhun heard this, he sent out from Kum-chapghan and Abdal two relief expeditions, with asses carrying food and water. I was consumed with the keenest anxiety about Faisullah, for he had all the old wood-carvings from the ruins, and all the photographic plates I had taken, together with other valuable possessions, packed away in his boxes.

After resting two days, we set off for Tokta Akhun's hut, a journey which it took us four days to accomplish. Now the most remarkable thing of all was, that at the point where we turned back, and were very nearly surrounded by the water, we were not more than two miles from the camp of the rescue party. But between our two camps there were several new arms and lakes, which, issuing northwards from the Kara-koshun, formed in the middle of the desert a large lake, and this we now had to go round—that is, we had to march four days in order to advance two miles.

At Tokta Akhun's camp we again rested, and I made a couple of splendid canoe trips before we finally set off for the shore of the Ak-köl, where Numet Bek, one of my old friends, met us with the good news that Faisullah was safe and waiting for us at Abdal. Late that evening I ate my supper beside that peaceful lake amidst the worst swarm of gnats I have ever fallen in with; but what did I care about gnats now that all my people were safe, and my recent labours were crowned with success? At length we heard the voices of the fishermen and the splashing of paddles, and five canoes shot up, come to take us up the Tarim to Abdal. This trip proved to be one of those fascinating, never-to-be-forgotten moonlight journeys on the still, bright river, amid Venetian-like surroundings, such as I had already experienced once or twice before. Upon reaching Abdal we found there Faisullah and his two companions safe and sound; but they considered it was a perilous commission I had given them when we separated at the ruins of Lôu-lan. They had crossed the desert without difficulty, but upon reaching the newly-formed lakes they completely lost their heads. Faisullah —as was indeed natural—failed to recognise the country again, although he had been there the year before. He was persuaded, too, that my compass was an arrant deceiver, and that the best place for it was at the bottom of one of my boxes. Anyhow, they had finally turned their backs upon the treacherous lakes, and after making a wide sweep round into the desert had landed, exhausted and half-famished, in the neighbourhood of the Tarim. To make matters worse, all three horses died at once, and for two weeks the men lived entirely upon horse-flesh.

Now, however, all their, and all our, toil and hardship were alike forgotten; and after yet two other days' rest we set off for Charkhlik, saying good-bye finally to the Tarim and its lakes. Whenever I think of those places, so far away in the heart of the desert, there always comes over me a feeling of sadness, coupled with the desire to go and see them again.

## CHAPTER XIX.

### THE GREAT START—SHEREB LAMA.

THEN, whilst I was making preparations for my last great expedition to Tibet, the most difficult part of my entire journey, I enjoyed a delightful, and indeed much needed, rest in the little town of Charkhlik. We occupied a comfortable and roomy *serai*, which had a large orchard of mulberry and plum trees, and under the shade of these my Mongolian yurt was pitched. My companions were a handsome stag, which had been caught in the woods of the Cherchen-daria, and now roamed freely about the orchard, and Yoldash; whilst outside Yolbars helped the night-watchman to keep guard. The stag was quite tame, and often used to come and eat bread out of my hand.

We were now in no hurry, for we had to wait for the grass in the mountainous regions, and it would be several weeks yet before it began to sprout up. Our animals therefore were able to obtain a thorough good rest, and so fit themselves for the tremendous hardships which awaited them. Almost every day Islam Bai bought one or two camels, so that by the time we started we had 39 in all, though three of these were born in Charkhlik. The youngest of the three was born on the 6th May, and when I went to look at it the little creature was hardly able to stand; but in the course of a few days it was roaming freely about the stable-yard, full of play. It accompanied us the greater part of the journey through Tibet, and long out-lived both its two comrades and its mother.

Meanwhile, stores were being bought to last ten months, and were being divided and packed up, and lashed to the pack-saddles, ready for starting. By the end of April the courtyard of the *serai* was crowded with long rows of heavy packages. In fact, the sight of them filled me with dismay. Had all that to be dragged through the wilds of Tibet? But Turdu Bai assured me that the loads were not too heavy, and besides their weight would grow less every day. One row consisted of sacks of rice, each sack crammed to the very top; another row of maize; a third of roasted flour and ready-made bread. Then there were big bales of skin coats for the men and of white felt rugs for the camels. Besides, there were numerous cases containing my instruments, clothes, books, preserved foods, ammunition, implements, weapons, articles intended as presents for the Tibetans, and a thousand and one other things that are required on a long journey. To feed our large force of camels and horses we needed a great store of maize. This I arranged should be carried up by 70 asses, which I hired from an old fellow, named Dovlet, from Bokhara, who was assisted by half a dozen men. After six or eight weeks the camels' loads would be so far reduced that we should be able to transfer the maize from the asses to their backs, and then Dovlet and his convoy were to return home.

In procuring and arranging all these stores my four Cossacks rendered me most valuable assistance, each of them having his own department to look after. But for the two Buriats, Shagdur and Cherdon, I had a special errand. I had got it into my head that I would not leave the mysterious land of Tibet without making at least one attempt to penetrate to Lassa in disguise. For this purpose I required a complete outfit and equipment of Mongolian clothing and Mongolian utensils, crockery, travelling boxes, and so forth—in a word, everything that Mongol pilgrims are wont to carry with them when they pilgrimage to the Holy City. Shagdur alone was, however, initiated into my plans; Cherdon was led to believe that the purchases which they two were about to make in Kara-

Sirkin and Chernoff with the two Baby Camels.

shahr were for their own use. Shagdur was also to bring back with him to Charkhlik a Mongol who had been in Lassa and could speak Tibetan.

When the time approached for their return, we set about making the final preparations for the start. Not wishing to carry with me through Tibet a greater amount of baggage than was absolutely necessary, and having as it was already an exceptionally large caravan, I determined to leave behind a portion of my belongings. What was the use of dragging all through Tibet the skeletons and heads of the animals and the geological specimens I had collected, or the heavy carved woodwork we had brought from Lôu-lan? All these made up nine camels' loads, and would have to be unloaded and loaded up again every day for the space of nine months. Better send them, therefore, I thought, to Kashgar by the great caravan road through Aksu. But of all the Mussulmans there was only one to whom I felt I could entrust such a very important mission, namely, Islam Bai. It was indeed hard to part from him, but the programme I sketched for him reconciled us both to the separation. He was to carry my collections to Kashgar, and having handed them over to Mr. Petrovsky, Russian Consul-General, he was to take five months' leave of absence, and go and visit his family at Osh. After that he was to return to Kashgar, lift my post-bag and a sum of money, and carry them to Ladak, where he was to await my arrival. Old Faisullah, who had felt severely the hardships he had recently undergone, would accompany him to Kashgar.

Another important task that I entrusted to Islam Bai was to carry to Kashgar my own post-bag, and a heavy one it was. The most important of the letters it contained was one addressed to Lord Curzon, Viceroy of India, in which I begged him to allow me to lift a loan of a few thousand rupees at Leh, in Ladak, and at the same time I hinted at the possibility of a short visit to India, and if I did visit that country, I requested permission to take with me one of my Cossacks. The kind answer which I received to this letter on my arrival at Leh belongs to a later chapter of this book.

On the 5th May Islam Bai set out on his journey to the north and west, with eight camels and some horses, and servants to look after them.

Three days later our caravan was all ready to start,

At Charkhlik, the Day before the Start.

and a very long string they made. It was, in fact, the biggest caravan I have ever led; the biggest, indeed, that any European has ever led with a peaceful object into the interior of Tibet. It marched in several detachments, each under the command of a separate leader, the string filling the whole of the road in front of the *yamen*, where Jan Daloi, the Chinese *amban*, or governor, and a special friend of mine, resided. All the animals were in the pink of condition. In fact, the horses were so fresh as to be half-wild, and no sooner did they get started than they began to play the maddest pranks, flinging off their loads and galloping away. Fortunately they carried nothing but sacks of grain and so forth, which, the sacks being strong and well-tied, suffered no hurt.

It was in truth a magnificent spectacle to see the long array of caravan animals winding away from the quiet *serai* and the shade of its willows to the tinkling of the camels' bells and any amount of shouting and screaming, neighing, roaring and barking. The dust hung in clouds along the highway. And yet I feared, nay I knew, that the greater part of these noble animals would leave their bones in the inhospitable wilds of Tibet. It is not without reason that my route is marked on the map with red: the journey was at the price of blood.

Chernoff was appointed commander-in-chief of the whole caravan, while Turdu Bai was nominated captain of the camel corps. Their orders were to march by way of Abdal and Tatlik-bulak, the easiest road that existed, up into the highlands, and there await my arrival beside the lake of Kum-köl. They also took with them seven dogs and the stag, and were to buy fifty sheep in Abdal.

After they had disappeared amongst the orchards, our *serai* felt very lonely and silent; stables and courtyards were all empty, and I was left alone, except for the three men whom I kept back to wait upon me—namely, Sirkin, my "chamberlain"; Li Loyeh, my cook; and Mollah Shah, to look after our horses. But I am forgetting—I still had Yoldash, for he never left me.

On the 13th May the ass caravan was ready to start,

Shereb Lama on Golden Ears, with Yolbars on a Cord.

and set off under the command of old Dovlet. He expected soon to overtake the main caravan, for he was going up by a shorter route. My strength was thus more scattered than it had ever been before. Here was I in Charkhlik; the main body of the caravan was on the road to Abdal; the ass caravan was marching up the Astyn-tagh; Shagdur and Cherdon had not yet returned from Kara-shahr; and Islam was wending his way through the worst of the summer heat to Kashgar. I felt like a general who has to keep the threads of his forces in his hands, and I had to manœuvre them in such a way as to make all their movements fit together at the right moment.

A messenger came on the 14th May to tell me that the Buriats were approaching. Thereupon, I sent a courier to meet them, with a command to Cherdon to ride up by the nearest road, and go and join the main body under Chernoff. I need not say that Shagdur had accomplished his mission in an exemplary way. He brought with him a complete Mongol outfit, and Shereb Lama, a Lamaist monk of 27, who was born at Urga in Mongolia, but now belonged to a temple outside Kara-shahr. He was dressed in his red priestly robe, which was more like a long night-shirt than anything else, and was fastened round the middle by a yellow girdle, and on his head he wore a small Chinese skull-cap. I gave him a very friendly welcome, so that from the first moment he might feel himself at home, and I at once began to brush up my rusty knowledge of the Mongol language. Ere many weeks had passed I was able to talk pretty fluently with the Lama, for so we quite simply called him. This man, the Lama, became the most interesting figure in all our company. In me he soon came to repose the utmost confidence, and used to confide to me all his troubles. He was ready to lay down his life for his master, and of a truth it was a very great wonder he did not do so.

Shereb Lama, when approached by Shagdur with the invitation to accompany him and Cherdon to Lassa—for being Lamaists they both enjoyed the right of visiting the Holy City—Shereb Lama had at once shown himself willing. But he had made it a condition that no "Russian" (*i.e.*, European) should accompany them, for if so he could not go, it might cost him his life. Shagdur assured him that no Russian would accompany them. During the journey to Charkhlik the Lama talked so much about the glories of Lassa, that Shagdur was simply dying with impatience to see it. Putting aside the visit to the Holy City, the Lama was willing to accompany me anywhere I chose, and duly received leave of absence from the prior of his monastery.

Once more there was life and movement in our *serai* after Shagdur arrived with his three companions; for he had brought two other persons with him. One of these was our old friend Ördek, who begged and prayed that he might accompany me to the world's end; the other was Khalmet Aksakal, a Russian subject from West Turkestan, though then living in Korla, an old man whom I had known for many years. The last-named, however, brought me intelligence which it was anything but a pleasure to hear. When he sold horses and provisions to Islam Bai at Korla, Islam, he complained, had cheated him, and he advised me to examine whether I too had not been robbed. I did not understand what the man meant. Islam Bai a deceiver! Islam Bai, who for five years had been faithful to me unto death, who had shared with me toil and tribulation, adventure and danger, among the burning sands of the desert—Islam in whom I had reposed the utmost confidence, and whom my King had in 1897 rewarded with a gold medal for his fidelity and honesty—Islam a thief? Impossible! I could not, I would not, believe it.

Let me be brief and spare both you and myself the details of this painful episode. Upon investigation I found that Islam Bai *was* a thief, that he had in fact stolen right and left, yet in such a way that there was no trace of it in my accounts. The people who suffered were those from whom he bought supplies, for none of them had been paid the full amount due to him. Islam threatened that if anybody complained he would shoot him, and that was why no whisper of his frauds ever reached my ears. It was very hard to have the unlimited confidence which I put in this man abused in this fashion. After this blow I felt a difficulty in breathing in Charkhlik, and longed with burning impatience to get away up into the crisp air of the mountains, where I hoped these gloomy memories would soon be blown away. But before starting I sent a special messenger to Consul Petrovsky, who arrived at Kashgar a fortnight or so before Islam did. Islam Bai, therefore, upon his arrival, was at once arrested, and his baggage overhauled. After that he was set at liberty, but on condition that he was not to leave Kashgar before I arrived there, which happened to be a year later. When I saw him again he was old and broken, and notwithstanding the many witnesses who came to speak against him at the trial, he could not be induced to confess his offences. After that he was taken to Osh, and sentenced to Siberia, though I was able to get his punishment reduced to two weeks' imprisonment, for the Russian authorities absolutely refused to let him off scot free. I have never seen him since then, nor do I wish to see him again; he is to me as one that is dead. I felt terribly sorry for him, for had he conducted himself properly he would have been a distinguished man in his native town, whereas now he had ruined himself and utterly spoiled his career.

In comparison with this disagreeable history, another *contretemps* which happened in Charkhlik was a mere trifle. It was this. On the afternoon of the 16th May there arrived a caravan of ten Mongol pilgrims from Tarbagatai (in Western Mongolia), and encamped in a grove just outside the bazaar. Now, as it happened, Shagdur and the Lama had met these people in Kara-shahr, and knew that they were travelling to Lassa. We could not, therefore, very well make a start without their getting to hear of it, and they would then soon have ferreted out that we were bound for Tibet. They would be pretty sure to reach the neighbourhood of Lassa before we did, and would consequently warn the Tibetan authorities of our approach. When, therefore, we left Charkhlik on the morning of the 17th May we made a detour in the opposite direction, before we durst bend our steps towards the mountain-ranges that shut in Tibet on the north.

# CHAPTER XX.

## ON THE WAY TO THE ARKA-TAGH.

THE caravan with which I myself now started for Northern Tibet consisted of the following: the Russian Cossack Sirkin, the Buriat Cossack Shagdur, the Mongol Shereb Lama, the Mussulmans Mollah Shah and Li Loyeh, the dog Yoldash, and twelve horses. The mountains, towering up before us in all their overwhelming majesty, drew us on with the magic of their attraction, and early on the second day we entered the first of their glens. How delightful was their sublime scenery! After our long monotonous journeys across the desert in the winter, how stimulating their ever-changing panoramas! And how pleasant the sound of our voices echoing against the cliffs, and pleasanter still to fill our lungs with pure crisp mountain air, in which there was not one particle of dust or drift-sand!

On the bank of the river Charkhlik-su, then greatly swollen, we had to wait a day for the arrival of a supplementary caravan of 10 asses, which I had hired to accompany us to Kum-köl and carry maize for our horses. When they did arrive, we set off beside the stream, marching up the glen, or, rather, ravine, for the stream had cut its way deep through the grey granite, and the cliffs, undermined by the tumultuous flood, often hung right over the track like a canopy. We knew that we had to cross the river no less than 16 times, and would therefore have to keep a sharp

**Our Camp in the Glen of the Charkhlik-su.**

look out and be perpetually on the alert. A shepherd whom we met gave us news that was anything but encouraging. His horse had come down in the middle of the torrent, and he had lost the whole of its load, consisting of bread, maize and clothing. And, in truth, it was an exciting ride. The bottom of the stream was full of huge blocks of granite, rounded and water-worn, amidst which the torrent thundered and boiled amid tossing showers of spray. If a horse trod on one of these bare slippery stones he had hard work to keep his footing, and if he stepped between them he ran a risk of getting stuck fast. What caused me the most uneasiness were the cases containing my instruments, photographic apparatus and photographic plates. At every ford a couple of the men used to strip themselves half naked and go into the water bare-legged to find out how deep it was. Then the horses were led across one by one and with the utmost caution by three men. Upon reaching a ford that was easier than usual one of our two mules refused to follow the horses, but tried to go at the side, where the water was flowing in a deep channel. She was, however, caught by the current, which carried her a little way down the stream and then flung her on a bank of gravel. Without a moment's hesitation the two Cossacks plunged into the water with their clothes on and succeeded in rescuing her, though we lost the whole of the load she was carrying, namely, flour and bread.

The fourth day brought us up to the pass of Yaman-davan, a very suitable name, for the word means "bad pass." The glen we were following contracted to a narrow gorge, and the ascent grew so steep that we all preferred to get off and walk. The loads kept slipping first to one side and then to the other, and then back to the horses' tails, and we had to stop incessantly to put them right. The summit of the pass was as sharp drawn as a knife-blade. From the pinnacle of an adjacent crag our ascent was watched by *arkhari* (wild sheep), but, fortunately for them, they were out of range.

One more day's march, and we emerged from this fantastic border-range, and once more found ourselves upon the lofty plateau of Northern Tibet. Our arrival was greeted by heavy, black clouds, which every now and again shook out their contents—rain and snow—over us—the sort of weather we had had more than a taste of the summer before.

In his fiery red robe, his yellow girdle and his blue cap, over which in rainy weather he used to draw a skin *bashlik* (hood), Shereb Lama was like the good-natured brownie of our caravan. The only people with whom he was able to talk (Mongolian) were Shagdur and myself, though he gradually learned to speak Turki. During our long rides he used to be very meditative. No doubt he was wondering what strange company this was his destiny had made him acquainted with. I had no end of difficulty to make him understand the object of my astronomical and topographical observations. In his eyes I was, I am sure, a very extraordinary sort of person, and yet he attached himself to me with a confidence and devotion that were quite touching. He understood perfectly well that we foreigners entertained none but friendly feelings towards him. I have seldom had a more zealous and insistent teacher than he was; he was *determined* that I should learn his mother tongue, so that we might be able to discuss freely the subjects which especially interested him.

One day when we were forced to mark time beside the Upper Charkhlik-su because of the bad weather, I took the opportunity to make the Lama acquainted with my plans. Whatever their ultimate issue, I did not wish him to believe or suppose that I had by deceit tricked him into any mad sort of enterprise. I thought it better to tell him frankly what I proposed to do, so that he might, if he chose, return to his own country with his honour unsullied. Accordingly I now told him that it was my fixed purpose to try and enter Lassa disguised as a Mongol, and accompanied by him and Shagdur. For a while he sat speechless, staring at me, and then ejaculated that the plan was absolutely impossible. "They will not dare to touch you or Shagdur, Sir, but I am a lama and should lose my head. And if they did not kill me, my future would certainly be ruined; I should be looked upon as a traitor and a renegade if I guided a European to Lassa. The Dalai Lama, the Mongol pilgrims, and the Chinese *amban* are not dangerous; but think of all the Tibetans who guard the roads leading to Lassa, and of all the priests in the temples who knew me when I was there studying in the university."

As I still persisted in my plan, the Lama suggested that it would be much better if the entire caravan were to march straight towards the capital of Tibet, for in that case we should only at the worst be politely, but firmly, turned back; and he might then disguise himself as a Turk, and none of his friends would ever suspect that he was in our company. At present, however, he would go with us as far as the Kum-köl, and if he then decided to return he could do so with the ass-drivers, for by that time we should certainly be able to do without their caravan. I proposed, therefore, that he should remain with the caravan, whilst I and the two Buriats rode towards Lassa, but this compromise did not jump with his ambition. "I cannot desert my master just when he requires me most," he said. During the days that followed he sat buried in his deep Mongol saddle, moody and full of thought. He considered it was mean of Shagdur not to have told him what I wanted him for, until I explained to him that Shagdur was only acting according to orders. We discussed the question as we rode up and down the glens, and again every evening when it grew dusk; and during all this time Shereb Lama suffered

Our Camp at Unkurluk, Looking up the Side-Glen.

tortures of mental agony. His mind was torn between his duty as a Lamaist and his personal devotion to me. For piety, for humility, and for real goodness, he reminded me of his colleague in *Kim*, one of the best characters that Rudyard Kipling has ever drawn. At Kum-köl, then, he was to make his decision, choosing whether he would prefer his safe quiet cell in the temple monastery at Kara-shahr, or the dangerous uncertainties and risks of keeping company with me.

At Unkurluk we bought twelve sheep from some shepherds, and then, climbing over a pass 13,000 feet high, we rode down into the valley of Chimen, where we had been the year before. Here Shagdur was seized with a species of mountain-sickness, with high fever and extraordinarily rapid pulse. For two or three days I was extremely anxious about him, but he soon recovered sufficiently to allow us to proceed.

On the 1st June we encamped on the left shore of the lake of Kum-köl, and had nothing else to do except to wait for the main caravan. This was almost the last quiet restful time I enjoyed during the remainder of the journey. The silence of the waste was unbroken, save for the east wind that blew, and the monotonous beat of the waves against the shore. I now dismissed the asses which had brought up the maize for our own horses. The grass was, however, so poor that the horses ran away, and Mollah Shah had no end of trouble to catch them and bring them back again.

The 4th June was a beautiful bright day; the men were asleep in their tent, all except the Lama, who, having fallen in love with my telescope, was sitting outside my yurt sweeping the horizon with it. All at once he rushed in and announced that he saw something which must be the expected caravan, of the existence of which he had hitherto had rather hazy ideas. Quite right—at the foot of the mountains I could just make out six thin dark lines and several dots. They were evidently our people, but the distance was much too great for them to be able to see us. We watched their progress with great interest, expecting soon to see them wheel and steer straight for our camp. But no, nothing of the kind. Instead of that they halted, and very soon the lines disappeared and became converted into dots. I understood then that they were encamping, having found tolerable grazing; therefore I sent Mollah Shah to them with instructions to come on and join us. It was a long time, however, before the little dots began to gather together; but eventually we were able to make out that the animals were being loaded up again, and soon after that we saw them start and come marching straight towards our camp.

After a while two horsemen detached themselves from the head of the column and galloped forward to where I stood. They were Chernoff and Cherdon, and they reported that all was well. Next came the ass-caravan, with old Dovlet at its head, and behind his grey column a confused and terrified kulan made off amid a cloud of dust. The next in the string was Turdu Bai, at the head of his magnificent camels, all wearing white *chapans*, or "felt rugs," which the men had made for them in their leisure hours on the way up. The three young camels looked very comical in their white rugs as they played about their mothers, while the youngest, which was scarcely a month old, frolicked about without showing the slightest sign of fatigue. The stag also was thriving.

The procession was closed by the horses with their drivers. Each column passed in review order before the spot where I stood, surrounded by the Cossacks, and answering the respectful greetings of the men as they marched past. The loads were arranged four-square so as to make a fold for the sheep, which faithfully followed the ram Vanka, an exceptionally trustworthy and tame animal. Vanka had already been with us two years, and was as faithful and obedient as a dog, while he looked after the other sheep with so much sense and cleverness that they scarcely needed any other shepherd. Of all the animals which passed before me that day Vanka was the only one left when we reached Kashgar a year later. Before starting again it was necessary to re-inspect all the loads, and make various alterations and rearrangements, and this took a whole day. During the journey up the Cossacks had made for me a remarkably comfortable little yurt, and this I now substituted for the old one. The shore of the lake was like a busy mart, what with the yurts and the tents, and the bales of goods, the animals grazing all over the locality, mounted men going to and fro, and other men sitting round the fires talking. Meanwhile, the breakers tumbled upon the shore, while the rain pattered thick and fast about our ears.

The hour had now come for the Lama to make his final decision. I let him settle the matter himself, and was very pleased when of his own accord he came to my yurt, and declared that it was his intention to follow me wherever I might go ; only there was one favour he begged me to grant him, and that was, if he fell sick I would not desert him, and this of course I readily promised. It was nothing short of a blessing that he agreed to go with me, otherwise I do not know what would have happened.

Finally, I called together all the Mussulmans, and publicly nominated Turdu Bai *Tugachi-bashi*, or Captain of the Camels, while Hamra Kul, a big, loosely-built fellow, was appointed *At-bashi*, or Superintendent of the Horses. His son, Turdu Akhun, a lad of sixteen, was the Mohammedans' "maid-of-all-work." The other men of my little troop I will introduce as occasion offers.

At last the morning dawned when I had the whole of my strength collected together in one place, and had no longer any need to bother myself about rendezvous and signal-fires. I superintended the start from the saddle, being again mounted on my favourite grey nag. The work of taking down the tents and loading up the animals was accomplished quicker than I expected. The first to start were the camels, arranged in five strings, each with a separate leader, the first string being led by Turdu Bai.

The horses and mules, to the total number of 45, were also led or driven in separate groups, and were followed by men on foot, to see that the loads kept their balance and did not slip off. The flock of sheep followed obediently behind Vanka, and seldom needed looking after. The dogs chased one another in and out amongst the troops of animals, and thought it all fine fun. The stag, however, was of a different way of thinking, for he sickened badly, and had to be killed. The asses, about 60 in number, were soon left behind; in fact, they never reached the camp at all that night.

The long caravan made a varied and interesting picture as it wound at slow and heavy pace beside the blue-green waters of the lake—the Cossacks in their now threadbare uniforms, and with their skin coats strapped on their saddles behind them; the Mussulmans, in their variously-coloured *chapans* and skin caps; the ass-drivers, resembling a troop of Oriental beggars; the priestly profession represented by Rosi Mollah, learned in the Koran, and Shereb Lama, who every day entertained Shagdur and me with stories of the secrets he had discovered in the temples of Holy Lassa. The whole reminded me of an invading army, and such we indeed were, though we were on our way to conquer new provinces of unexplored Tibet for the science of geography. I was perfectly alive to the fact that we had now burnt our ships behind us, and that the greater part of the large and imposing caravan which had just defiled before me was doomed to almost certain destruction. Yet whatever might happen, we should certainly not turn back north again; our route ran south and west, and I was resolved that I would not deviate from it before I had made an attempt to penetrate to Lassa, nor return until I had heard the surf of the Indian Ocean thundering on the beach.

Our first day's march from the Kum-köl was full of difficulty. The route led us over some barren hills and across a river deeply excavated below the level, the bottom of which consisted of red ooze, while its water was excessively salt. The surface of the earth was shaped in a most capricious way, like towers and walls; it was as though we were riding through the ruins of an ancient town. When evening came, we had difficulty in finding anything like a suitable spot to encamp in, and Camp No. XII. was formed in the wretchedest region it is possible to imagine. Grass and fuel we scarcely expected to find, but worse than that—there was not even a drop of water to be had. Fortunately it began to snow, and we made haste to put out all the receptacles we had and to spread tent-cloths on the ground. We let the animals eat their fill of maize, for the asses would be unable to go with us very far, and it would be better to consume their loads in this way than to throw them away. Dovlet turned up towards morning, but with only one-half of his caravan; the rest would overtake us, he said, if we were not in too great a hurry. Next day, therefore, we made only a short stage.

And whilst we are waiting for the asses, it may perhaps interest you to learn how our camp was arranged. We always adopted the same plan. The loads were deposited in long rows, and at one end of them Turdu Bai had his tent, which he shared with Hamra Kul, Mollah Shah, and Rosi Mollah. In the same locality was the tent which served as a kitchen for preparing my food and that of the Cossacks; it was occupied by Kutchuk alone, for he was assistant to Cherdon, who in the meantime

Scanty Grazing.

acted as my house-steward. Chernoff was the Cossacks' cook. Our kitchen was thus separated from that of the Mohammedans, for they will on no account eat with unbelievers, and have a horror of pots and pans into which by any chance a piece of pork may have found its way.

Then there was a big dome-shaped yurt, occupied by Sirkin, Shagdur and the Lama, each having his own bed, consisting of felts, skins and a pillow. Sirkin was my assistant in taking observations. He was able both to read and to write, and of an evening he used to read aloud to the other Cossacks Prschevalsky's description of his journeys, for I had the book with me. Shagdur was for the present resting after his illness. I had instructed the Lama that he need not take part in the coarser work of camp-life; all I expected of him was to give me lessons in Mongolian, and later on to act as Tibetan interpreter. But it was no use; he was always helping, nor did he consider any work too rough for his tender hands, which had been more accustomed to handle the volumes of Holy Writ than to do labourer's work. It was a treat to see old Turdu Bai chuckling to himself when he saw the Lama lugging the heavy boxes down off the camels' backs, or lifting them up again in the morning. This made the Lama popular in the caravan, and stirred the Mussulmans to emulation, for no true believer could of course let himself be beaten by a *kaper*, "a heathen" that ate swine's flesh.

Further, there was the little yurt, occupied by Chernoff and Cherdon, and at the extreme opposite end of the loads stood my yurt, guarded by Yoldash and Yolbars, sometimes all too zealously against imaginary enemies, such as our own horses and camels. The rest of the men had to content themselves with bivouacs of a more makeshift description, by stretching felt carpets across the camels' loads and creeping in underneath them. They used to cook their food over various fires made in the "streets" and "squares" of the encampment. Some of them had, however, to go on sentry duty and watch our animals at night, and see that they did not stray too far away. In this irksome task they all took their turns, while it was Chernoff's business to see that nobody played tricks or shirked his turn. Sometimes he would mount his horse in the night and ride to the various troops of animals to make sure that their guardians were not nodding.

No sooner was the signal given to halt than the camp was arranged and the tents up in a very few minutes. Every man had his own appointed duty to perform, and the camp very soon settled down to peace and quietness; the animals were led away to the best grazing that the neighbourhood afforded; fuel—*i.e.*, the dried dung of yaks and kulans—was collected, and the men gathered round the various fires to prepare their suppers. We had a valuable reserve supply of wood in the pack-saddles to which the grain sacks were lashed. As the sacks were gradually emptied, the pack-saddles, which were then no longer required, were mostly used up to eke out the natural supply of fuel, which often burned badly.

My bed used to be made like that of everybody else on the bare ground, and of an evening I used to sit on it with a light in front of me, and make my maps and write up my diaries.

On the 8th June old Dovlet went back to see what had become of the other asses which were still missing. Meanwhile we proceeded south through a country of soft, moist red clay. In front of us was a glen, which, though rather deep, nevertheless looked promising. The long black procession marched in and began to follow its windings. As we advanced the ground grew softer and the camels began to sink into the mire. The voices of the men rang out incessantly, warning or encouraging. A camel capsized, a horse flung off its load, a mule stuck fast in the mud and had to be pulled out by main force as you pull a cork out of a bottle. Everybody was marching on foot. One of my boots stuck fast in the quagmire, and I went in with my stocking-foot right up to the knee. Two camels became exhausted and had to be relieved of their loads, which were transferred to the backs of horses. At last it was utterly impossible to advance a step further in that abominable mire. Right about, march! The space was so narrow that each animal had to turn round on the spot where it stood, so that what had been the head of the caravan now marched last. The retreat out of that treacherous trap was even worse than the entrance into it, for the ground had been ploughed up still more by all the animals that had trampled through it. We found a little pass to the west, by means of which we reached more favourable country. I sat on horseback at the top of the pass and watched the whole of the caravan march past. And what a business it was to get one of the two tired camels over. He had literally to be pushed up step by step by five men. After this experience I made it a rule to reconnoitre the country ahead before starting, and from our next camp Mollah Shah and Li Loyeh were ordered to go and spy out the land.

The grass at this camp, which was formed around a little spring, was exceptionally good. At three o'clock we had a storm, accompanied with snow, from the west, and in the evening another from the east. I was sitting, working in furs, and leaning over a brazier. During the night the thermometer dropped to 8.°5 Fahr., and yet this was the middle of the summer and we were on the parallel of Seville; but then we were also more than 13,000 feet above the level of the sea.

The next day we followed the track of our pioneers, climbing steadily into higher regions, and pitched our camp on the sloping western bank of a big river, the loops of which were filled with hummocks of ice. The river flowed at the bottom of a deep cutting, the camp being 75 feet above the stream; and as the bank at last shot perpendicularly down, and I was afraid that the camels might fall in and be drowned if they ventured too near the soft, crumbling edge, I had them sent back to a safer valley.

Here we sacrificed three days in restoring order in the caravan and resting the animals. A great part of the ass-caravan had never once yet put in an appearance. I, therefore, sent Cherdon back with some horses and mules, that he might at least save the maize; and on the third day he returned, having successfully accomplished his errand. But the poor asses had had a very bad time of it: nine of them had died one day and thirteen another, so that out of the thirty there were only a few left, and they were fit for nothing. We had also left behind one of the two exhausted camels, and as the ass-drivers were to return home from this camp, I told them they might keep the camel, if they would promise to try and get him down to a warmer climate, and this they undertook to do.

# CHAPTER XXI.

## A KILLING JOURNEY OVER THE ARKA-TAGH.

CONTINUING our journey south, we marched in the usual order, sometimes beside the stream, sometimes in its bed. For the most part the ground was firm, though in places it was very soft and treacherous. Chernoff, who was piloting the way, very nearly came to grief, for his horse literally disappeared underneath him in a quagmire, and was only rescued with the greatest difficulty. For a long distance we kept to the top of the scarped terrace, with the stream boiling below us. Down beside the water we observed a flock of wild-geese; a shot echoed. Most of the birds spread their wings and took to flight; but two or three were unable to rise, although they fluttered away across the mud-banks. With amazing agility and daring Ördek scrambled down an almost perpendicular escarpment, and chasing the wounded birds caught them and drew his knife to kill them. But all at once over he went headlong, and remained lying on his back motionless, like a man that is dead. What was the matter with him? was it a stroke? I at once sent two of the Cossacks down to see. After they shook him a little he came to himself and sat up; but when he tried to walk he staggered and reeled like a drunken man. However, he was soon able to sit on horseback, and after about an hour was quite well again. In that attenuated air it is not wise to run or in any way exert yourself. Our heart and lungs are not adapted for it.

Before us we now had an immense mountain range, capped with snow, and were tempted to halt in the mouth of a small glen from which there issued a little brook. Just at the spot where it debouched from the glen it had formed a large sheet of ice. The men proceeded to put up the tents on the near side of this, while over on the far side of it was a block of stone; but—what? Why, the stone is moving! Then it cannot be a stone; it must be a yak calf. Then I heard cautious, but eager, whispering in the Cossacks' yurt, and a minute or two afterwards, Chernoff stole into my tent and whispered excitedly, "A bear!" And sure enough there was Bruin marching quite calmly straight towards the camp, perfectly indifferent to the fact of our presence. The dogs were hurriedly caught and led behind the hill, so as not to spoil sport. I watched the clumsy movements of the lonely hermit through the telescope as he walked with his toes turned in. The Cossacks were lying in wait for him with their rifles at full cock, and their cheeks burning with excitement. Bruin, however, must have been both blind and deaf, for he was marching deliberately to his doom. Upon reaching the further edge of the ice, he stopped a moment to consider, and then stepped upon it, keeping his muzzle the whole time close to the ground, as though he were searching for a pool of fresh water. He appeared to be tired, for his gait was slow, and every now and then he would stop and gaze up the glen. At length the shaggy wanderer dipped down into a hollow in the ice, and as it was some time before he reappeared the Cossacks began to lose patience. I advised them to seize the opportunity to creep forward to the edge of the hollow, for I wanted to take the skeleton of a bear home with me. But Bruin soon showed his grey coat again, climbing up out of the hollow. Bang! three shots rang out simultaneously as though they were one. Off went the bear at a wild trot up the slope above the camp. The horses were ready, and after him went the Cossacks. A fresh salvo awoke the echoes of the mountains, and down came the big brute, rolling like a ball down the steep declivity.

After I had perpetuated him on a photographic plate in an attitude as near life as possible, we set about preparing the skeleton. In his stomach we found a variety of herbs and a marmot which he had just swallowed. He had consumed his victim, skin and all, and had adopted a cunning device to make him slip down. After flaying the marmot to its toe-ends, he had swallowed the body and the legs, and then, rolling the skin into a ball with the hair inside, had gulped it down at a single gulp.

On the other side of the range we found a small lake, and beside it made Camp No. XVIII., at an altitude of 15,530 feet. The surviving asses were now in such a pitiable condition that it was impossible to take them any further. I therefore dismissed Dovlet, paying him well, and he set off for the north, accompanied by his five ass-drivers and three of my men whom I no longer needed, especially as they were not good for very much.

Immediately in front of us we now had our old enemy the Arka-tagh, and our next serious business was to climb over it. The glen by which we elected to make the assault was hard at the bottom, with a thin sprinkling of grass. Grass? Yes! But do not imagine it was anything like a soft green carpet of meadow; it was the reverse of that. The separate blades were about an inch high and of a yellow colour and as hard as thorns; that's what is meant by grass in Northern Tibet. If you happen to sit down on it you make the very greatest haste to get up again without being told to do so. And yet that was the only

The Tibetan Bear.

food we were able to get for our animals in that inhospitable country.

Shagdur and Sirkin shot two antelopes; but when Sirkin was galloping after his victim to secure it, his horse suddenly put his nose between his fore-legs and over he went, head foremost, flinging his rider, so that he rolled over two or three times on the ground. The horse was stone dead, though we could not make out whether he had broken his neck or had a stroke of some sort; anyway, Sirkin had always looked after and tended him with the greatest attention.

Up in the mountains where we were there was no longer grazing of any description. Since we had sent back the asses, our loads were very heavy, and we were of deliberate purpose spendthrift with our provender. The load must somehow or other be lightened, so every evening we gave each camel a big portion of grain. Artan, the camel I rode in the desert, was here seized with a sort of cramp, and I spent the whole evening massaging him, though it is hard work massaging camels at an altitude of 16,000 feet above the sea. But Artan recovered, and was one of the last surviving camels which reached Ladak. He always marched at the head of the caravan, with one of the biggest of the bells hanging round his neck.

On the 22nd June the camp was astir early, for we were now to make the great attempt to climb over the Arka-tagh. The caravan began to march slowly up towards the pass we had pitched upon to cross by. Barely a stone's throw from camp one of the camels lay down and refused to get up again. We relieved him of his load, and having at length induced him to rise, started to lead him without one; but at the next slope he fell again. He was evidently done for, and a resolute slash set his life's blood flowing.

I now set off to ride after the caravan, which had passed me. Just as I was overtaking it a tempest burst, the very

A Wounded Orongo Antelope.

worst, I believe, that I have ever experienced in Tibet. The hail and snow fell literally in sheets. The cold was intense, and it was no use trying to shelter ourselves against the stinging blast. The ascent was not difficult, though the altitude and the weather were both murderous. Two more camels stopped and refused to proceed. Woe to the man that beat them! they did perfectly right to mutiny. They were uncoupled and left behind with a man to look after them. Before we reached the top of the pass two others were left behind with their loads, and were brought in afterwards.

Although the sun was then at its highest, we were marching in darkness. The snow was swirling thickly all round us, filling the entire glen with blinding, smothering, spinning, clinging snow-flakes. The landscape was one uniform white, except for the winding ribbon of the brook, which tinkled and rang with a metallic sharpness in the attenuated air. I rode leaning forward in my saddle, scarce knowing where I was going to; in fact I was simply following the sound of the nearest caravan bell. Suddenly there was a scream of pain. A camel had stopped, and one of the men took pity upon him, released him from the string, and began to lead him after us at a slower pace. In less than a minute he was lost to sight amid the welter of the falling snow.

It cut me to the heart to hear and see all this suffering; so I rode on ahead with the Lama to the top of the pass, and soon reached its giddy height, where the great, impassive silence shares dominion with the everlasting snow and the never-ceasing storms. The pass itself was not difficult; but just think of the altitude, 17,000 feet above the level of the sea! and the deep snow! Securing what shelter we could behind the horses, we pulled our cloaks about our ears and waited—waited, shivering with cold, for on the summit of the pass we were exposed to all the unbridled fury of the blast. At length its deafening roar was pierced by the saddening clang of the bells and the warning cries of the men. The first of the string emerged like spectres out of the darkness, and like spectres they glided away again into the gloom of the falling snow. Slowly—painfully slowly—the long string of the caravan defiled past me over the summit of the pass. I counted them as they came. Thank God! that is thirty out of our thirty-four camels. Two had given up even before reaching the actual ascent to the pass, and two had fallen just under its crest. Amongst those that were missing were the oldest of the young ones and its mother—a good thing that they were not divided in their deaths! The horses, mules, and sheep all stood the ascent remarkably well.

The descent on the other side consisted of one broad flat pudding of soft clay, down which we had to zigzag and make many detours to avoid sticking fast in the mire. Although we were all dead tired, it would have been madness to think of encamping there: all the loads, boxes, packages and what not would have been swallowed up before morning. Long after dusk we continued to pick our steps under the shade of those white unholy mountains. All we wanted was a dry spot big enough for our camp. No thought of grass or fuel; who would be so foolish as to dream of such things on the very verge of the endless immensities of space? At length we did discover a hard gravelly slope, and there we pulled up for the night. Turdu Bai and several of the other men failed to turn up, nor did they come in until the night was far advanced, leaving behind them finally four camels. At daybreak next morning they went back to fetch them, taking some of the horses with them, so that if things were at the worst they might at any rate save the camels' loads and the straw in their pack-saddles. All four were, however, too far gone; in fact, one was already dead, and lay stiff and cold just beneath the pass. Whenever they were reduced to this condition, I always had their throats cut to save them from further suffering, and also from the wolves which prowl about these mountains in considerable numbers.

Five camels in one day! The strength of the *élite* of the caravan diminished to the extent of one-seventh in a single stage! As the loads would now be far too heavy for the survivors, I gave orders that all the animals should be allowed to eat as much maize and flour as they liked. After that we marched on for about six miles, until we found a tolerable site for the camp; there we decided to rest and recover from the fatigues of the last two or three days. A horse which showed no visible indication of anything being wrong dropped down and died, there and then, between the tents. From that time it seemed as though scarcely a day passed but we lost one or other of our animals. In fact, the route taken by the caravan might have been traced by the skeletons left behind it. Assuredly it is a *via dolorosa* when the milestones of your road consist of bleaching bones. The greatest possible attention was now paid to the care of the animals, and Turdu Bai was unwearied in his efforts to pull them together. He was able to tell when any of the camels was approaching its end. When you see a weak camel begin to weep, you may be quite sure it will not live long. I have often seen the big bright tears gush out of their eyes when they were no longer able to get up on their feet.

Midsummer Day morning opened with brilliant sunshine, and the whole of our company, men, tents and baggage alike were spread out to dry, after the thorough drenching we had got in the Arka-tagh. I had now been on the tramp for two years, but I knew that the third would be the hardest of all, and that the enterprise which I had in view was of a perilous nature. After breakfast I made a

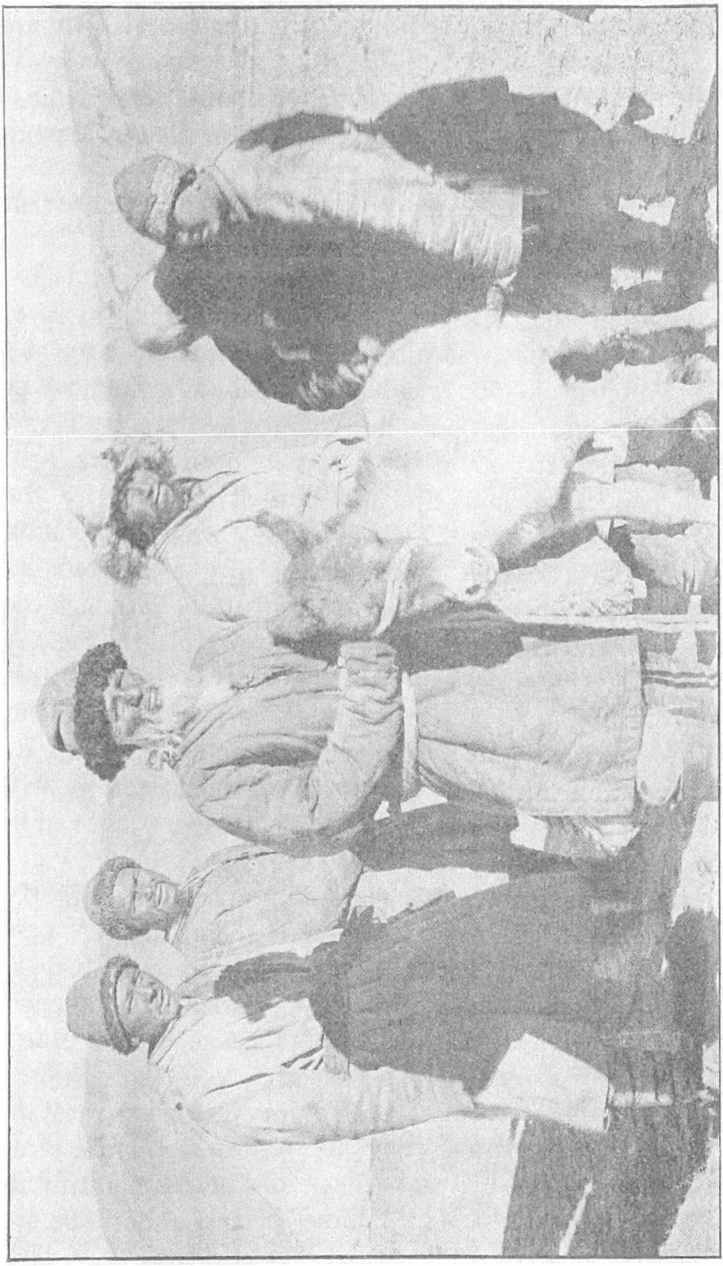

A Young Kulan Wounded.

thorough inspection of the whole of the caravan. Hamra Kul, the superintendent of the horses, was seriously ill, so I gave him a dose of quinine and allowed him a horse to ride on. When crossing the Arka-tagh, all the Mussulmans had been reduced to travelling on foot, because we wanted the horses to carry the loads of the camels that we had lost.

My favourite nag, a handsome, good-tempered beast, came now on the sick list. Shereb Lama, like most of the Lamaist priests, was also a clever medicine-man, and carried amongst his baggage a chest filled with more or less well-proved drugs. He now offered to cure my horse, and proceeded to open the veins in both its fore-legs; then he bandaged them up, and himself carefully led the animal the next stage. That evening, amid the pelting hail-storm with which Midsummer Day celebrated its close, the Lama continued his treatment by bleeding the horse again, and giving him a long foot-bath in the nearest brook. There must have been something in this primitive method of cure, for the horse was better, and soon began to eat, and munched away the whole evening at his maize, or rather at his maize and rice, for of the latter we had such a large supply that we were able to spare some even for the horses.

During the last days of June the ground was pretty favourable, and the weather good. The highest pass reached, however, an altitude of 17,510 feet; nevertheless, the whole caravan surmounted it in safety, although five camels turned queer and had to be relieved of their loads.

It now became a regular rule for my medicine chest to appear at every camp. Several patients came complaining of headache; I gave each of them an antipyrin powder, and they were of course better almost before they had got it down—imagination goes a long way with some people. Turdu Bai had something the matter with one of his eyes; I dropped into it two or three drops of cocaine, and he was tremendously impressed by its soothing effects. Hamra Kul had toothache; I prescribed some "drops," and he was instantly better. This so astonished Islam Akhun from Charkhlik and Kalpet from Keriya that they also thought they had toothache, and came moaning and groaning to the entrance of my yurt. Suspecting which way the wind blew, I put a few drops of tea on a tuft of cotton and laid it upon their gums, with the result that they declared it was an instantaneous cure. The only one of my patients who was really ill was Mohammed Tokta, a man of fifty, who belonged to the camel corps; he complained of his heart, and suffered from sleeplessness, so I allowed him to ride, and set him free from all duty. My medicine chest was looked upon generally in the light of a wonder-working talisman. No sooner was it brought forward than all who were not actually on duty used to gather round my yurt; and many were the suppliant glances cast at its metal lid during the months of our long journey. For my own part, I am happy to say, I never had occasion to draw upon its resources.

We travelled due south, except when the lofty mountains barred our way and compelled us to make a detour. We were now anxiously longing to reach lower and warmer regions, where we might find fresh young grass. This was indeed the question of the day, for our camels were growing thinner and thinner, and as Turdu Bai justly said, if we were to save them, we must find grass and let them have a month's rest. But could we find grass before it was too late?

It was only by the rarest chance that we now managed to travel as far as we did on the 2nd July, namely, sixteen miles at a stage. Fortunately for us the downfall had been very much less of late, so that the ground was dry and hard, and at times actually a cloud of dust hung upon the track of the caravan. Between two small lakes flashing in the sunshine, Yoldash caught sight of an orongo antelope, with a young one; this last he easily caught and killed. Thereupon I sent Shagdur after the mother to shoot her too; but he failed to find her. A little further on, however, Sirkin shot a magnificent specimen of the same species. I should say that all hunting for mere pleasure was strictly forbidden, and no animal was ever killed unless we wanted it for food. Besides, we had to husband our cartridges, for nobody could say what sort of a reception we should meet with at the hands of the Tibetans.

Upon reaching a small pool containing a slight impregnation of salt we found the grass sufficiently good to rest beside it for over a day. In so far as one may apply the word idyllic to a Tibetan landscape, then this was the place to apply it to. On every side of us was nature, primitive and uncontaminate. Nature? Nay, it was the bare-bones of Mother Earth. Here we had been travelling for weeks and even months, and had not seen a single human being except ourselves.

That night the sun set with a purple after-glow that lingered in the west. In the east, against a purple-blue back-ground, the full moon rose pale and chill, its light veiled by a transparent mist, giving rise to magical effects. Across the orb of the moon lay a ribbon of cloud, perfectly horizontal, and as black as pitch. It was like a crape scarf flung across a silver shield, in fact it made me fancy that Saturn with his ring had somehow lost his way and was coming to visit the earth. The night was so still and quiet that I was able to take my supper, or rather dinner, with the tent-door open and a light burning inside. But shortly after eight o'clock there swept over us one of the maddest storms I ever remember, drowning all other sounds except an occasional shout from one or other of the men, when any of our lighter belongings was caught up by the wind.

According to my calculation, the valley in which we were now encamped was the westward continuation of that in which, the autumn before, we had buried poor Aldat. It was about twenty miles away that the black yak's tail was fluttering above his lonely grave.

Immediately before us rose another lofty range, up to the summit of which, 17,100 feet high, we slowly and painfully scrambled. Looking south, we had an uninterrupted vista across the highlands for fully four days' journey, but from the north, whence we had come, the prospect consisted of nothing but a chaos of mountain ranges, exhibiting every shade of colour. Here and there we caught a glimpse of perpetual snow, the whole arched over by the turquoise blue dome of the sky.

On the 4th and 5th July we rested beside a little spring, where the Cossacks shot two yaks and twelve partridges. We now endeavoured to live as far as possible upon meat, so as to spare as much rice as we could for the animals. At twilight on the second day the whole of our sheep were missing. Everybody jumped to the conclusion that they had been attacked by wolves, for these creatures were very plentiful in that region; we used to hear their blood-curdling howls every night. The discovery of our loss threw the camp into a state of great excitement; at once a hue and cry was raised, but the searchers all returned about nine o'clock, tired and dispirited, having found nothing. They waited until midnight for the moon to rise, and then tried again, and this time found the wanderers lying snug and comfortable in a deep ravine. After this Vanka was cashiered, and his place as commander-in-chief of the sheep corps was given to Kalpet.

I used at this stage to do the reconnoitring myself, and generally took with me the Lama, to acquire practice in speaking Mongolian. On the 6th July we crossed over another pass, which brought us to a sandy region with tolerable grass. Farther on, having pitched on a place for the camp, we had to wait for the caravan to come up, for the animals were going slower and slower in proportion as their strength gave out. On this occasion we were waiting beside a little spring, and when after a couple of hours we at length heard the caravan bells, we found that two of the camels had been left behind, though they were brought in later on during the evening. One of them was the veteran of 1896, being one of the three which in that year accompanied me all the way down the valley of the Keriya-daria, for considerable distances across the desert of Takla-makan, and then down the Tarim to the lakes of Lop-nor and the Kara-koshun. Finally I had sold him in Charkhlik for a mere trifle, and five years later bought him back again at a high price, though I did not mind that, for I looked upon him as an old friend and travelling companion. But he was now doomed, and he knew it himself, for when Sirkin led him forward that I might photograph him, his legs trembled under him, and the tears welled out of his big bright black eyes. However, he did not give up just yet.

## CHAPTER XXII.

### FIRST CONTACT WITH THE TIBETANS.

ON the 8th July we travelled through a broken region abounding in yaks and kulans; but although we did not cover much more than 8½ miles, only 27 camels were able to reach the next camp, No. XXXIII., situated at an altitude of 16,540 feet. The other three had as usual been left behind, one of them being the 1896 veteran. However, he and one of the others managed to struggle in next day.

It was evident we could not go on in this way any longer. So I made an alteration, and separating out the eleven worst camels, five of which had for some time been travelling without loads, as well as six of the horses, decided to leave them behind. With the rest of the caravan I resolved to push on south at a faster rate, letting those we had weeded out follow on at their leisure. These I left in charge of Rosi Mollah, Mollah Shah, Kutchuk, Khodai Kullu, Almaz, and Chernoff, with Chernoff as chief. We also left with them four of the dogs, namely, Malchik, Hamra, Kalmak, and Kara Ilt, as well as half of the dozen sheep that still remained alive. Chernoff's orders were to rest where he was for a few days, and then march slowly on in our track. We promised, wherever it seemed necessary, to build up a mound of stones for his guidance. It was not, indeed, altogether prudent to divide our strength just now when we were approaching inhabited regions, perhaps hostile regions; but it was absolutely necessary, and I left Chernoff's party as well armed as we were.

Accordingly, on the morning of 10th July our division set off alone. For the last two days it had rained and hailed and snowed without intermission. This made the loads heavier, the ground soft, and the animals evil-smelling. The camp we were turning our backs upon looked inexpressibly wretched in the wet and mire, with the eleven camels lying about amongst the hills, actually despising the scanty wretched grass. But Chernoff and his men would, I knew, do their best. But should we ever see them again? I did not doubt that they would reach our new headquarters camp; but when they did reach it, they would not find me and the other two Lassa pilgrims, and it was more than doubtful whether we should return from the adventure we were now about to embark upon.

We started in the pouring rain, and the camp with its damp smoky fires soon disappeared behind an intervening ridge. I and the Lama rode on ahead. At length the rain stopped, and the sun came out, but before we got thoroughly dry we received another drenching. After going a little more than fourteen miles we found a suitable spot for the camp and waited. Whilst waiting we got a third wetting to the skin, although I wrapped myself in a camel-hair cloak, which I always carried rolled up behind my Hungarian military saddle. The Lama just sat still, indifferent to the rain, and let the 108 beads of his rosary glide restlessly through his fingers as he murmured the holy formula, "On maneh padmeh hum," meaning, "Oh, jewel of the Lotus Flower!"

The grazing at this camp consisted of moss and wild garlic, although it was rather scanty. The last-named was greatly relished by us all; with it I seasoned my soup and my everlasting cutlets; the Mussulmans ate it raw; while the camels just revelled in its sappy lusciousness. Whenever Turdu Bai came to a spot where this herb was growing at all thickly, he invariably used to stop and let the camels enjoy it for a while.

The next day, too, we had more rain and hail than we really wanted. The thunder rumbled in the valleys, making the horses restless and alarmed, while the camels tried each to get behind the other, which of course brought their loads into disorder. Meanwhile the mountains around us were streaked with glittering snow. Notwithstanding all the rain, we actually had difficulty in finding water to drink that evening. The rain ran away into the ground as fast as it fell, and the water in a little pool there was near the camp was intensely salt. Shagdur, therefore, taking a couple of copper vessels in his hands, went to look for a spring. After a while he came back, running fast and tremendously excited. He had been attacked by a wolf, which had twice flown at him with great determination, and he had had nothing in his hands to defend himself with except the copper vessels. He had now come to fetch his rifle, and to ask Sirkin to help him hunt the wolf down. We saw it running off, a big shaggy beast, almost white, and very soon it disappeared over a neighbouring hill.

On we went across the low ridges, through the valleys, and through the streams of salt water, on towards the south-east. At length we saw on the right of our route a big yak bull grazing alone. There was no need to shoot him, but the Cossacks could not resist the temptation of setting the dogs upon him. They, nothing loth, danced round the yak, barking themselves hoarse. They were careful, however, to keep at a respectful distance, though whenever the yak made a rush at Yolbars, Yoldash, the rascal, would rush in and give a sly tug at his long side-fringes. Round and round danced the yak, snorting and stamping, with his feathery tail in the air, while the clods flew for yards. In the thick of this performance up came Turdu Bai and informed us that we were in need of meat. That was the yak's death sentence. The next moment two bullets whistled through the air; but the yak took not the slightest notice either of them or of the reports. For a few seconds he stood motionless; but when the dogs again approached him, he turned "ugly," and made a dash after them down the slope. I was waiting about twenty or thirty yards away with my photographic apparatus ready, and was just beginning to think it was high time to be moving, when down went the yak, and after rolling over once or twice down the incline he lay stone dead.

At times during the last few days we had seen, far away in the south, the snow-capped peaks of a gigantic mountain-range, peeping over the tops of masking hills of a lower elevation. That was now our goal, for we could scarcely hope to find satisfactory grass until we got over it, and it was only on the other side of it that we were likely to find human beings. We already began to look out for a suitable notch in the crest of the range, for we were now quite unable to attempt any very lofty pass. On the 15th July we forded a big river divided into a number of arms. The hills on its left bank were black with yaks—we counted at least 75 of them. Then, in another direction, we perceived what we took to be a solitary traveller. I at once commanded halt, and scrutinised the mysterious figure through my glass. The Lama declared it was a Tibetan collecting yak-dung. Perhaps, then, the yaks we had seen were tame ones after all; if they were, their owners had already caught sight of the caravan, for the yaks were now gone. Soon afterwards the lonely traveller turned out to be nothing more formidable than a kulan.

A little bit further on the following incident happened. Yolbars put up a leveret, and would certainly have caught it had it not at the last moment, after two or three cunning turns, managed to slip into a little hole in the ground. Shagdur pulled the frightened creature out and wrapped it in his neck-handkerchief; and when all the caravan, and the dogs, had gone safely past I set the trembling little thing at liberty, and away it hopped across the steppe. But before it had gone very far a hawk, which we had not seen, darted down upon it like an arrow. Off ran Shagdur to the rescue; but though he frightened the hawk away, he found its victim with its eyes picked out and in the last convulsions of death.

Camp XXXVIII. was made on the left bank of a fresh river. The next day, the 16th July, was a rest day, and while Turdu Bai and Hamra Kul went up the valley to see if it led to a suitable pass, I sat in my tent working. All at once I heard a hubbub and the men shouting. Looking out I saw a big bear waddling towards the camp, followed by Sirkin and Shagdur. But perceiving his danger in time, Bruin turned off to one side, plunged into the river, forded it with a tremendous amount of splashing, and then scrambling up the bank on the opposite side, continued his flight over the hills, closely pursued by the two Cossacks on horseback. No sooner had the chase passed than a shot rang out from Cherdon's tent. A big old whitish-grey wolf had ventured too near and was now made to pay dearly for his inquisitiveness.

When at length the Cossacks returned at a smart trot, I saw at once from their countenances that they had important news to tell me. The bear had escaped, but whilst pursuing him they had plumped into the middle of a Tibetan camp. As they did so a man armed with a gun ran and hid himself behind a hill, leaving a score of yaks and some horses grazing in the vicinity. The Lama was quite alarmed, now that he was face to face with the unavoidable reality; for so long as we did not come across traces of human beings, he had not, I fancy, thoroughly realised the actuality of my plan. Perhaps after all the kulan that we saw the day before really was a man ; at any rate, it was a warning that we had not now very far to go before we should come to human habitations.

We held a short consultation, but one thing was clear at once : there was no time to lose. The Tibetans were pretty certainly yak-hunters, and they would soon be returning home ; it was, therefore, absolutely essential that we should get hold of them if we could. They might give us valuable information, and perhaps we might arrange to travel with them, for amid the labyrinth of mountains which now lay before us a guide was indispensable. That they had seen us did not admit of a shadow of doubt. If they escaped us now, they would make haste to report what they had seen, and the news would travel swiftly from mouth to mouth all the way to Lassa, and so we should be prevented from reaching the Holy City. I at once ordered Shagdur and the Lama to go to the Tibetans' camp, which was only two miles distant. The former, who was already attired in his Mongolian dress, took with him tea and tobacco to convince the Tibetans that we were friendly disposed towards them. I also gave him some money (silver), so that he might try to buy two or three horses. Thus equipped, they plunged into the river again and disappeared behind the hills on the other side.

It was dark when they returned. Upon reaching the Tibetans' camp they found nothing left except the smoking embers, and two or three yaks' skulls and bones. The trail of the Tibetans' caravan led to the east, and the question was, should we try to catch them up or not ? We decided not to follow them, owing to the poor condition in which our horses were, especially as the Tibetans would be pretty certain to travel all night and all the next day without stopping, so as to put as great a distance as possible between themselves and the unknown strangers whom they had seen riding about shooting bears.

This put an end to the peace and quietude of our camp life ; we were no longer alone amongst these desolate wastes of Tibet. From this time onwards I had sentries or guards posted every night, and all the animals were closely watched. Our main concern now was to find, and the sooner the better, a suitable place for the head-quarters camp, for after consultation with Shagdur I had determined that he and I and the Lama alone should undertake the ride to Lassa, while Cherdon should remain behind to guard the camp, though he would, of course, soon be joined by Chernoff.

At this momentous camp we remained yet one day longer, so that we might get all our Mongol equipment in proper order, ready to hand in case of a hurried separation from the caravan. At dusk we perceived the outlines of our two pioneers returning from their reconnoitring trip. They had found no insuperable obstacle to the south, and next day they led us up the tumultuous stream that we had crossed several times already. Upon reaching an expansion of the glen, where there were a few blades of wretched grass, we made our next camp. One of our eighteen camels had, however, hard work to get thus far, and when next morning came we could not induce him to go any farther. Accordingly I resolved to leave him behind, trusting to the rear caravan to pick him up. Turdu Bai assured me that he would be in no danger from wolves, for they never touch a camel that carries a pack-saddle. However, we set up, on a little hill in the glen, a spar of the tent, and fastened to the top of it a preserved-food tin with a strip of paper inside it, on which were written the following words in Turkish : " We have left a camel here ; if you don't find him, follow his trail till you do." As it happened, the rear caravan for some reason or other made just here a detour, and consequently they never saw our signal box, nor the camel either; hence we never knew what became of him.

We saw any quantity of yak-signs, but we never saw the animals themselves. It was as though they had all been spirited away. Three times, too, we passed indications of recent fires, namely, circles of stones with a heap of ashes in the middle.

The 20th July was a hard day, leading us up to higher and more inhospitable regions, for we now had to cross the stupendous mountain-range I have spoken of. Its summit was rounded, and the pass itself was bordered on both sides by broad glacier arms, from which brooks of clear water radiated, making the ground soft and treacherous. On the way up we were met by a terrific hail-storm beating directly in our faces, so that our bashliks afforded us very little protection. Below the glaciers there was a small army of yaks grazing, over three hundred altogether, but they retreated as we approached. Slowly but surely we worked our way up to the summit of the pass, where the instrument showed an altitude of 17,920 feet. Over on the other side, that is, to the south, was nothing but a tumbled confusion of mountain-ranges. A brook led down from the pass, gathering tributaries from both sides as it went, until finally it swelled into a pretty big river. Here the dogs made a reckless attack upon seven old yaks; four of these at once took to flight, though three stood their ground with their noses down to the earth and their horns ready for instant action; but when the dogs concentrated their attack upon one of the three, the other two retreated. The last of the seven had no end of trouble to shake off his assailants, and only managed it at last by adopting the cunning tactics of taking up his station in the middle of the rushing stream, where the dogs were completely non-plussed. After a while two of the yak's companions came back to see how he was getting on; but by this the dogs had grown tired of the game, and were sitting on the bank panting and watching their enemy.

After picking up a tributary from the right, the river turned to the south-east, traversing a distinctly marked valley, which we hoped would eventually lead us to a region with better grass. In this glen we came across a highly remarkable formation, namely, two thick shelves of ice, one clinging to each bank. We elected to travel on that

Hewing a Path Down off the Ice.

which bordered the right bank; it was there six to seven feet thick. But we were soon stopped by a gap in the ice, and to get over it were obliged to go down into the bottom of the glen, which was filled with rushing water. It took us a fearful time chopping out a path with axes and spades, and strewing it with gravel and sand, before we could venture to lead the camels down one by one. Meanwhile, Shagdur had proceeded down the gorge to reconnoitre, and when we at length met him he explained that we might easily continue for three miles or so, but after that the glen contracted into a ravine, which the river, churned into foam, filled from side to side. At the spot where he had turned back, the water was three to four feet deep. I saw at once that it would be madness to continue, for at noon the river would swell, and if we were then compelled to turn back, we should meet the flood coming down from the glaciers and should inevitably all be drowned.

Right about turn and all the way back again! We must just try the glen by which the tributary descended from another pass. But upon reaching the foot of this last we had had quite enough for that day, for all this time the storm was still raging. With the view of sparing the rear caravan this extra and fruitless deviation, we built up several mounds of stones by way of landmark.

Next morning I and the Lama spent two solid good hours in climbing up to the top of the new pass, and then another two hours waiting for the caravan. Imagination can hardly conceive worse ground for travelling over. At every step the animals sank deep into the mire, while rain and hail vied with one another as to which should make the ground still softer. We were now approaching regions which gather the precipitation brought by the clouds from the Indian Ocean. The immense altitudes, the horrible weather, the steep slope and the abominable quagmires—all these things taken together were enough to effect the ruin of any caravan.

But the southern slope was ten times worse. We had a pilot on in advance, walking and leading his horse, in order to test the ground. Turdu Bai hurried the camels faster so as to prevent them from sinking in so deep. But it was all of no use; we had a repetition of the scene I have so often described, the camels getting stuck fast in the mire, screaming with pain, and having to be cut out of the string, unloaded and left behind; only this time, to make matters even worse, it rained incessantly. In truth, a wretched country! Human beings fled from us, and even the very elements conspired together against us! How on earth will Chernoff make his way with the feeble animals of the rear caravan?

Just under the pass we lost another camel, one of the best in the caravan. He was unable to get in that night, and next morning we found him stiff and frozen, half buried in the mire. Perhaps you will now understand that it is anything but a pastime or an exhilarating sport to travel across Tibet. In fact, there were times when the prospect looked so desperate and so gloomy that we should hardly have rebelled had the earth opened and swallowed us all up, and in that way freed us from all our troubles.

At last! At last! we made our way down from those terrible altitudes and reached yet another river. Where it came from and where it went to we could not see, for the blinding snow and the driving rain were conspiring together to fill the glen with an impenetrable mist. It was, however, a relief to find that the bed of the river—for we marched in the water—was strewn with gravel, and firm enough to bear the weight of our animals. But we were not only dead tired, we were wet to the skin, when we formed Camp No. XLIII. on the right bank of this stream.

# CHAPTER XXIII.

## STARTING FOR LASSA—TIBETAN ROBBERS.

DURING the much needed day of rest which I here granted to the exhausted caravan, several of the men went out to explore the neighbourhood. A few miles down the glen the Cossacks discovered excellent grass growing on and amongst some sandy hills. Turdu Bai at once led down his camels, and was followed by Hamra Kul and the horses. My resolve was now taken. The next morning, the 24th July, we would march on to the newly discovered grass, and there form a permanent camp. It was high time to be starting for Lassa, for two or three of the men, who had been out reconnoitring, had heard gun-shots at a distance. Here, then, we had neighbours; but were they friends or were they enemies? Anyway we must be on the alert.

On the 24th July, therefore, we rode down the glen, which descended so steeply that the river formed boiling cataracts. The grass improved at every step, until at the spot which the Cossacks had chosen for the camp it was actually luxuriant, especially on the slopes which faced the midday sun and were protected against the icy winds of the north. And yet the altitude was no less than 16,820 feet above the sea, though the latitude was of course southerly. From the strategic point of view, however, the site of the camp was not at all well chosen, for it was commanded by all the encircling hills, and if any band of thievish Tanguts should take it into their heads to make a midnight attack the men would find great difficulty in beating them off.

During the two days that we remained in Camp No. XLIV. we were busy completing our final preparations for the start. We were to take with us five mules and four horses, and these were now tended with the greatest possible care. We let them eat the very last of the maize, and had them shod, and their saddles and rugs overhauled and repaired.

All our baggage was packed into two Mongolian boxes. I took with me some of the smaller instruments, so as not to suspend my geographical observations, besides a small camera, three pairs of coloured spectacles, writing materials, a razor and soap, for we should have to shave the whole of our heads. Other toilet requisites were not needed; on the contrary, it was a *sine qua non* to get as filthily dirty as possible, so as to acquire the proper Mongol complexion. A pair of scissors, a lamp, an axe, a dozen stearine candles, some boxes of matches, pipes and tobacco, and finally ten *yambas* (£100) of silver, were likewise indispensable. Our provisions consisted of flour, rice, *talkan* (roasted flour) and meat. For the first few days we should use tinned food, and sink the tins in water so as not to arouse suspicion. Our weapons consisted of a Russian magazine rifle, a Berdan rifle, and a Swedish officer's revolver, together with fifty cartridges for each weapon.

Our equipment was genuine Mongolian throughout. I, too, wore a rosary and a *gavo* (talisman), with an image of the Buddha, round my neck, while hanging from my girdle I had a sheath-knife, with grooves in it for the usual Chinese ivory chop-sticks, flint, steel and tinder, tobacco pouch and a long pipe. All our pots and pans, plates, jugs and cups were genuine Mongolian. We had two suits of clothing each, for we were certain very soon to be wet through. We used the smallest and lightest tent to live in, and the Lama made out of white felt a very decent cloak to be worn whilst keeping watch at night. I carried my watch, compass, aneroid and thermometer in specially-made inside pockets, which only a very close and, indeed, an impertinent examination could have discovered. Everything that bore the stamp of European origin was hidden under the provisions in one of the boxes, and most of them were of such a character that they could very readily have been sunk in a river or lake in case our position grew desperate.

I appointed Sirkin chief of the camp I was leaving behind, and straightly enjoined everybody to render to him the same obedience that they rendered to me, and impressed upon each and all that they should do their duty. Turdu Bai, however, being a sort of expert, was to have the right to propose a removal to other grazing grounds when the grass at Camp XLIV. was all consumed. But every time they moved they were to leave in a heap of stones at Camp XLIV. a document, written by Sirkin in Russian, telling us where we should find them when we returned. Then I took Sirkin aside, and made him understand the full gravity of the adventure I was embarking upon. He listened in silence, shaking his head. "If we are not back within seventy-five days," I said. "you may look upon us as lost. You must then lead the caravan back to Charkhlik, and from Charkhlik on to Kashgar." I did not for one moment think that the Tibetans would take our lives, but it was of course necessary to be prepared for the worst. In any case, I wished my maps and notebooks to reach home in safety. Finally I locked all my cases and boxes, but gave Sirkin the key of the box containing the silver, so that in case of need he might at Charkhlik equip a fresh caravan for the return to Kashgar.

The Author in Mongolian Dress.

In the evening one of the men told us that in a neighbouring glen he had seen fresh footprints of Tibetans, both on horseback and on foot, and during the preceding night the dogs had barked furiously in that direction. It was already whispered in the camp that we were being watched by spies. At length I turned in for my last night's sleep under "civilized" conditions, slept soundly and well and did not wake till Shagdur came and called me next morning.

I made haste to dress, and in the course of a few minutes stepped forth a full-fledged Mongol. My long dark-red coat fitted me comfortably, and round my waist I had a yellow girdle and on my head a little yellow cap, with the lappets turned up. For a couple of weeks or so I had already been wearing the clumsy Mongol boots, so as to get accustomed to them; their turned-up toes and thick soles make them especially suitable for soft, wet ground. The high Mongol saddle, with its framework of wood and its soft seat, was easy to ride in, although the stirrups were buckled up high, in the Mongol fashion, so that my knees were drawn up. Behind the saddle was my yellow sheep-skin overcoat; at the moment of starting I did not require it, for the sun was warm and pleasant.

At length our little caravan was ready; we mounted and were off. I wished the honest Mussulmans had not made quite such a fuss; it led me to think of a funeral. But they, no doubt, honestly believed they would never see us again. For my own part, I did not doubt that the Almighty hand, which had watched over my footsteps through the deserts and over the mountains during so many years of solitary wandering in the vast wilds of Asia, would be with me still. As for Shagdur, he was delighted to know that we really were at last on the way, and the Lama sat in his saddle as grave as an owl. I asked him whether he had any hesitation about the journey,

Our Start from the Headquarters Camp.

and would prefer to remain behind with Sirkin and Cherdon. "No," he replied, "even though it should cost him his life, he would go with me." I rode my good old grey horse, which was in the pink of condition. Shagdur rode a cream-coloured animal, likewise in excellent condition; while the Lama contented himself with our little mule, Yellow-ears, the one which had very nearly died, but was now one of the best animals we had in the caravan. For canine sentries we chose Malenki and Yolbars; the other dogs were kept tied up when we started, and poor Yoldash howled dismally at being left behind. Ördek went with us to watch our animals the first night.

Now why did I expose myself to the perils which must inevitably attend a forced ride to Lassa? Ever since Father Huc visited the Holy City—likewise in disguise—the Tibetans had jealously guarded their country against European visitors. The American Rockhill had twice unsuccessfully attempted to reach Lassa in the disguise of a wandering Lama. Bonvalot and Prince Henry of Orleans, Dutreuil de Rhins and Grenard, Littledale, Bower and several others, not to speak of Prshevalsky and Kozloff, had all attempted the same thing, but all alike had been politely but firmly turned back. It was part of my programme to explore geographically and map as large a part of unknown Tibet as possible, and as in pursuance of this object I should naturally penetrate to no great distance from the Holy City, I felt the temptation too strong to be resisted. What benefit did I hope to derive from it? Did I perhaps think that I might be able to describe Lassa, and give photographs and a plan of the city and its temples? Not at all. Lassa is in every respect far better known than any other city in Central Asia, just because it has for so long been the object of such keen curiosity on the part of Europeans. The Russians have sent their Buriats and the English their

Shagdur, the Author, and Shereb Lama in Pilgrim Attire.

Indian pundits, all learned and able men, equipped with the best instruments, so that not only do we possess detailed descriptions and maps of the Lamaists' Rome, Jerusalem and Mecca, but we also know exactly what life there is like.

Then what in the name of wonder, you may ask, did I want to go there for ? Well, frankly, in one word, it was the ancient Viking blood that was stirring in me. After the dull, quiet, monotonous days of tramping through the desert, I longed for something with a spice of danger in it. I was ambitious to find myself in a dangerous and precarious situation, out of which I might work my way by courage and manhood. A victory won through difficulty and danger is more precious than one gained in placid security. I resolved, therefore, to push on with only two attendants as far as I could, and not to turn back until I was absolutely forced to do so. And if I were turned back by a force I could not resist—well, I would simply march back contented; my ambition would be satisfied. I should have done my best and who could do more ? Whether I saw the Holy City or not was of little importance. I was already in a way perfectly familiar with it : the Lama had described to me its streets, its markets, and its temples, again and again. Moreover, of temples we should see plenty in Western Tibet, supposing we got so far.

Off we went, then, at a smart trot, down beside the river, and found the remains of camp-fires dotted here and there all the way down. In one place we came upon the shrivelled-up body of a yak, which had been shot some time before ; and round it were the tracks of a bear, which had paid it a visit either that day or the day before.

At length we reached a wide open valley beside a small bright spring, with good grass ; then, whilst the other two put up the tent and looked after the animals, I went and collected fuel and lighted a fire. We took our supper in the

Mongolian fashion, for, as we were determined to play our parts thoroughly, there was nothing like beginning in time. We three pilgrims turned into bed early, leaving Ördek to watch the animals. There was a bright moon, and it was fortunate for us that there was these nights.

On the 28th July I decided to take Ördek with us one day further, partly that we might get another comfortable night's sleep and partly because the Lama was of a sudden turned so ill that he could hardly sit upright in his saddle, and I expected nothing but that he would have to return to headquarters. I took council with Shagdur, and we agreed that if the Lama did go back, we two would nevertheless push on alone. But, fortunately, the Lama recovered during the ride of twenty-four miles we made next day. The ground was hard, and we made good progress; but though there were plenty of yaks and kulans everywhere, we saw not a single human being. Every now and again one or other of us would ride to the top of a hill and search the horizon with a glass. Had we seen a nomad encampment, we should, like the honest pilgrims we were, have ridden quietly towards it; but in that case Ördek would have had to turn back instantly.

We encamped that night on a low narrow neck of land between a salt-water lake and a smaller lake of fresh water. Whilst gathered round the fire, we discussed the plan of the journey. I calculated how far we had already come, and how far we still had to go. The Lama painted in vivid terms the strictness and severity with which the Tibetan authorities at Nakk-chu examined all the pilgrims from Mongolia. In consequence we decided that it would be wisest to avoid Nakk-chu, and strike into the great Lassa road, further south, where we hoped we might mingle with the stream of pilgrims unobserved.

The time was now come for my outer man to undergo a tragi-comical transformation. After I had taken my seat beside the fire, Shagdur committed vandalism with the scissors upon my hair. Then, after my head was well lathered with soap, Ördek came forward with the razor, and in the course of a few minutes my head was as bare and as bright as a billiard ball. Finally, I laid hand myself upon my moustaches, and, sacrilege though it was, cut them off root and branch. My brothers, the Mongol and the Buriat, who were both beardless, now began to think that I looked like the real thing, though I confess I myself thought it sinful to destroy such a handsome ornament. Luckily I was not required to pull out my eye-brows and eye-lashes, and yet what did it matter how I looked? There was not a soul to see me.

I had, however, one consolation in that I bore a certain resemblance to Cæsar's bust; and yet that satisfaction was not long vouchsafed to me. The Lama, like an old and practised quacksalver, began, with an expert's mien, to rummage amongst his medicaments, and then, having with a light touch well greased my face with mutton fat, he rubbed it over with some sort of brown stuff, and finally, stepping back a few paces, scrutinised me with the air of a connoisseur, and said "Ikeh sän baneh" (That's fine!) But when I looked at myself in the polished inside of my watch-case, I confess I was quite unable to agree with him. Was that greasy, shiny, copper-brown, clean-shaven Mongol scare-crow really and truly identical with my own self? Gradually the grease dried, and under the influence of wind and dust turned a greyish colour. Every time I laughed, or had occasion to use the muscles of my face, the skin pulled terribly; but very soon laughter became a rare guest in our little caravan.

The camp lay, as I have said, on the tongue of land between two lakes, but was otherwise quite open on every side except towards the south-west, where there were some low hills. We saw no signs of human beings; the dogs

An Encampment of the Three Pilgrims.

kept quiet, and the neighbourhood appeared to be perfectly secure. At five o'clock a violent gale set in from the north, driving clouds of sand and dust across the salt lake towards our camp. Upon this we took shelter inside the tent, and sat and talked and smoked until eight o'clock, and then, having nothing better to do, we turned in and went to bed. Ördek was guarding our animals a couple of hundred paces to the west of the camp. He was to keep watch all night so that we might get a good rest, the last we were likely to have for some time to come, and in the morning he was to take one of the baggage-horses and ride back to the head-quarters' camp.

At midnight the tent-flap was opened, and Ördek, creeping on his hands and knees, stuck in his head and whispered in a terrified voice, "There's a man—there's a man." Without waiting to hear one word more, we at once seized our weapons and rushed out into the night. The storm still raged with undiminished violence; the moon shone wan and pale amongst the ragged, hurrying clouds. Ördek led us to the horses that were farthest distant, where he had seen a dark figure stealthily moving amongst them. Upon this our hero, whose courage only flourished in the silent deserts, lost his head completely, and instead of giving the alarm hurried to the tent to tell us. We arrived, therefore, upon the scene too late. In the faint moonshine we detected the dark forms of a couple of horsemen hurrying over the hills, and driving two unbridled horses before them. Shagdur sent a shot after them, but it failed to take effect. Then he and Ördek and the Lama mounted and rode after the robbers whilst I remained with the other animals, for, for all we knew, we might be surrounded by an entire band of robbers. But at the end of an hour the men returned without having either seen or heard anything suspicious.

Thereupon we went back to our little troop, which was

still quietly grazing. We found the five mules and the two worst horses left; it was my favourite nag and Shagdur's cream which had been stolen. The way in which the robbery had been effected was made clear to us afterwards from the tracks. Three Tibetan horsemen, either professional robbers or thieves through opportunity, had evidently dogged our footsteps all day, and made themselves accurately acquainted with the position of our camp. Then, when all was quiet, one of them, cleverly taking advantage of a concealed hollow, had crept towards our quietly grazing animals in the teeth of the hard northerly gale, and then rising to his feet at a suitable moment he had rushed in behind the two outside horses and frightened them off to the west, where the other two Tibetans were waiting with their horses ready, and all three had then galloped off over the hills, driving the two stolen horses before them.

I do not think I was ever so annoyed in my life as I was then. At first I had but one thought, namely, to track the thieves down and make them pay dearly for their exploit. Shagdur was mad to be after them; his rifle just burned in his hands. But I soon swallowed down my wrath sufficiently to take a calm survey of the situation. With our tired horses we had not the slightest chance of catching up the Tibetans, who would, of course, take good care to ride hard for a couple of days without pulling rein. If two of us pursued the robbers, while two remained at the camp, we should only divide our strength, and that would have been excessively unwise now that we were evidently being watched by enemies. I concluded, therefore, that there was nothing to be done: we had had a proper lesson, and must just make the best of it. The game had now begun in earnest, and we might any moment expect a fresh attack. We ought not for a single instant to relax our vigilance.

We got no more sleep that night, but crouched round a little fire, huddled in our cloaks, and smoked and discussed the situation. Then we boiled the kettle and made our breakfast out of tea, rice and bread. At daybreak we saddled the two remaining horses and the mule, and packed up our belongings and were off again.

When the rising sun tipped with red the unknown hills in the east, we saw Ördek sitting crouched over the embers weeping. He begged and prayed that he might go with us instead of returning to the camp alone through that treacherous country, where robbers seemed to spring up, as it were, out of the very ground. But when he saw that I was inexorable, he asked that he might at least have the revolver; but, unfortunately, I wanted it myself, it was my only weapon.

Owing to my having been kept awake all night the bright sunshine made my eyes smart. Tearing a page out of my note-book, I wrote a few lines to Sirkin, urging him to exercise the utmost vigilance. Further, I commanded Cherdon, Li Loyeh, and one other man to spend a week in pursuing the thieves. Ördek stuffed the letter into his girdle with the mien of a man who has but a few minutes more to live before being led out to execution. Hardly were we in the saddle than we saw him running beside the lake. He was so terrified that he found his way back by the ravines and river-beds, not daring to follow our track in the open. All day he kept longing for the night, and when the night came, he was afraid of the darkness, thinking he saw an enemy in every shadow. A couple of peaceful kulans nearly frightened him out of his wits, then for a time he curled himself up like a hedgehog in a hole in the rocks; but the pelting rain filled his imagination with fresh terrors. At length, however, he reached the entrance to the valley in which the camp was situated, and there all other sounds were drowned in the rush of the river, and he kept fancying all the time that he heard stealthy footsteps creeping up behind him. How he managed to find his way in the dark he could not explain himself: he stumbled, he fell, he got up again, he raced down the hills like a madman, he waded through the river with the water up to his waist, and when he finally came near the camp, he was as near as possible shot by the man on sentry. Upon getting into camp, he collapsed completely, and could not be induced to open his mouth. The other men were filled with consternation; they believed that he was the only survivor of our little band, and that we three pilgrims had been killed. Some little time elapsed before the men were able to revive him, and he then told them what had happened, and delivered my letter to Sirkin.

Cherdon's pursuit proved fruitless. All we learned from it was that the robbers had travelled for about twenty-five miles without stopping and had then been joined by several other Tibetans, who were waiting for them, and after that the whole body rode so far in a river that their trail could no longer be picked up.

## CHAPTER XXIV.

### TIBETAN NOMADS—A DANGEROUS RIVER-CROSSING.

After Ördek left us, we rode twenty-four miles towards the south-east. On our right was a low saddle in the hills, on which hundreds of yaks were grazing. As they showed no inclination to take to flight, we concluded that they were tame, and expected every moment to see the herdsmen in charge of them; but when we approached nearer, they moved away. This showed that they were after all wild yaks; from which we inferred that we still had at least a couple of days to travel to reach the nearest nomad encampment. We all felt that we should be glad when we got there, for we should then feel a good deal safer.

We made our camp that night in a perfectly open locality, with an uninterrupted view in every direction, and with plenty of grass, water and yak-fuel. As we three pilgrims were now left to ourselves, I had to lend a hand in unfastening the loads and putting up the tent and in gathering fuel. The last time I did this sort of work was in 1886, when I twice rode to all intents and purposes alone through Persia. The arrangement between us was that Shagdur was to act as leader of the party, and neither of the other two was to show me any special mark of respect; in fact, I was to be treated as the groom. Moreover, we were not to speak Russian; not a word of any other language except Mongolian was to be heard amongst us. We soon learned to play our respective parts admirably, though at first Shagdur rebelled against ordering me to go and gather *argol* (yak-dung); but after a day or two everything went like clockwork.

After I had done my duty to the satisfaction of my chief, I had a good sound sleep, and slept right on till eight o'clock. When I awoke, the other two were out bringing in the animals. After letting them graze for another hour quite close to the tent, we drove two stout stakes into the ground, and tethered them to the rope that was stretched from stake to stake. We always, both then and afterwards, picketed our animals in this way on the lee side of the tent, close to its entrance, which we left open. As soon as it was dark, we let the fire die down and carried inside our boxes, saddles, and cooking apparatus. Yolbars was chained on the farther side of the horses, so that it was from him we might expect to have the first warning of the approach of danger; whilst shaggy Malenki was tied up a little way from the opposite end of the tent. We divided the night into three watches —9 to 12, 12 to 3, and 3 to 6, and, as a rule, I took the first and the Lama the last watch.

Both Shagdur and the Lama appeared to me unusually out of spirits, and when I asked what was the matter, they told me that whilst I was asleep three horsemen had approached our camp from the south, and after taking council together on the top of a hill had ridden off, and never showed themselves again. This struck me as being very suspicious; it could only mean that they were waiting for night to make some sort of attempt against us. There could no longer be any doubt that we were surrounded by spies and mounted patrols, though whether they were watching us of their own initiative or by command of the authorities we did not of course know.

Some time before nine both my companions were fast asleep and snoring, for they were of course tired after the exertions of the previous night. Meanwhile, I was doing my first "sentry go," marching backwards and forwards, now close to the tent and then a little way from it. I had no difficulty in keeping awake, for every moment I expected an attack. But oh! how slowly the minutes passed! Yolbars barked with joy every time I went near him, while Malenki quietly wagged his tail.

It had rained several times during the preceding day, and now the sky became covered with inky black clouds, which were lit up from the inside by vivid flashes of lightning, while the thunder rumbled in the mountains all round. The rain came down in torrents, leaping up from the ground, and pattering upon the tent as if it meant to beat it flat. Everything inside the tent was wet, for a fine spray like that from an eau-de-Cologne bottle penetrated through the canvas. But the sleepers cared not a rap for the rain; they only pulled their cloaks closer about them and went on driving their pigs to market. The rain-drops clattered noisily on a saucepan which had been left outside; the dogs expressed their discontent in low muffled growls; and the horses and mules switched their wet sides with their tails when the rain-drops tickled them.

I lighted the candle and sat in the tent opening and wrote, but at every the least suspicious sound up I jumped and took a turn round. Oh! those long dark nights, with the slow, leaden-footed, crawling hours! They seemed as if they would never end! As long as I live, I shall never forget them, those solitary pacings to and fro in the rain between Yolbars and Malenki and Malenki and Yolbars. That night the moon gave very little assistance, for the clouds were so tightly packed she could not get through; there was, however, a faint diffused light, just sufficient to make the animals stand out somewhat darker against the background of the night.

All at once I heard a long-drawn, plaintive howl, though

it was scarcely audible owing to the monotonous patter of the rain. Were the Tibetans beginning to howl like hyænas, as the band of Tangut robbers did who threatened to attack me near the Kuku-nor, or Blue Lake? Out I slipped with the revolver cocked under my cloak. I stood still and listened, waiting in the rain. The same weird, complaining sound reached me again. Pshaw! it was only Yolbars expressing his discontent at the weather. Another time it was a distant rumble of thunder which caused me to rush out ready for instant action, and on yet another occasion an innocent switch of a tail. It was no use trying to smoke, everything was wet through. The mules were sleeping as they stood, and their regular monotonous breathing began to make me feel sleepy. But I should have despised myself if I had slept at my post.

At half-past eleven I began to stroll about in the darkness, firmly resolved that I would not go into the tent before midnight struck and the hour of my deliverance came. And when my watch was done, I sat down beside the candle-end, thinking that it was a pity to wake up Shagdur, he was sleeping so soundly. I had just persuaded myself to let him have an extra half-hour, when the dogs began to bark furiously—madly. This woke up the Lama, and he came hurrying out with his rifle, while I blew out the light and followed him with the revolver. We crept stealthily towards the direction from which the suspicious sounds came, and distinctly heard horses moving and dogs barking in the distance. Our camp was being spied upon by mounted men from a couple of hundred yards away! I then sent back the Lama, and Shagdur now joining me, we two walked further in the same direction, stopping and listening every few yards. Very soon we heard, and heard quite distinctly, the sound of horses moving rapidly away. After that the dogs gave over barking, and everything was quiet. It was now Shagdur's turn to keep watch, and it was to the echo of his slow tramp, tramp through the rain and the mud that I at length dropped off to sleep.

The Lama called us at five o'clock, and we rose and started at once. After a night such as we had just spent we all felt cold and dispirited. We longed for the sun, but no sun came; the day remained dull and clouded, and the clouds hung so low down that we kept expecting every moment they would fall upon us. At frequent intervals they pelted us with their contents, sweeping so low down that we felt as it were almost suffocated. In a valley that we came to we found the body of a sheep, with its load lying beside it, namely, salt sewed up in a sack; for in Tibet sheep are used as well as yaks for beasts of burden. Upon reaching a dominating pass in a range that was entirely covered with snow, we found a large cairn of stones; and from that point we could trace a much-trodden road leading towards the Tengri-nor, the lake that lies a little north of Lassa.

We pitched our tent again on a neck of land, about a furlong wide, between two small lakes. Then, after the routine duties were performed the other two slept, whilst I sat listening to the incessant patter of the rain. And at eight o'clock, when we tethered the animals, the rain was still descending as though all the spouts of the skies were turned upon our devoted camp. But, then, it was the rainy season in that country; consequently, rain was the thing to be expected, and we had no right to complain. For four hours I kept watch, sitting sometimes in the tent-opening, where I got a certain amount of shelter. But the mules' pack-saddles might as well have been in a wash-tub, for the water ran off them in streams, and whenever any of the animals shook itself it made a perfect shower-bath of spray all round it. Every now and then the horses would prick their ears, and the dogs would growl suspiciously. At last I let Malenki loose, that he might go and look for a bone, for the Tibetans had been there, and had left the remains of their dinners behind them. The yak-dung which was lying about had been turned over, so that it might dry better; evidently, therefore, the Tibetans intended to come back to fetch it.

The dogs began to bark again. But it was only a false

A Tame Yak, the Animal I Rode from Leh to Kara-korum in 1902.

alarm—confound them! One of the mules had broken loose from the rope and gone off up an adjacent hill. Her escapade, however, completely demoralised one of her fellows, and I had an awful business to catch the two of them again. For that half-hour, at any rate, I could not complain of not having anything to do.

After giving ourselves a couple of hours' extra sleep, we proceeded again next day, the 31st July, towards the south-east, through a very broken country. As I rode, the saddle was so wet, it flop-flopped against me at every step, and after a couple more showers had fallen, my top-boots echoed back swish, swish! When I lifted my arm it was like wringing out a wet rag. What would we not have given for an hour's warm, bright sunshine?

To the east we saw a large winding river; but the track we were following crossed successively over five easy passes and then joined another route from the left, which had recently been used by a yak-caravan.

A little bit farther on we perceived in the distance a number of black dots, which eventually revealed themselves in the all-pervading gloom as a flock of sheep. On the bank of a brook we saw a tent; whereupon the Lama went to pay it a visit. Meanwhile, Shagdur and I continued steadily on, he leading the little caravan and I driving on the animals behind. The people at the tent turned out to be a caravan of Tangut pilgrims, travelling from the temple of Kum-bum (in the Chinese province of Kan-su) to Lassa. They had with them fifty yaks, two or three horses and three dogs; these last had a short but disastrous tussle with Yolbars and Malenki. The pilgrims showed themselves interested to a suspicious degree in our movements.

The flock of sheep consisted of seven hundred head and was in the charge of an old woman, who showed not the slightest trace of fear. But then we were now so horribly dirty from the mud and the rain that the raggedest tramp would not have blushed to be seen in our company. The old woman pointed out to us a nomad's black tent, and said that we could get there any information we wanted. Accordingly we pitched our own tent not very far from it.

No sooner was our new camp in order than the Lama went over to the black tent, and found there two women and a young man; the master of the house was, they said, away from home, but would soon come back. They excused themselves from being unable to sell us sheep, milk or *tsamba** on the ground that it was the day of a religious festival; but if we would wait until the morning, we might have whatever we wanted. But there was one thing that they could give to two or three poor Mongols and that was a sack of dry *argol*, which the Lama brought with him. Whilst we were kindling our fire, the master of the tent appeared on a hillside, whence at a safe distance he stopped and scrutinised us. Thereupon the Lama went and fetched him in, and without hesitation he came and squatted down on the wet ground beside our fire.

This man, the first Tibetan we saw, was probably forty years of age, and his name was Sampo Singhi. His face was almost black, beardless, and wrinkled; his hair, raven-black and dirty, hung in draggled, disorderly ends about his ears, and the rain-water kept dripping off it upon the sack-like cloak he wore. His boots were made of white felt, though then nearly black, and from his belt hung his tobacco-pouch, pipe, and various other useful articles—all inconceivably filthy. Sampo Singhi, like almost all Tibetans, went bare-headed and bare-foot, except for his top-boots. In other words, he was minus the usual nether garments of man—pretty cool and airy, I expect, riding in that condition in such rain as we had had. Sampo Singhi kept incessantly blowing his nose with his fingers, and did it with such *éclat* that we thought Tibetan etiquette demanded we should follow his example. Many were the longing eyes he ostentatiously cast upon our Mongolian cups and so forth, but we pretended not to notice his interested admiration. To me he paid not the slightest degree of special attention; but then I was just as filthy as he was. Shagdur and the Lama were in the habit of taking snuff, and when they offered it to Sampo Singhi he helped himself to a pinch, which caused him to sneeze

* A Mongol dish; see p. 364.

violently. But he was not in the least put out by our laughing at him; he only asked, quite innocently, whether we put pepper into our snuff.

All at once, Shagdur, like a genuine Cossack hetman (chief), cried to me, "What are you sitting there for, boy, with your mouth open? Go and drive in the horses." Up I jumped, and like an arrow sped off up the hillside; but I confess I was greatly relieved when I saw Sampo Singhi waddling off back to his own tent; for had he stopped to watch my proceedings, he could hardly have helped saying to himself, "A precious lot that fellow knows about driving in mules!"

That night we felt a good deal safer than we had done before. After our unexpected meeting with the yak-hunters, we had not encountered any further natives, although we knew perfectly well that they were hovering around us like evil spirits; indeed, one night they had, as I have said, actually attacked us. Sampo Singhi assured us there were no robbers in that part of the country; nevertheless, we did not trust to that, but kept watch all night as usual.

When I was called early on the 1st August, amazing to say, it was not raining! Our neighbours, two men and a woman, were already on their way to pay us a visit, so that we had to hustle away various small articles which might possibly have betrayed the presence of a mysterious stranger. Sampo Singhi was again the spokesman, and he began to praise the various dainties he had brought with him to sell to us—a big piece of greasy fat, a bowl of sour milk, a dish of powdered cheese, a can of fresh milk, a "lump" of cream, and a fine sheep. My word, but we should just fare like princes! said he. Powdered cheese is one of the ingredients in *tsamba,* the others being flour, tea, and lumps of fat or butter, with occasionally a few pieces of raw dried meat added, all stirred together in a bowl, into which every man dips his dirt-plastered fingers. The sour milk was a long way the best; it was thick, white and sour. I am not, as a rule, a *gourmet*, but I do not think I ever tasted anything better than *sho*, as the Tibetans call it; cham-

A Tibetan Woman.

pagne and oysters are not to be mentioned in the same breath with it.

Breakfast over, it was time to pay Sampo Singhi for the good things he had brought us. The honest Tibetan weighed in his hand with manifest pleasure the Chinese silver money which I offered him, but he said that he could not accept anything except Lassa money. Of that we had of course none; but fortunately there were stowed away in one of our boxes two or three rolls of Chinese silk. You should just have seen how the little piggish eyes of Sampo Singhi's better-half glistened with covetousness when she saw it! She stroked the rustling material with her big black paws and feasted her eyes upon it lovingly, as if she intended to make a ball-room dress out of it. After that the price was settled in a jiffy.

Besides this, I told Sampo Singhi that he might keep the sheepskin in return for the hospitality he had shown us. Upon hearing this he rose at once, and eagerly set about killing the animal, though I confess I never saw a sheep killed in a more barbarous way. After tying together three of its legs, and binding a rope tight round its mouth, he knelt upon its horns, which were stretched out flat on the ground. In this way he held the poor beast as in a vice, and then thurst his thumb and forefinger into its nostrils to suffocate it. The sheep struggled and kicked to get loose, and its eyes started out of its head, while Sampo Singhi gabbled desperately fast, "On maneh padmeh hum." At length his victim was quiet and its legs collapsed. Thereupon the Tibetan got up and cut its throat. This scene was very painful to witness; but I did not dare to move a muscle, or in any way interfere, for fear of betraying myself.

Madam Sampo Singhi was dressed in precisely the same way as her husband. Her coarse black hair was gathered up into two plaits, besides which there were any number of rats' tails and matted locks sticking out at all angles. The felt top-boots which she wore were adorned with parti-coloured embroidery of a simple pattern, and had no doubt been rather handsome when new. But how in the world the woman had managed to accumulate such an amount of dirt upon her countenance was a complete puzzle to me. My fine skin, upon which I in vain attempted to maintain the proper degree of incrustation, was continually being

In the Pouring Rain and Mire.

washed "clean" by the rain, and had to be "made up" two or three times a day; but I defy anybody to have made that Tibetan beauty presentable in decent society even though they had turned a fire-hose upon her.

Honest Sampo Singhi made no effort to detain us beyond the one day; on the contrary, he was anxious to get rid of us as soon as possible. And perhaps he was right. Anyway, when we came to his grazing grounds again on our return, he had disappeared. Perhaps his hospitality had got him into trouble; and amid the tremendous commotion occasioned by our entry into Tibet proper, he may somehow have been made to suffer. When we left him, he wished us a successful journey, deceiver that he was, and told us it would take us two days to reach the next nomad camp.

It was pouring with rain when we resumed our journey beside the river Gar-chu, which flowed down Sampo Singhi's valley. Beyond the last low pass we reached, the country appeared to open out before us, at any rate, there were no mountains or hills; but then we could not see very far because of the rain, which was literally coming down in sheets. Our saddles were so wet it was like sitting in a pool of water, while our own clothes clung to us like wet sheets. The track now led down between deserted Tibetan encampments to the right bank of a river, so big and broad that we at first took it for a lake. It was the Saju-sangpo, one of the largest streams in the interior of Tibet. The loud pattering of the raindrops on the water was, however, soon drowned by the dull rumbling that a vast body of water makes when pouring on at a swift rate.

The river was divided into twenty arms, four of them so big that I was afraid it would be impossible to ford them. Our Lama, who always led the way, rode quietly down into the water as though he had not observed the greyish-brown tumultuous torrent, and we of course followed close at his heels. I confess I expected every moment to see him

A Young Tibetan Shepherd.

disappear. With the water in that condition it was impossible to form an idea of the depth ; as a matter of fact, we found that in two or three places it exceeded three feet.

At length we managed to struggle across ten of the arms, and then stopped to rest on a mud-bank, where the water was only about one foot deep. There we were then in the middle of the tossing, rushing flood, which came sweeping down the valley without let or hindrance, and so swiftly that the entire scene began to spin round before our eyes. There was not a glimpse of the banks to be seen, nothing but water whichever way we looked. After the heavy rains the stream had swollen tremendously.

Without a word the Lama dug his spurs into his mule and plunged once more into the torrent. Down, down he went, until the water reached to his stirrups—to the mule's crupper. Her rider drew up his knees to prevent the water from getting into his boots. At the same moment a second mule that he was leading, and which carried our leather-covered boxes, began to struggle alarmingly. The boxes, acting like floats, were lifting her off her feet. She spun half-round and was swept down by the stream. She is lost, she is lost! But no, wonderful to relate, she recovered her feet, regained her balance, and scrambled up the opposite bank, with both boxes safe and sound.

At the moment that the baggage-mule was caught by the current we shouted loudly and excitedly to the Lama to turn back ; but he did not hear us for the thunder of the water racing past him. But calmly and collectedly he continued to rise higher and higher in his saddle, until at last it was entirely under water. Is the man mad, for we knew he could not swim ? In a moment I had my belt unfastened and was preparing to fling off my overcoat, when I saw the little priest would pull through all right, for his mule was beginning to rise out of the water, and in a moment or two I saw that our Lama was safely out of danger.

The last arm was the worst, for although it was not more than a hundred feet across, it was deep and swift, and churned into foam. The other two got safely across, and then it was my turn. Putting my horse into the water, I headed him straight for the point where Shagdur and the Lama were standing on the opposite bank. I felt the water rising up the legs of my boots. Splash, splash into them it went. Then it was over my knees; then my saddle was under water, and there was nothing visible except the horse's head and mane. The Lama and Shagdur flung themselves upon their knees, screaming and gesticulating, trying to point out to me which way the ford ran; but I could not hear a word, owing to the rushing of the flood. At length, however, thinking it was time to part company with my horse, I kicked my feet out of the stirrups and wriggled out of my skin-overcoat, and prepared to strike out, when I felt my horse lose his footing and begin to swim. At the same time he was being carried rapidly down-stream, though luckily towards the bank. Instinctively I clutched at his mane and went with him. In less than half-a-minute he got his feet again, and making desperate efforts, succeeded in scrambling up the bank.

But, Saju-sangpo, we had conquered you! For my own part I was like a drowned cat, and yet that did not matter much, for the rain had already soaked us to the skin. For some little time I felt my knees trembling under me; for no matter how strong a swimmer a man may be, a situation like that I had just been in is anything but a comfortable one. My boots were remarkably waterproof, and after riding some distance it occurred to me that there was really no necessity for me to carry so much water with me, so I stopped and pulled them off, and having emptied them slung them across the saddle behind me, and then rode barefoot.

Our camp that evening presented a queer spectacle—not a dry stitch throughout the entire caravan, several of our things destroyed, water drip, dripping incessantly from the boxes, the animals, our own clothes! After many desperate attempts we at length succeeded in lighting a fire, which, however, hissed and spluttered and filled the tent with foul reek. Nevertheless, I stripped from head to foot, and wrung out my dripping clothes, and spent the night trying to dry them a little; to expect to dry them completely was not to be thought of, for the rain still continued to pour steadily down.

Grim and pitiless, night settled down upon the earth, while the moon did not condescend to cast even the most fugitive glimpse upon the rain-drenched mountains of Tibet. Out on the hillsides it was windy and dark, and the rain pelted down drearily, dismally, without a moment's cessation. The tent canvas flapped like a sail with a hole in it, and we kept fancying we could sometimes hear stealthily footsteps, sometimes mounted men, stealing towards our tent. Twice, and from different directions, we heard shouts during the night. Could it be the pilgrims from Kum-bum? Surely they would not be so mad as to attempt to cross the Saju-sangpo with their yaks? The night-watching was making us nervous and unstrung; we started at every sound. Our journey was no longer a secret, for we had already been in contact with the Tibetans. But we were already well on towards the heart of the mysterious land of Tibet, and I thought that surely we should now be allowed to reach Lassa, seeing that we had safely weathered the attack of the robbers and the dangers of the Saju-sangpo. It was almost like a fairy-tale, in which the hero has to go through fire and water to deliver his bride from the power of the dragon—in this case, the fair city of Lassa! But we were all horribly tired; I almost wished we might be seized, if only to get a real sound good sleep. Both my companions were splendid fellows; namby-pamby folk are no use in such adventures.

The moment midnight came I shook up Shagdur without compunction. He examined his rifle and crept out, while I flung myself down without a moment's delay upon the bare ground from which he had risen. He was too wide awake, and I was too tired, for us to talk; we simply exchanged places without uttering a word.

## CHAPTER XXV.

### PRISONERS!

On the 2nd August the elements were favourable, and it did not rain; but both our horses were foundered and two of the mules had sore backs. After passing a solitary black tent, with twenty yaks and 400 sheep, we came to a tea-caravan encamped beside a spring. It consisted of 300 yaks in charge of 25 men, and the loads, which consisted of cube tea sewed up in sackcloth, were stacked in a dozen rows. Some of the men came forward to look at us. As usual their first question was, "How many of you are there?" Then they asked, what was the object of our journey, where we came from, whether we had anything to sell, and so forth. The men looked for all the world like highway robbers. Many of them had their long black hair gathered into two pigtails, and all had the upper part of their brown body bare, their sheepskin coat being flung back so that the sleeves trailed on the ground behind them, while the coat itself was held fast by the belt round the middle. They invited us to encamp beside them; but we preferred to proceed to more open grazing-grounds which we saw a little bit further on.

The next day was a rest day. At nine o'clock the yak-caravan marched past in exemplary order. The animals were divided into troops of 30 to 40, with two or three men to look after each troop. They drove and guided the yaks by means of loud whistlings and short shrill cries. Although they went close past our tent, they were so engrossed with their business of yak-driving that none of them took any notice of us, nor did one of them show the slightest curiosity to peep in. The entire company were black as pitch; yaks, dogs, men, their clothes, their guns—all were black; so that it was like a procession of grimy demons marching

Our Lama in Conversation with Tibetans.

past. They were bound for the temple of Tashi-lumpo, the seat of the influential Lama, Banshing Bogdo, and for the bazaars of Shigatse,* where they were going to sell their tea.

We spent the day in drying our belongings, spreading them out on the ground in the sun, and filled our top-boots with warm sand to absorb the moisture. Whilst the Lama was examining into the condition of his various drugs and

* On the Brahmaputra, west of Lassa (Lhasa).

medicaments, he produced, to our surprise, a packet of raisins, which he had bought in Charkhlik. After baking myself well in the sun, I was painted afresh by the Lama, and practised the answers it would be prudent to give to the inquisitive questions which sooner or later were bound to be addressed to us. This was, however, a ticklish matter, for according to our Lama the Dalai Lama knew everything, he even knew what we were talking about at that very moment; but he was good, said our Lama, and would not let any harm happen to us, especially as he knew that we had no hostile intentions with regard to his holy land and city.

On the 4th August, after a still, quiet night, with a bright moon in a star-strewn sky, we continued our journey towards Lassa. Soon after starting we met a big yak-caravan, the leaders of which wore tall yellow hats with wide brims, and carried long muskets fired from forked supports. We had no occasion to speak to the Tibetans and intended to pass them quite quietly; but our mules, which had made the most of the good grazing during the past few days, were of a different way of thinking, for they suddenly turned tail about and ran in amongst the yaks, which, resenting their company, scattered in a panic and went off in headlong flight. The Tibetans whistled and screamed, we shouted and halloed, Yolbars and Malenki got up a private prize-fight with their Tibetan associates—in fact, the greatest confusion reigned. At length, however, after no end of trouble, each party succeeded in getting hold of their respective runaways, and we parted good friends.

After crossing over another low pass, crowned by a cairn of stones with the inscription, *Om maneh padmeh hum*, we came to a tract in which there were several black tents with herds of yaks and flocks of sheep grazing round about them. Human beings were, however, few and far between, and when we at length got hold of an old man and asked him to sell us some sour milk, he replied, that though he had plenty of milk, it was not for sale, he wanted it himself; nor would he sell us anything else, the curmudgeon!

The tents now grew more and more numerous, and in front of each was a big heap of *argol* for winter fuel. However, not wishing to be annoyed with inquisitive visitors, we continued until we reached four tents standing by themselves. Here the Lama succeeded in buying a *domba*

A Group of Tibetans.

(bowl) of sour milk. Meanwhile Shagdur and I were visited by a young Tibetan, whom we took for a spy. He talked straight on end without stopping, though we did not understand a word he said.

On Monday, the 5th of August, we rode 21 miles to the south-south-east until we reached Camp LIII., counting from Charkhlik. It was here we got our first taste of summer, and in the neighbourhood of the Tso-nekk (the Black Lake) the temperature rose to 68° Fahr. The tents and flocks and herds of the Tibetans were abundant in every direction. We halted for the night not far from twelve tents in a pretty extensive plain, surrounded everywhere by lofty mountains. We had by this travelled 162 miles from our headquarters camp.

As the Tibetans paid no attention to us, but remained sitting round their fires, while their children played with the puppy-dogs and lambs, we felt perfectly at our ease. But no sooner was it dark than we saw three Tibetans approaching our tent on foot. The Lama and Shagdur went to meet them, and remained such a long time absent that I grew uneasy. At length, when it was quite dark, Shagdur came back alone. He was calm and collected as usual; but when he addressed me in Russian, I understood that something serious had happened. "Things look bad for us," he said. "I didn't understand a word; but they were talking all the time about 'Shved Peling,' 'Buriat,' and 'Lassa.' The Lama is quite humble and his voice almost tearful."

Heated and completely dispirited, the Lama at length came back and told me that one of the three Tibetans was a chieftain, or officer, who had spoken to him politely enough, but at the same time in a stern commanding tone. He had said without circumlocution, that they knew a "Shved Peling" (Swedish European) was on the way to Lassa, and some yak-hunters, who had just reached Nakkchu, had reported that they had seen a large and powerful European caravan advancing over the mountains towards the south. A thousand questions were rained down upon the unhappy Lama: "Did he know anything about these Europeans? Were any of them with him? How many did his party consist of? How many animals had we? Were we armed? Where did we come from? Where were we going to? Why had we chosen this by-road instead of following the usual highway by which the Mongol pilgrims travel?" "Now speak the truth," the chieftain added, "and tell me how you, a Lama, dare to travel with these unknown strangers?"

Our Lama replied, that the European caravan had halted nine days away, but that, whilst the animals of the caravan were resting, we three had been given leave to go to Lassa. With regard to the constitution and numbers of the caravan he gave perfectly accurate answers, for he gathered the impression that the Tibetans already knew all about it through their spies.

The chieftain's decision was given in these words: "You stay where you are over to-morrow. I will then come to your tent, and we will discuss the matter further. I will bring a Mongol interpreter with me, and we will see what we can make of the other two." That night we sat up a long time discussing what we were to do. That the road to Lassa was now closed to us was pretty evident; but would they let us leave the country without molestation? It puzzled me to understand where they had got the expression "Shved Peling" from, unless they could have learned it from the Tangut pilgrim-caravan which visited us at Temirlik the autumn before. What had the morrow in store for us? One thing was certain, we should be examined and cross-questioned, but how should we come through it? Anyway, whatever the result was, our fate would be decided, and I confess I drew a sigh of relief now that the die was finally cast and all uncertainty was at an end.

All night the dogs were barking in the nomad encampments around us. Evidently the Tibetans were going from tent to tent, spreading the news of our arrival, and preparing for what was going to happen. In several places we saw their fires gleaming through the darkness of the night.

Scarcely had the sun risen next day when three fresh Tibetans came to visit us. Stopping at a respectful distance, they hobbled their horses' forelegs and left them, and then came and sat down beside our fire and lit their pipes. Their real errand seemed to be to examine my eyes, for no sooner had I squatted down between two of them than they begged me to take off my coloured goggles. They were no doubt persuaded that all Europeans are fair and have blue eyes, and consequently they were unable to conceal their amazement when they found that my eyes were as black as their own. Greatly taken aback, they nodded to me in a friendly way, and went on talking eagerly and without stopping.

Next they asked to be allowed to look at our weapons, and Shagdur, with a great deal of ostentatious display, showed them the points of his Russian magazine rifle, and then I demonstrated to them the advantages of my Swedish officer's revolver. No sooner was the exhibition concluded than they shook their heads and begged us to put the murderous things away. At the same time they rose, evidently thinking they would be safer at a distance, for they returned at a slow and watchful pace to their horses, which they did not mount until they thought themselves safe out of range.

Half an hour later we were honoured with the visit of four fresh guests, three dirty nomads, with long black hair, and with a sword and long metal pipe hanging from their belt, and a tall old Lama with short clipped hair, wearing a red robe and a yellow cap. The only thing this good man wanted to know was the strength of our main caravan, and that we told him. On both sides there was no lack of the customary forms of politeness, and neither party was chary in its assurances of friendship and esteem. The old man told us what was his own priestly rank, and whatever it was it immensely impressed our modest Shereb Lama, for he rose to his feet, placed the palms of his hands together and touched the old man's forehead with his own.

Finally the old man said, with disconcerting assurance, "You will stay here for three or at the most five days. This morning we sent messengers to the chief of Nakk-chu, to ask whether you may go on or not. In answer to our writing we shall have either a letter with an order for us to detain you, or Kamba Bombo, the chieftain, will come himself; in any case, you are until then our prisoners." So saying, he took his leave.

After that we hoped we should be left in peace, but before five minutes were past something happened which filled us with uneasiness. Around the little encampment nearest to us there gathered from every quarter small bodies of horsemen, armed to the teeth with spear, lance, sword and long black musket. Some wore tall white felt hats, others dark scarves wound round their heads, and every man carried a black or red cloak. They looked more like bandits than soldiers, though they had been called to arms to protect Tibet from an imaginary hostile invasion. They sprang up like mushrooms out of the ground, and soon we counted fifty-three of them as they gathered round their scattered fires in the open air.

We watched their every movement with the keenest attention. The Lama was convinced that our last hour was come; but I thought that if they really did intend to make an end of us they would not have collected quite so many people, as also that they would be more likely to massacre us at night-time. But after a while it really did begin to look as if the Lama were right. Seven horsemen set off east towards Nakk-chu, and others started riding hard for Lassa, to carry the news of our arrival to the Dalai Lama. But the rest, who were being constantly reinforced, charged in a solid body and at full gallop straight down upon our tent. Resolved not to be slaughtered like cattle, we sat or stood in the tent-opening with our weapons ready, prepared for the worst. The Tibetans were coming on like a whirlwind; we could hear the thud-thud of the horses' hoofs on the bare ground. The men were uttering blood-curdling war-whoops, and brandishing their spears and lances over their heads with threatening gestures. On they came with reins dangling and spurs digging into their horses' sides. In two minutes, in one minute, they will be upon us! We shall be crushed as by an avalanche! But no; at a given signal—two of them waved their swords in a particular way—the troop divided, one half wheeling sharply to the right, the other half to the left. But they were so near to us that the foam from the mouths of the leading horses dropped at our feet. Then they returned to the point from which they had started.

Twice more they repeated this unpleasant manœuvre, the object of which plainly was to inspire us with a proper degree of respect. Upon reaching their tents, they dismounted and began to shoot or practice with their long black muskets. At two o'clock they again mounted, and pulling their cloaks about them, for it was raining pitchforks, they rode off in the direction from which we had come. At this I grew decidedly uneasy, for I feared they were going to attack the headquarters camp. I was just burning with impatience to be up and after them, and share in the defence of the camp; but, unfortunately, we were prisoners, and unable to move from the spot.

As soon as the field was thus clear, two nomads came to visit us, bringing with them fat and sour milk. They were forbidden, they said, to take payment for what they brought. The most pertinacious of our visitors were, however, four old men, who appeared as if they meant to stay for good. As we could not get rid of them in any other way we went and lay down, and pretended to sleep; but as just then the rain began to come down again, they all four crept into the tent after us, notwithstanding that there was scant room enough for the three of us before. One old man showed his

The Tibetans Charging Past Our Tent.

friendliness by giving us the comforting intelligence, "Don't you know that it may cost you your heads for having come this way? Everybody who attempts to approach Lassa from this direction has his head cut off."

A little torrent of rain was trickling through the middle of the tent, and eventually it grew so big that it drove us to the sides. In fact, to prevent ourselves from being flooded out, we had to go outside and dig a trench above the tent to carry off the rain-water, for as it happened we were standing on sloping ground. That night we turned our animals loose and left them to graze where they chose, without troubling ourselves further about them. We ourselves were watched by thirty-seven vedettes; we saw their bivouac fires gleaming through the blurr of the rain, especially in the direction of Lassa.

All day on the 7th August the Tibetans were rather troublesome with their attentions. First came the old man who had talked about our having our heads cut off; but he brought us a bowl of sour milk, a sack of *argol*, and a pair of bellows, this last an especially welcome gift. Another Tibetan, whose name was Ben Nursu, and who remained for over three hours, said without scruple that he was sent to spy upon us. He was, however, so complaisant as to furnish us with much valuable information, so that we did not much resent his intrusion. From the place where we were, which he called Jallokk, he reckoned it was five days' journey to Lassa, although a mounted man could reach the capital in a day; and shortly afterwards we did ascertain that a special messenger went to Lassa and back in two days. But these fast special couriers change horses, of course, several times on the way, for the distance was about 120 miles.

Another of our visitors, an old long-haired man called Dakkyeh, remarked to his comrades, at least so our Lama said: "These three men are very suspicious characters.

They will, of course, not continue to Lassa. Kamba Bombo will come in two or three days' time, and then we shall see. In the meantime let them want for nothing, and see that they have everything they wish, but nobody is to take anything in payment. If they attempt to escape, the watchman must let me know at once. Amgon Lama has consulted the holy books, and found that these men are

A Tibetan Soldier.

dangerous individuals, who must not be let go to Lassa. The hunter Onji saw them not very long ago amongst the mountains, and he says they have an alarmingly big company of men with them. This news was at once sent on to Lassa." Then, pointing to me, he added: "Amgon Lama was unable to determine whether this man was a Buriat or not." His companions answered simply, "Lakso! Lakso!" an expression which signifies reverence, respect and obedience. From this conversation it appeared that it was in especial the yak-hunters of Camp No. XXXVIII. who had got us into this fix.

All day mounted patrols were riding to and fro across the plain. The Tibetans had mobilised to meet and check the enemy who was invading their country from the north. One of our visitors said frankly that they had been called to arms because of our main caravan; another that they were only concerned to defend the holy land of Tibet.

On the 8th August I awoke half-suffocated by the horrible smoke that filled the tent; for as it was still raining hard, Shagdur was baking bread inside. I found that a thick coating of soot was adhering to the grease with which my face had lately been smeared. The people brought us far more mutton, butter, fat and milk, fresh and sour, than we were able to consume, even with the dogs to help us.

When the everlasting cross-examination began again I lost my temper, and told them that if they did not stop their inquisitive questioning, I would drive them all outside, and not let one of them come in again. They at once stopped their questions, bowed politely, and said simply and modestly, "Lakso! Lakso!" The Lama informed me that they stood in terrible awe of me. It was evident they had been commanded from Lassa to treat us with the greatest possible respect, and that no harm would be done to us. In a word, we were both their guests and their prisoners, their friends and their enemies. The only one of us who was uneasy was the Lama, ever since he had learned that Kamba Bombo himself was coming to examine us. The Lama had seen Kamba Bombo in Nakk-chu, and knew that it was that chieftain who searched with such close and strict jealousy all the caravans that go to Lassa, and was responsible that no European passed him. Moreover, he called to mind that on one occasion a Mongol Lama for some fault or other had forfeited his right to visit Lassa, and in order to atone for his fault was made to travel all the way from Urga, in Mongolia, to the Holy City on his knees, flinging himself forward with his hands on the ground at every step, a penance which took him six years to perform, and then at the end of it he was not allowed to enter the city. Our Lama feared, therefore, not without reason, that similar hard measures might be meted out to him, and "even if I escape with my life," he said, "my career is ruined and I shall never see Lassa again."

Meanwhile I was beginning to weary of sitting still and doing nothing, except sleeping, preparing meals, eating, and watching the coming and going of the Tibetans. On the other hand, it was a relief to rest without having to mount and ride through the everlasting rain, for it was so cold, and grey, and raw, and wet, and dark. All the same the loss of liberty was irksome. I hated to be at the beck and call of the Tibetans, and looked forward eagerly to Kamba Bombo's arrival; for when he came something decisive would be done. Meanwhile Jallokk seemed to have been converted into a military rendezvous, for scouts, messengers, couriers and convoys were coming and going all day. However, the nomads had a fine time of it, for Tibetan soldiers, when called to arms, possess the right of demanding from the natives whatever they want, and pay them by credits upon the capital.

In the afternoon we were sitting talking to seven Tibetans, when we perceived a troop of horsemen approaching our tent from the east at a rapid pace. Ah! here comes the Bombo (Governor) of Nakk-chu! It turned out, however, to be not the distinguished chieftain himself, but only his Mongol interpreter, an easy-going, good-natured Tibetan. The moment Kamba Bombo learned of our arrival, he had ordered the interpreter to ride night and day to Jallokk, and he himself was to follow as speedily as he could.

Then the old round of cross-questioning began again. All suspicions as to my nationality were swallowed up in the fear that our main caravan was but the advanced guard of the big invading army which the Tibetans seemed to expect from the north. They had a panic terror of this imaginary army, and I am perfectly certain that the highest authorities in Tibet never even dreamed of putting themselves under Russian suzerainty and protection. The interpreter declared that no matter who we were, we should never get into Lassa, but at the same time, by command of the Dalai Lama, no harm was to be done to us.

Shagdur and I now began to ride the high horse, and lectured the poor interpreter right and left. "What did they mean by stopping us? We had the permission of the Russian Czar to make the pilgrimage to Lassa. Had the Dalai Lama ever before refused to allow peaceful Buriats to go there? Kamba Bombo's head was in danger; if he did not restore us our freedom, he might lose his life. The interpreter and his attendants looked very grave. Of Russia they knew nothing whatever and of India they had but the faintest idea. What we said about the extent and power of these empires made not the slightest impression upon them. At length we agreed that a special messenger should be sent to Kamba Bombo, with the request that he would hasten his arrival, and the interpreter promised that he himself would send a courier to Lassa to lay before the Dalai Lama everything that I had just said to him.

## CHAPTER XXVI.

### KAMBA BOMBO.

THE 9th August was an important day for us. In the morning a number of mounted men and patrols drew off to the south-west, driving all the flocks and herds before them, so that the plain echoed again with the shouting of men, the trampling and neighing of horses, the bleating of sheep and the angry grunting of yaks. Shereb Lama, who still continued to look at the dark side of things, got it into his head that they were clearing the course for the charge with which they intended to overwhelm us.

At ten o'clock our friend the interpreter appeared again, and told us that Kamba Bombo, chief of Nakk-chu, had arrived with a large following, and wished to see us at once. And in fact quite a village of tents had sprung up a mile or two away on the road to Lassa. The chieftain's tent was very large, and blue and white, and columns of smoke were already curling up from the others. Our Lama, upon seeing all the newly-arrived horsemen, and men on foot swarming about the airy village, became a prey to the keenest disquietude.

The interpreter's errand was to invite us, in the name of Kamba Bombo, to remove our tents to the immediate vicinity of his own and to join him at dinner. In one of the tents, he said, dinner was already being served: in the middle was a sheep roasted whole, surrounded by dishes for tea and *tsamba*, and as soon as we set foot within the tent we should each be honoured with a *haddik*—that is, a thin light-blue scarf which the Mongols and Tibetans are wont to offer to distinguished guests as a token of respect.

My answer was, that if Kamba Bombo possessed the very smallest knowledge of the usages and customs of civilization, he ought to know that it was his duty to come and visit us before inviting us to go and dine with him.

If he desired our acquaintance there was plenty of room for him to put up his tents beside ours. We did not send for him; we wanted to have nothing to do with him. We did not even know who he was, or what authority he possessed to speak in the name of the Dalai Lama. All we desired to know was whether we should be permitted to continue our journey to Lassa. If not, we should return to our main caravan, and Kamba Bombo would have to answer for the consequences.

The poor interpreter wriggled and writhed like a worm. He begged, he prayed, he bemoaned himself. "If you do not come, I shall fall into disgrace and be dismissed." For two mortal hours he used every art of persuasion he was master of to induce us to go with him; but when he found that I was not to be moved from my purpose, he mounted and rode away. "Tell Kamba Bombo," I called after him, "that unless he has the good sense to come and visit us, he will never see a glimpse of our faces."

Now to give such an answer to the governor of a province is rather impolite; but then this was not the first time I had had to deal with Asiatics. There is only one method of dealing with them if you want to get your own way with them. At the same time, I will confess that I recognised we were in an awkward situation. We knew that the Tibetans were called to arms, and we had pretended to be Buriats; nobody, therefore, would have had any right to reproach them, had they chosen to make an example of me,

Tents of Tibetan Chiefs, White with Blue Borders. (Photographed on a Later Occasion.)

a European who was trying to steal into their country in disguise. And if they had killed me, and afterwards been called to account for it, they would readily have been able to answer, "We did not know that he was a European; he said himself he was a Buriat." We all three were afraid that the invitation was but a trap to get us into their power, for when people go to dine they usually lay aside their weapons, and that it was meant as a pretext to separate us from them. The Tibetans had, we knew, the profoundest respect for our fire-arms; but, no thank you, we were not going to be outwitted. We were resolved we would not let them take our lives before we had used up our last cartridge.

The next two hours were a period of great suspense. The critical moment had come. All this time we were left alone. But the decision was now close at hand. I remember those long hours of waiting as if it were but yesterday. Men and horses were swarming around the chieftain's tent. What were they talking about? What were they preparing to do? Was Kamba Bombo annoyed by the curt answer I had sent?

The troops in and about the tent village now drew closer together, and after getting their weapons ready, mounted on horseback. Then arranging themselves in one long black line, they started to gallop towards us. It was not raining, and we were able to enjoy freely what was in truth a magnificent spectacle. In the middle rode the chieftain on a big, handsome grey mule; all the other men rode horses. Immediately behind Kamba Bombo was his staff of military, civil, and ecclesiastical officials, all wearing handsome gala dresses. The wings of the company consisted of soldiers armed to the teeth with gun, sword and lance. We counted altogether sixty-seven men, while we were but three poor pilgrims! We had taken our station just outside the tent, and our weapons, ready loaded, were

Tibetan Cavalry.

within easy reach. On they came at an easy gallop. First we heard a confused rushing sound, and then the quick hoof-beats of the horses upon the ground. When they came near enough, the interpreter dashed forward and announced the arrival of Kamba Bombo. The great man advanced quite close to our tent and drew rein, whereupon some of his servants leapt out of their saddles and spread upon the ground a carpet and some cushions, upon which he took his seat, accompanied by Nanso Lama, a distinguished Lama of Nakk-chu.

I stepped forward and invited him quietly, but firmly, to enter our tent, and after some hesitation he accepted the seat of honour I pointed to—namely, a wet sack of maize standing amongst other evil-smelling belongings. Kamba Bombo was a man of probably forty years of age, small and pale, with a tired, worn-out look; but he chuckled, and looked sly and cunning. Evidently he was delighted at having us in his toils, knowing very well that his vigilance would prove greatly to his own advantage. His dress was tasteful and elegant. His outer garments, namely, a red cloak and a *bashlik* of the same colour, were taken charge of by his servants, and he then appeared dressed from head to foot in yellow silk, with wide sleeves to his cloak; his head was covered with a small blue Chinese skull-cap, and his Mongolian boots were of green velvet—in a word, he was got up as if for a great occasion.

As soon as writing materials were produced, our cross-examination began; but Kamba Bombo was far more anxious to know details about our main camp and caravan than he was to know about ourselves. It was clear they were afraid of an invasion from the north, and believed that our caravan, which was waiting in the mountains, was the advanced guard. For us, however, it was a great advantage that we had left the caravan behind us, for the Tibetans understood that if they did us any harm, they would bring

"Not Another Step Towards Lassa."

the main force down upon them, and they seemed to think that there were thousands of soldiers lying hidden amongst the northern mountains.

They examined such of our belongings as were lying about, but Kamba Bombo never once asked to look inside the trunks; the information that they contained provisions satisfied him. All our answers were written down, and the protocol would, he admitted, be sent direct to Lassa. With regard to myself, he appeared to have already made up his mind, for he did not ask me a single question. When Shagdur was questioned, he gave his replies in a loud, ringing voice, and asked how they dared to stop a Russian Buriat.

But Kamba Bombo laughed and said, "I am not to be frightened. I have had my orders from the Dalai Lama, and I shall do my duty. Not another step towards Lassa! If you advance it will cost you your heads," and he drew his hand edge-wise like a knife across his throat. "It doesn't matter who you are, you are under suspicion. You have come by a by-road, and must go back to your principal camp."

Shagdur, who posed as the most important person of the three, bore himself very creditably, and made an impression upon the Tibetans. But when he could make nothing more of the request to continue to Lassa, he demanded compensation for the horses that had been stolen from us. Kamba Bombo prevaricated, and said that he could not be answerable for what happened outside the boundaries of his province. Thereupon Shagdur cleverly scored off him by quickly exclaiming, "Quite so, it is not your country. I suppose, then, it belongs to Russia!" Upon this Kamba Bombo grew angry, and answered curtly, that the whole country belonged to the Dalai Lama. We should have a couple of horses next morning.

Finally, the peremptory Governor announced that we

might stay there as long as we chose, and start when we liked, but that he should not return to Nakk-chu so long as we were at Jallokk. He would give us a special escort as far as the Saju-sangpo, the boundary of his province, and whatever we required by way of provisions should be placed freely at our disposal; and by way of proving that he was in earnest, he gave us at once various edibles and a couple of sheep.

On the whole, Kamba Bombo was friendly and polite, and not the least bit annoyed at all the trouble we occasioned him. He was a capital fellow to have to deal with; he knew exactly what he wanted. Who I was, I suppose, he never knew exactly; but anyway he must have thought that I was somebody out of the common, or else he would not have come with all that pomp and ceremony. Whilst the cross-examination was proceeding, the other Tibetans crowded round, making their various remarks and observations. They carried their swords in silver-mounted scabbards, decorated with corals and turquoises, brought from Nepal and Badakshan; *gavos*, *i.e.*, talisman cases of silver filagree, handsome bracelets and rosaries, while the long plaits of their hair were full of ornaments—precious stones, pearls and silver jewellery, all from Lassa. In fact, every man carried upon his person the most valuable things he possessed, and their saddles and bridles exhibited the artistic skill of the Mongols. The more distinguished of Kamba Bombo's attendants wore big white hats, with plumes in them; others had scarves wound round their heads, while the soldiers were for the most part bareheaded, their hair sticking out in rats'-tails in every direction, so that they looked like North American Indians.

Shereb Lama was subjected to a severe examination in Tibetan. His name was enrolled in the temple books, and he knew perfectly well that Europeans were forbidden to visit Lassa. Yet he had brought with him two suspicious strangers, and had disgraced his priestly office. He was a traitor; he should never more set foot within the holy precincts.

Eventually I proposed to Kamba Bombo that I should write a letter, which he should send to the Dalai Lama. But he answered, that it would be as much as his place was worth to offer counsel to the Holy One. Nor was there

Tibetan Soldiers.

any need to send a messenger; orders were despatched to himself direct from Lassa every day, and he knew precisely how he had to deal with us.

After that he got up, politely took his leave, swung himself into his highly-decorated saddle, and rode away, followed by his large staff. By this it was twilight, and the whole troop soon disappeared from sight, and with it vanished my hope of seeing the Holy City. That night the stars twinkled bright and still above the mountains of

Tibet; not a breath of air stirred, not a sound was audible, except the occasional barking of a dog in the distance.

Almost three years have passed since that evening, and many other changes have taken place in the interval. I myself am hard at work in my quiet cosy study at Stockholm. Shereb Lama has written to me that he has left Astrakhan, where he settled when the journey was done in a lamaist monastery of the Kalmucks, and has returned to his birth-place, Urga. Shagdur—perhaps he is bleeding on some battlefield of Manchuria, slain by a Japanese bullet? Who knows?

Next morning I bade our Tibetan guards bring our two horses and four mules to the tent, for I was not minded to lose any more time than was necessary. Yet it would not do to ride away quite in an unceremonious fashion. I resolved, therefore, to go alone and visit Kamba Bombo in his own tent, although Shagdur and the Lama both sought to dissuade me. When I got about half-way there I was surrounded by a score of mounted horsemen, who without a single word arranged themselves before me and behind me; but at about half a mile from the Tibetan tents they stopped and dismounted, and signed to me to do the same.

After waiting barely a quarter of an hour, I saw approaching at the gallop the same troop of cavalry who had visited us the day before, Kamba Bombo in his yellow robes riding in the middle. Then, taking our seats on a couple of cushions laid on a carpet, we had a long talk together, the interpreter being the intermediary. But all my arts of persuasion were fruitless. Kamba Bombo had no desire to lose his head in order to please me; and when I proposed to ride alone and unarmed to Lassa, he laughed and shook his head, and pointing towards the north, repeated, "Back! Back!" Then, closing one eye with a knowing air, he ejaculated the word, "Sahib!" using this word as it is used in India, to indicate a European, especially an Englishman.

"No," I answered, "I am not a Sahib, though I will confess that I am a European. I come from a country far away in the north, a long way beyond Russia." But he only reiterated again, "Sahib! Sahib!" And when I pointed out to him, thinking to convince him, that I had four Cossacks with me who had been lent to me by the Czar of Russia, his reply was, "They are all Sahibs"; and from this conviction I was unable to move him.

After that two horses were led forward, which he offered me as compensation for those stolen from us. I asked him to let me see them tried, when they turned out to be such wretched jades that I turned round and asked him whether he didn't want them for his own artillery; I wouldn't have them. Immediately two others were brought forward, useful animals of a white colour, and these I accepted.

An hour later we were all sitting once more in front of my tent, Kamba Bombo being entertained with *tsamba*, raisins, and tobacco, while we exchanged our Chinese *yambas* for Tibetan money. Once more we exhibited our weapons, and I remarked seriously, "Remember, if you had attacked us, we could have shot down thirty-six of you before you would have had time to load again."

The Governor declared that he had never intended to begin hostilities; all he wanted to do was to protect the frontiers against intrusive foreigners.

"Why are you, then, so afraid of me that you dare not visit me without an escort of sixty or seventy men," I asked.

"Why, you are a distinguished Sahib," he answered, "and I have been ordered from Lassa to show you the same respect that is shown to the highest authorities in our own country."

Finally he introduced to me the three officers and twenty

men whom he had commissioned to escort us back over the frontier, and who were to be at the same time answerable for our animals and our commissariat. Then we climbed into our saddles, and after mutual polite farewells, we turned our backs upon this friendly, but inhospitable, Tibetan; and I remarked to Shagdur, "Well, we haven't seen Lassa, but we are still alive, and that's something to be thankful for!"

## CHAPTER XXVII.

### ESCORTED BACK.—A FRESH ATTEMPT.

FOR four days we were accompanied by the Tibetan escort, the leaders of which, Solang Undy, Anna Tsering and the old man Dakkyeh, were exceptionally pleasant and agreeable fellows, and from the very first evening we were on the best of terms with them. At first we were, of course, closely watched. Horsemen rode behind us, horsemen rode in front of us, while there were others on both sides, and when we encamped they pitched their tents quite close to ours; but gradually they allowed us more freedom. It was, I admit, irksome to have to retrace our steps; but our escort amused us immensely, and we never grew tired of watching the ways and doings of these half-wild mountaineers, with their long black muskets and forked supports, their spears and lances, and swords. We frequently met small patrols of cavalry, who no doubt had been making a reconnaissance towards our main caravan, and they sometimes turned and accompanied our cavalcade. Amongst them were two or three venerable lamas, who as they rode kept swinging their *korlchs*, or prayer-wheels, and mumbling in a singing, flowing sort of rhythm their everlasting *On maneh padmch hum!*

When the time came for pitching the tents, they always asked me politely whether I was ready to stop, or wanted to go on further. But as a rule I let them choose the camping-ground for the night, for they knew, of course, better than we did where the grass and the water were best. They used to show wonderful skill and address in setting up their tents; then with their swords they dug

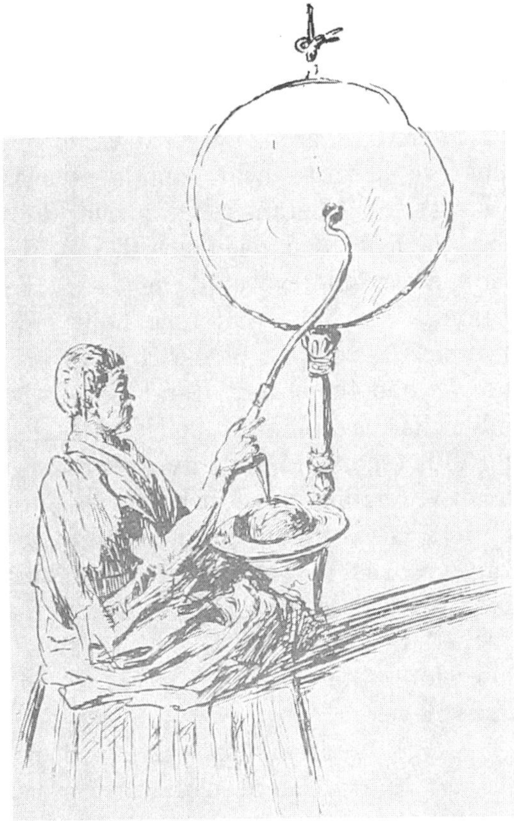

A Lama Playing on a Drum and Metal Plates.

three sods out of the ground to put the cooking-pot upon, kindled the *argol*, and blew it into a flame. Saddles, sacks, guns, swords, lances, and cups and platters, all used to lie scattered about here, there and everywhere, so that the camp had an air, not only of picturesqueness, but of comfort. I used to go and take my supper with the Tibetan officers, who never grew tired of looking at my watch and hearing it tick; in fact, I never took it out of my pocket but what they began to repeat, "Tick, tick, tick, tick!"

"It is my *gavo*" (talisman-case), I said, "and the god inside it goes on repeating his *On maneh padmeh hum* day and night without stopping."

At this they would look at one another earnestly, and evidently considered that I was a wonderful person. Every evening we used to hear sounds of swishing and mumbling: it was the Tibetans reciting their daily prayers, an occurrence which filled our lama with sad, if not bitter reflections, for never more would he hear the growing volume of prayers which at the same hour always swells up from the numerous temples of the Holy City.

By day, too, we had the sleepy sound of bells in our ears, for each soldier had a collar of bells fastened round his horse's neck. Our escort did not travel very fast, and made only short stages. Against this I had no objection to offer, for after they left us we should push on by forced marches and long stages, so as to get across the robber-haunted zone as quickly as possible. Solang Undy advised us, if we were attacked again at night, just to shoot at once. Evidently, therefore, the Tibetans were not in collusion with the horse-thieves.

Old man Dakkyeh became a special friend of mine. It was killing to see him when he came and greeted me by sticking out his tongue as far as he could, jerking both thumbs upwards, shrugging his shoulders, and nodding his head. And when I returned his greeting in the same way, I did it with such energy that Shagdur almost split his sides with laughing.

By this the Saju-sangpo had dropped so considerably that we crossed it without the least difficulty; but then the Tibetans knew accurately how the ford ran.

A Lama with a Prayer-wheel.

The 15th August was the day our escort was to leave us, and it was with real regret that we said good-bye to them all. They turned back at the same spot where we had fallen in with our friend Sampo Singhi on the journey out.

A Lama Reading.

The five stages which remained between that point and the head-quarters camp were both hard and gloomy, though the nights were the worst, for we no longer had the Tibetans to look after our animals for us. The very first evening we had a foretaste of what was to come. Threatening, fiery yellow clouds loomed up across the mountains in the south-east, and massed themselves together as they do before the onset of a sandstorm in the desert. A furious blast was sweeping across the highlands, and the thick darkness which accompanied the hail-squalls made the night fully two hours longer than usual. All night it rained violently, and the moon, our best friend on the way out, never once showed herself. This time I was to take the middle watch, and at 11 o'clock I went out to see how Shagdur was getting on. I found him sitting amongst the animals in the mud and the rain, and as I approached him he bade me in a cautious whisper, "Listen!" Then he told me he had just heard footsteps, and thought they were the footsteps of a man. I walked in the direction from which the suspicious sounds came, and found that it was only Malenki who had given occasion to the false alarm. On a pitch-dark night like that, when you can't see your hand before your face, you have nothing to guide you except sounds. Nor were things made any the more comfortable when our good Lama began, as he often did, to talk in his sleep, and in a tone of complaint to call upon Sirkin, as if he were in distress and needed help.

With the view of seeing as much of the country as I could, I chose a different route from that which we had followed on the journey out. But this led us into a tangle of hills, where the ground was marshy and treacherous. Once it took us several hours to get over a wretched little height on which the animals sank in up to the saddle-girths. We were getting quite worn out by this night-watching, these long marches and the incessant rain and hail.

On the 18th August we gave ourselves a couple of hours' rest on a hill-side. The air was quiet and still, and the temperature rose to over 66°; in fact it was so hot that we were almost afraid of sunstroke. It was terribly hard work to get up and start again, for we lay stretched at full length in the sun while the animals grazed. But we had barely got started when another hail-storm burst, and in a moment summer was changed into winter, and we had to don our furs.

The principal diversion that day was occasioned by a bear which Malenki surprised in the act of digging a marmot out of his burrow; and when Bruin set off at a fast trot the dogs followed him, and kept dancing round him barking like mad.

Then came the night again with its hateful watching. But we now had only twenty miles to go, and we were anxious to do them at one stage. But after their three-hundred miles' journey the only two of our horses that were at all fresh were the two Tibetans, and them we had to watch closely lest they should break back south to their former haunts. The Lama kept imagining all this time that our main camp was besieged by the Tibetans; but then the strain was beginning to tell upon him, and he was getting unstrung.

At length, from the top of a low pass, our eyes were gladdened by the sight of the broad open valley we had ridden across the first day of the journey out. But it was silent and deserted, not a sign to indicate that there were human beings anywhere near. Here unfortunately one of our horses came down, and was unable to get up. That settled it; we must perforce spend another night on the road.

The next day was the 20th August, and it was of course—pouring with rain! We had already passed the first encampment we made on this trip when we heard rifle shots and saw a yak come galloping up a hill. We at once directed our steps towards him, and soon became aware of two black dots, which ere long we made out to be men on horseback. Were they Tibetans we wondered? No, they were riding straight towards us, and after a while we recognised them; they were Sirkin and Turdu Bai. Upon this we dismounted, and waited until they came up, overjoyed to see us.

An hour later I was sitting in my comfortable yurt; but to describe the pleasure of being once more home again—well, it is a feeling that really cannot be described.

Chernoff had, I found, joined the main body with the rear-guard; and so well had he succeeded that he had lost only two horses and two camels, one of them being my faithful veteran of 1896.

After I had inspected the camp, I ordered Cherdon to get me a warm bath, for I had not had a wash of any sort for a month; and he had to change the water no less than three times before I got even tolerably clean. Then I took an eternal farewell of my Mongol rags, and once more stood forth in European garb. The dash for Lassa was only a memory, a transient episode in the greater and bigger journey.

Next day we started again to return to the point from which we had set off for Lassa. Here and there on the hill-sides as we went we saw the skeletons of horses which had died whilst we were away. The camels, on the other hand, had picked up wonderfully. Old Mohammed Tokta was, however, in a bad way, and still complained of his heart; so I recommended him to keep perfectly quiet. That night everybody was in high spirits. The Cossacks made themselves a *balalaika*,* and with it and a Tibetan flute, and a temple bell, and a couple of saucepans used as cymbals, and the musical-box and four strong voices, we were entertained to a tolerable concert, and that despite the rain which was coming down as usual in a deluge.

On the 25th August we finally left the site of our main camp in Northern Tibet and started upon our long journey to Ladak. Nevertheless I did not direct our march towards the west, but towards the south. We made, however, a

* A guitar-like instrument with three strings, used in Russia to accompany songs.

bad beginning by losing three of our horses. Two gave up directly we left camp, and the third only succeeded in getting over the first pass; but then that day's march turned out to be one of the very worst we ever had. During the night it had snowed, and in the morning it turned to rain, and the rain came down in torrents. The country looked as if it were the dumping-ground for the street-mud of all the cities in the world. Every man was

A Camel Sinking in the Quagmire.

forced to walk, even at the risk of losing his boots in the mire. Had we been a smaller company we should infallibly have lost a large proportion of our camels, for they kept falling incessantly, and when they did so it was no end of a business to get the beast up again. In the first place it was hard work to find tolerably firm ground on which to place the load, whilst we gave our attention to the camel. Then we moved aside the mud with spades, pulled the camel over on one side, and putting felts under his feet, hauled at him by main force until he condescended to get up. And all this while the rain continued to stream down in torrents.

When I was called early on the 28th August Kalpet of Keriya was reported to be missing. He had lingered behind the night before, but everybody assumed that he had come in after dark. I now, therefore, sent back two men on horseback to see what was become of him. They

Sirkin's Kökkmek Goat.

returned at the end of a couple of hours, bringing Kalpet with them. The poor fellow was ill; but we at once gave him the best care we could.

Every night I now had vigilant watch kept, and the Cossacks took it in turn to sit up with the animals that were grazing. Camp No. LXVIII. was situated 16,630 feet above the level of the sea. Thus the lofty table-land showed no sign of decreasing elevation. Every night the thermometer fell several degrees below freezing point, nor during the day did it rise above 50°. Autumn had begun; yet how little did we realise the terrible winter that lay ahead? Camping-grounds both old and new were numerous everywhere, nevertheless there was still an abundance of game, especially of yaks, wild sheep and hares, and as we approached the camp I have just mentioned a troop of fifty kulans drew away from it. The men shot two *köttmek* goats, and a beautiful little

A Frozen Deer and Goat.

*yureh* antelope. In the evening the Cossacks fixed them up with the help of sticks and string against two or three packages, in the attitudes the creatures adopt when leaping, and in the morning they were frozen stiff and stood of themselves. This was done to give me an opportunity to photograph them. Every night the mountains around echoed with the dismal howling of the wolves. Eagles were also numerous. We found quite a colony on the shore of a little lake. The young were not yet fledged, but all the same when our dogs attacked them they defended themselves so valiantly with beak and claw that the assailants were forced to beat a retreat.

At length from the summit of a pass which we crossed on the 1st September we had the welcome sight for which we had been looking so long—a flat open country, stretching several days to the south. The grazing also was good, in fact the earth assumed a verdant tinge, so that we stopped at the first spring we came to.

That afternoon the camp was all excitement. We saw what we at first took to be a herd of wild yaks, but upon a closer inspection through the telescope we found that they were horses. The Cossacks rode out to reconnoitre, but failed to detect any people with them. Next morning, however, we saw on some distant hills a flock of probably 1,000 sheep, and the Lama, Shagdur and Sirkin at once went towards them. At the end of some hours the first-named came back, bringing with him a *domba* (bowl) of milk. At the end of another hour the two Cossacks turned up, driving before them three Tibetans on foot, leading their horses and a sheep. The Cossacks had discovered a tent inhabited by a dozen people, who when they saw the strangers approaching took to their heels; but as they went off without their horses they were easily overtaken and caught. But although they were in a state of abject terror, they stubbornly refused to sell us any eatables, because they had been commanded by the Bombo or governor not to help us in any way. But after Shagdur gave one of the old men a taste of his riding-whip they proved more amenable to reason, and brought forward a sheep and a bowl of milk. They informed us that they belonged to the district of Jansung, and were subject to Banshing Bogdo of Tashi-lumpo, and had nothing to do directly with the authorities at Lassa.

We entertained them with tea, bread and tobacco, paid

them for their provisions with sterling coin of Lassa, and gave them a present of a porcelain cup. When we had got out of them all we wanted we let them go. In a moment they were in the saddle, but as I wanted to photograph them the Lama skilfully detained them in conversation, at the same time carefully keeping a firm hold upon the bridle of one of the horses. The moment he let go the Tibetans galloped off like madmen, and only drew rein when they thought themselves safe out of range. Then, however, they pulled up, and began to talk and gesticulate with great energy. We had wanted to buy from them two or three horses, but they stubbornly refused to sell us any, alleging that they were only the keepers of the horses, not their owners. The Cossacks urged me to let them help themselves, but against this I sternly set my face.

When on the 3rd September we continued our journey towards the south through a country that was relatively thickly populated by nomads, mounted troops began to show themselves, now on our right and then on our left. They appeared to spring up out of the ground, and gradually drew together into larger bodies, and kept galloping round us, performing various rude evolutions. Their object was of course to hinder us from advancing, but in this object they found a more powerful ally in our old acquaintance the Saju-sangpo, for its swollen flood effectually barred our passage. We were therefore forced to encamp on its bank. The Tibetans lit their bivouac fires not far from ours.

Next morning the Bombo of the region appeared with his staff. He begged and prayed of us to turn back, promising to supply us with food, horses, sheep; in fact, anything and everything we wanted, if only we would direct our march towards Ladak. If it was our purpose, he said, to advance towards Lassa, he would have to send a courier there to get orders, and when I told him—

A Visit from the Shepherds of Jansung.

politely, of course—to go to the devil and not interfere with my affairs, he replied resignedly and without fear, "You may indeed take our lives, but so long as we live, we shall do our very utmost to prevent you from marching south."

Meanwhile the men were getting my little canvas skiff ready. Then, after ordering the Cossacks to lead the caravan down the right bank of the river, I embarked on the broad stream with Ördek for my boatman. Down we spun at a giddy pace. Now the Tibetans were encamped on the top of a cliff that shot down precipitously into the river. The current was carrying us to the base of the cliff. When the Tibetans saw this, they howled and shrieked and gesticulated violently with both arms and legs. What were they going to do? It was rather an anxious moment, for they might very easily upset us by rolling a big stone down upon us. But fortunately such an idea did not occur to them, and we safely weathered the point of danger. It was a delightful and refreshing trip sweeping round the curves between the high banks in that comfortable fashion.

After spending the night on the bank with the rest of the caravan, where we had the Tibetans for our nearest neighbours, I continued again in the same way on the morrow. Gradually the river widened out to nearly a mile. Towards the south there appeared what looked almost like an ocean, for land was not visible anywhere in that direction, except the mountains which shut in the expanse of water on the east. The weather was warm and delightful, but owing to the mirage the mountains seemed to be raised a little above the earth, while our camels, marching some distance away, seemed to be walking on tall narrow stilts. Meanwhile the river continued to widen out until it became nearly 1¼ miles in breadth, and at last its banks fell away, and through a magnificent trumpet-

Our Lama Detaining the Three Tibetans.

shaped estuary the Saju-sangpo emptied itself into the large lake of Selling-tso, about the middle of its northern shore. The panorama which unfolded itself as we entered the lake was magnificent. The turbid grey water of the river was perceptible a long way out into the lake, but everywhere else the lake itself was of a brilliant blue-green colour.

But the day was getting late, and there were big waves on the lake. Accordingly I deemed it prudent to put back to shore, where two of the men were waiting for us with horses to take us back to camp.

All the time that I was on the river, the Tibetan horsemen swarmed round the caravan and prevented the people in the tents we passed from selling provisions to the Cossacks, These last, who were more hot-tempered than I am, sent the Lama to warn the Tibetans that the first man who came within range after that would be shot down without further warning. For the rest of the day the brave national militia of Tibet kept at a respectful distance. This opportunity we at once seized to buy several sheep and all the milk food we could get hold of from our nearest nomad neighbours. And it was fortunate we did so, for next morning there appeared a fresh troop of over fifty mounted men, who came and pitched their tents quite close to us. Some of the newcomers met the Lama and negotiated with him on neutral territory; but I sent him back to tell them that unless the highest official amongst them came in person to visit me in my own camp they need not hope to make anything out of us.

Apparently that official found these conditions hard, for he took three full hours to reflect upon them before he could prevail upon himself to come and visit me. He arrived on foot, followed by a bodyguard of ten swordsmen. We entertained him in the cooking-tent. He was an old man with a very friendly and sympathetic face. With the idea of reassuring him I had the musical box set agoing, but even the *Marseillaise* did not avail to move a muscle of his features. He no doubt took it for a mitrailleuse or some other sort of toy, quite out of place in polite society. But when the instrument began to grind out the plaintive melodies of the *Cavalleria Rusticana,* he begged me in moving terms to go back; he would give

Two Shepherd Boys.

me everything I wanted if I would only do so. If I would not go back, then he begged me at least to wait until he sent a special messenger to Lassa to learn the orders of the Devashung or Grand Council. It would only take four days.

My answer was simply this: "We are going straight on to Lassa!"

"Then we shall follow you and prevent you," he interposed; "we have further reinforcements coming."

27*

"You cannot stop us without shooting; but remember that we also can shoot back."

Thereupon he shook his head. "We never thought of shooting," he said. "Such hard words ought not to pass between us." So saying, he walked away, depressed and full of trouble, towards his own tent.

# CHAPTER XXVIII.

## STOPPED BY TIBETAN CAVALRY.

WE started again with the object of advancing south by the west shore of the Selling-tso, and were closely followed by the Tibetans, between sixty and seventy in number. The old chieftain still continued to overwhelm me with entreaties to stop. Then he threatened that we should be met by a large army of men. I answered, that he might gather ten thousand men, but we should not stop until we were really forced. Thereupon with a gesture of despair, as though he gave it up as a bad job, he turned and went away to his own tent, and soon afterwards the whole troop disappeared. It was quite a relief to be left in peace from them.

Another river of pure bright water empties itself into the Selling-tso from the west; but we forded it without difficulty. As its waters swarmed with gulls, we inferred that they contained fish. Wild-duck also were plentiful, and the Cossacks shot some for our cooking-pots. We could not go past such splendid camping-ground as that, and accordingly we pitched the tents on the right bank of the stream, near the point where it enters the lake.

Hardly were we settled down, when we saw the black troops of the Tibetans coming galloping down from the hills on the north, bringing with them a number of baggage-horses. They had only retired to replenish their stores. On they came, dashing through the river, galloping past us, riding in and out through our tents as though, like an avalanche, they intended to sweep us before them, and as they rode they shouted and yelled and brandished their spears, but without taking the slightest notice of us—in fact, they appeared not to see us at all. With their decorated saddles, with the red and white bannerets that fluttered from the antelope-horns on which they rested their muskets, and with the silver scabbards of their swords, they presented a picture a battle painter would have given his eyes to paint.

Then followed a remarkable scene. Having encamped a few hundred yards beyond us, they gathered in small companies round their officers, who proceeded to teach them how to handle their weapons, and every now and again they would all unite in uttering a strange wild shout. Finally, they placed their muskets in position in a long line, with the muzzles pointing towards us. Their camp was placed on a little hill entirely commanding our camp, and the Cossacks wondered whether they intended to open fire upon us during the night. As soon as it was dark, I went to the chieftain's tent, accompanied by Shagdur and the Lama. In a moment the tent was crowded with Tibetan officers. After spending a pleasant evening with him, I promised that I would remain where I was on the bank of the Yagyu-rapga over the morrow, on condition that the Tibetans brought a fish to my tent at daybreak. For they had declared that the river was full of fish, and I could not resist the temptation of a change in our monotonous bill of fare. Some of my men were fishers from the Lower Tarim, and had brought two or three nets with them from Abdal; but I knew that the Tibetans detest fish, for they say you might just as well eat snakes and worms.

Well, next morning, almost before the sun rose, some of the Tibetans appeared in triumph at my tent, bringing with

Tibetan Marksmen.

them one miserable little fish! It had been an awful business to them to get hold of even that one; they declared it had almost cost them their lives. But our night-watchmen let the cat out of the bag. They told us that the Tibetans waited until they saw a gull rise from the water with a fish in its maw, and then flung stones at it until it disgorged its prey.

It was now our turn to show the Tibetans our way of catching fish. We put the boat together and set out our nets below a little cascade. I and Ördek manœuvred the boat, and at the first cast we drew up 28 "beauties." The Cossacks, who were angling from the bank, were equally successful. The Tibetans squatted like black crows on the hillsides, with their eyes and mouths wide open in amazement; they could not understand how anybody could eat such detestable things as fish. I lived upon fish for fully a week after.

It was a beautiful day and the country was charming. But the shores of the Selling-tso swarmed, not only with wild-duck, but with wild-geese. Kulans and orongo antelopes grazed all over the steppes; while eagles circled round the summits of the wild and rugged mountain range which lifted itself skyward immediately to the south; nor did the pretty little rock-pigeons exhibit any fear of them.

In the evening the Bombo came to my tent, followed by thirty of his soldiers. He brought me a present of two sheep and three pails of milk, and in return I allowed him to see the wonderful things we had with us; and he went away quite enraptured with the presents I gave him, namely, a revolver, a pair of scissors, a knife, and a piece of cloth.

The next day we continued southwards along the shore of the Selling-tso, passing through an imposing sort of rocky gateway. I had pushed on ahead, when two of the men came galloping after me to say that Kalpet was taken

Kalpet lying Dead on his Bier.

seriously ill. He had been anything but well for several days, although his appetite had still continued good. Upon reaching him, I found him lying on a felt carpet spread on the ground, but more dead than alive. His eyes were very bright, but rigidly fixed, his cheeks deeply sunken and pallid, and his lips ashen grey. We at once stopped and prepared one of the tents as a hospital for the sick man. Then we were visited by a squall, and it was so violent that it threatened to blow our light tents clean away, or else crush them flat under the beating rain and hail. Old Mohammed Tokta, who had so faithfully helped to look after the camels, was also on the sick list; his body had begun to swell and he had lost all sense of feeling in his fingers, so we put him in the hospital beside Kalpet.

The night passed, however, quietly, and in the morning I went in and talked to Kalpet for a while. He was convinced it was a serious illness he had got and he complained that one of his companions had beaten him two or three days before. He was a poor miserable wretch; he had been so lonely all the time, and now nobody cared for him one bit; he was deserted alike by God and his fellow men! He was so, so lonely! Whilst I was trying to comfort him and inspire him with courage, his consciousness darkened and he lay staring vacantly up at the top of the tent. I would gladly have remained there; but unfortunately we had neither water—for the Selling-tso was salt—nor grass. We had no choice, therefore, but were obliged to move. We made Kalpet as comfortable as we could on the back of his camel, and helped Mohammed Tokta to mount his horse, which he was able to manage himself, and on we went again to the dull and now ominous ding-dong of the caravan-bells.

Upon reaching the top of a low pass there burst upon our sight the most glorious scenery we had hitherto beheld in Tibet. Embedded in the arms of picturesque mountains was a lovely lake, its water dark blue and as bright as crystal. The lake penetrated the mountains in every direction, in deep dark fjords and bays, fantastic, yet grand, overshadowed by heavy rain-clouds, while the little craggy islets which dotted it were bathed in vivid sunshine. In places the cliffs shot straight down into the lake, the name of which was the Nakktsong-tso; but we were unable to proceed until the Cossacks went and reconnoitred, because the Tibetans refused to give us any information.

We were skirting round a wide bay. Kalpet had already two or three times asked for water, and complained that his camel was going too fast. Then for an hour or so he was silent; so I sent word to the ambulance, which was bringing up the rear, that we would halt and make up the sick man's bed again. But when they came to look at him, all was over. Kalpet was already dead and cold. After Mollah had reverently closed his eyes, the caravan continued its march. Up to that moment the Mussulmans had been singing as usual to relieve the monotony of the march; but now every voice was hushed and all one heard was the mournful jingle of the camels' bells. We encamped at the head of the bay beside the black tents of a nomad village.

The day we buried Kalpet, the 12th September, we had brilliant sunshine, and under the fresh breeze that blew off the lake the waves sang a melodious, but metallic dirge for the departed. The Mussulmans had requested me to allow them to bury their co-religionist with the ceremonies suitable to the occasion. During the night the dead body was put in one of the tents and watched by two of the men. In the morning it was washed and swathed in a white sheet by Ördek, Mollah Shah and Hamra Kul, who put bandages round their mouths to prevent them from inhaling the mortuary vapours. Outside the tent Mollah Shah read aloud passages from the Koran. After that they placed the corpse on a camel's pack-saddle and carried it to the grave-side. Then, whilst his companions lowered the body into the grave, Rosi Mollah addressed the dead man, speaking in a whisper as though he were only concerned that the dead man should hear him: "You have been an honest and faithful Mussulman. You have never done any harm to any of us. We shall miss you, and we weep for your departure. You have served Tura (your master) honourably and well."

After that they placed the pack-saddle over the grave and upon that laid a felt, and then heaped the soil all round it. At the head they raised a perishable monument of turves and small stones, then kneeling down around the grave they put their hands before their faces and murmured prayers for the peace of the dead man. Then they rose and left Kalpet in his lonely grave in a strange land, and now the nomads drive their flocks and herds over it, and in the dark winter nights the wolves howl in the mountains around.

The Tibetans, who watched our proceedings from a respectful distance, thought that we were giving ourselves a great deal of unnecessary and unseemly trouble, and asked us why we did not fling out the corpse to the wolves and vultures and ravens; for that is what they do themselves, as we saw with our own eyes later on.

Having loaded up, we once more started and soon came to a second magnificent mountain gateway, through which the country opened out with a wide sweep to the south. Close at our heels followed the Tibetans. On the open plain beyond the rocky gateway we perceived a group of black tents, with one or two white ones beside them. As we were passing the latter, a troop of horsemen trotted forward to meet me, and announced that two distinguished chiefs had arrived from Lassa and desired to speak with me. They came straight from the Dalai Lama, and brought his commands with them. They begged me, therefore, to stop and encamp beside them.

Ere many minutes passed the two distinguished chieftains emerged from the blue and white tents and mounted their horses. Then, each horse being led by four attendants on foot, the two Tibetan officers approached the spot where I stood, still seated in the saddle. The first thing they did was to ask me to stop and encamp beside them, and this

The Funeral Procession.

after some hesitation I assented to, for they both appeared decidedly friendly and good-natured.

After we had got our camp in order, a considerable time passed without the two red-robed messengers putting in an appearance. I therefore sent our Lama to tell them that if they did not make haste, we should strike our tents and be off again. This brought them at once, each accompanied by a large escort. After politely greeting me, they stepped inside the cooking-tent, which we were accustomed to decorate for such occasions with a gay Khotan carpet, at the same time spreading a table-cloth over the box which served as a table. Then we sat down for a talk, while a crowd of black Tibetans clustered outside.

The two messengers, Hlajeh Tsering and Yunduk Tsering, were governors respectively of the provinces of Namru and Nakktsong, and also, according to what they said, members of the Devashung, or Great Council, of Lassa. They were sent by the Dalai Lama to prevent me from advancing further. There we sat then and discussed and argued hour after hour, Shereb Lama acting as interpreter. I had made up my mind I would no longer resist the force of circumstances, for I had had enough of Tibet for that time, and was longing to get home; but just for the fun of the thing I disputed the matter with the old men for a time. I should not be allowed to take another step towards the south, they said, and if we nevertheless did attempt to force a passage, one of the parties, either we or they, would lose our lives. They had hosts of soldiers to stop me; and if nothing else would serve, they would have each of my camels held by main force by a band of Tibetans. They shouted, they gesticulated, they perspired; but I kept quite cool, and smiled, and told them that we were in the hands of a higher Power, which would protect us, and if the Tibetans did not keep off, I warned them they would have a hot time of it.

"It doesn't matter," they said, "we shall have our heads cut off in any case if we let you proceed; we have brought special orders from Lassa."

"Show me them," I answered, "and if they are correct, I promise I will march straight from here to Ladak."

Then they read to me a document of which the following is a literal translation:

"In the year of the Iron Cow, the sixth month, the nineteenth day, there arrived from the governor of Nakk-chu a writing (to the effect) that Lama Sanjeh, secretary of the Mongol Tsangeh Khutuktu, besides several pilgrims, was making a pilgrimage to Jo-mitsing in Hamdung, and that he, together with Tugden Darjeh, made certain communications to the governor of Nakk-chu (that is, Kamba Bombo).

"The Governor of Nakk-chu has communicated the said intelligence to the Devashung. Tsangeh's secretary said, when he was setting out on his journey, he saw European

Hlajeh Tsering and Yunduk Tsering.

men and travelled in their company a piece. After they bought a quantity of clothing, they travelled on further. In the bazaar he saw two Russian men. 'Where travel you to?' he asked them. 'Are you Lamas?' 'We are Lamas,' they answered. The Khalkha Mongol, Shereb Lama, the healer, was in their company, and was their guide. On the road we saw six Russian men travelling. A large number of camels and other men were also on the road.

"Let writings be sent with haste to Namru and Nakktsong that it may be known everywhere, that from Nakkchu inwards for as far as my (the Dalai Lama's) kingdom extends, Russian (European) men cannot be permitted to travel south. Writings must be dispatched to all the chiefs. Watch the frontiers of Nakktsong. It is necessary to watch the country closely bit by bit. It is positively unnecessary that European men should come into the Land of the Holy Books to spy it out. In the province which is subject to you both they have nothing whatever to do. If they say that it is necessary, then know that these chieftains shall not travel south. Should they all the same continue, then you shall lose your heads. Compel them to turn and go back the way they have come."

This document cleared up many points that had hitherto been obscure, and showed that we had not only the yak-hunters, but also the Mongol pilgrim-caravan to thank for it, that the frontiers had been so jealously and so strictly watched. After that I could not deny myself the pleasure of telling them honestly, that the policy of isolation which they were pursuing was the only one by which they could save their country from ruin.

"All round Tibet," I said, "north, south, and west, Europeans have either conquered your neighbours' territories or made them dependent upon themselves. Your country is the only one in Asia which they have not penetrated into."

"Reh! Reh!" (True, true) they exclaimed. "That's just how we want to keep it."

Shereb Lama's name was mentioned in the document, and now here they had him before them, alive and in the flesh, and they read him a very severe lesson, and told him that his name was written down in the book of the suspect. But our Lama now threw off all reserve, and abused the two messengers right and left, actually jumping to his feet and shaking his fist at Hlajeh Tsering, he asked him how he dared to talk of punishing a lama who was not a Tibetan subject. As the row looked like ending in blows, I brought out the musical box, and its soothing strains soon poured oil upon the troubled waters.

In the evening I returned the visit of the Tibetan officers, accompanied by Shagdur and the Lama, and spent no less than five hours with them, laughing and talking. We became the best of friends, as though we had known one another for scores of years. We were entertained with tea and *tsamba;* while at one end of the tent incense was rising before a small altar on which were several idols.

On the 14th September I set out with Kutchuk and provisions for three days for a sail on the lake of Nakktsong-tso, a small lake lying south-west of the Selling-tso. It turned out one of the most delightful trips I have ever made by boat.

We started from the east shore of the lake and sailed towards the west along the southern shore, which was thickly dotted with nomads and their flocks and herds, having arranged to meet the caravan at the north-west corner of the lake. At length Kutchuk rowed into a kind of bay, which narrowed rapidly. The rocks rose perpendicularly on both sides, and against them the echoes of the oar-strokes rang out sharp and resonant, and the water was a bright emerald green. It was like entering the temple of some mountain-king, with a glassy emerald floor. In fact, the water was so transparent that we could see the algæ and other water-plants distinctly growing at the bottom. The slightest sound trembled backwards and forwards from crag to crag. Altogether it was very impressive. We instinctively held our breath, for fear of disturbing the great and holy silence. A couple of eagles were circling noiselessly on motionless outspread wings, between the precipices, and their shadows flitted along the water like the genii of that so enchanted and so enchanting scene.

At length it grew dark, and it was time to think of rest. Having drawn the skiff up on shore we lighted a fire and prepared supper, and then wrapping ourselves in our overcoats, we slept the sleep of the just—and the tired. Early next morning Kutchuk dipped his oar into the water again, and our little craft continued her journey between the bewitching mountain-walls. Narrower and narrower grew the sound; it was like a river glen, a watery gorge. The most magnificent panoramas that I have ever seen in my life continued to unroll themselves before us one after the other. Would this winding water-way never come to an end? Should we have to go all the long way back again? If it were an island that we had on our right, then we must be not very far from the rendezvous. Some natives who came out of their tents, standing on the shore, stared at us in speechless amazement. A fresh scene! Perhaps there is still yet another? No; here is the end of the sound! Upon reconnoitring, we found that it was only a narrow neck of land which barred our way. Accordingly, taking all our belongings out of the boat, we first carried them, and then the skiff herself, overland, and started again on the other side. Here the lake broadened out and went down to a depth of 72 feet; but it is night again and we must stop. That evening there was a fresh breeze, and we were sung to sleep by the soft music of the waves lapping on the shore. Fortunately it did not rain on either of these nights that we slept out in the open, and lovely nights they indeed were—a silence that no words can describe, stars that sparkled like silver, and an air that was crisp and bright like pure wine!

Next day we arrived at the rendezvous. Before we reached it, we saw the caravan approaching, surrounded by a swarm of black cavalry. Before we came to land, the tents were already up. We had 5, the Tibetans 19; they numbered 194 men, we only 18—1 against 10, or, if I count the Cossacks only, 1 against 50.

Truly a remarkable lake—the Nakktsong-tso! It is like a ring of water, all the middle being occupied by a large island. It suggested a crater-lake or a fortress with a moat round it filled with water. The Tibetan emissaries had been greatly concerned at my disappearance; but by means of mounted patrols, they convinced themselves that I had not run away.

## CHAPTER XXIX.

### PULLING FOR LIFE ON THE CHARGUT–TSO.

THE Nakktsong-tso was thus the turning-point of our journey, the furthest point south that we reached in our attempt to penetrate into the land of the *burkhans* and the Holy Books. The reason Europeans are not tolerated is not that the lamas are more fanatical now than they were when they hospitably received the Jesuit missionaries. In fact, they are quite as tolerant as when in the year 1846 they allowed the Lagariste Father Huc, and his colleague Gabet, to spend two months in Lassa. Their jealous isolation during recent years is due to political motives. The objects of their peaceful, but effective, tactics are to guard their frontiers against Europeans, and to conduct the unbidden guests politely, but firmly, out of the country. So far the Tibetans have not yielded to the captivating prospects of a growing prosperity through trade, and the introduction of tobacco, spirits, opium, fire-arms, and other blessings of civilization! No, away, they cry; away with your luxuries, your steel, your gold and your silver, and leave us alone in peace in our own country. And yet Tibet's turn is bound to come.

Thus I wrote in my diary at the time on the shore of the Nakktsong-tso, and already, as I pen this present book the prophecy is fulfilled.

While the caravan marched back to our old camping-

View Across the Chargut-tso, Looking West.

ground beside the Yagyu-rapga, I got Ördek to row me there across the Selling-tso. Thence we were to start on our long journey to Ladak. The Tibetans willingly showed us the road; that is, they guided the caravan, for I myself chose a more southerly route, in the course of which I crossed over a pass so steep and so dangerous that, had a camel slipped and fallen on it, he would certainly have been crushed to a mummy. Camp No. LXXXIV. was pitched on the eastern shore of the Chargut-tso, a small lake lying west of the Selling-tso. Here nothing met the eye but what was delightful, not to say magnificent. Looking west, we had a view deep into the fjords of the lake as into the vistas of a forest of stone. The Tibetans, with their gay-coloured garments and warlike equipment, suited this wild scenery excellently. Along the shore, which was like a natural *corso*, we counted twenty-five tents, apart from our own, and yet by far the greater number of the Tibetans bivouacked around their fires in the open. Indeed, our escort now numbered 500 men.

Beside this magnificent lake, with its fjord-like scenery, we remained two days, arranging our programme for the further journey to Ladak. Hlajeh Tsering informed me that he had orders from the Dalai Lama to place at our disposal as many baggage-animals as we required. Accordingly I at once ordered 40 yaks to be procured as soon as possible. Then the old man gave me a present of two white horses, precisely as Kamba Bombo had done, as well as provisions; and other supplies would be furnished to us, he said, all the way to Ladak. Wonderfully nice people, I thought!

At noon on the 19th September the Tibetans treated us to a very fine spectacle. I asked Hlajeh Tsering to command a couple of hundred of his cavalry to arrange themselves in line, because I wanted to photograph them. But it was impossible to get them to stand still for even a

The Tibetan Emissaries' Guard at the Chargut-tso.

minute; and no sooner did I ask them to flourish their swords and lances in the air than their warlike instinct awoke, and the horses becoming restless, the entire troop charged straight ahead at the gallop, shouting and yelling as if they were about to make an attack. It was indeed a fine sight to see them racing across the steppe with their reins dangling loose on their horses' necks, and their weapons and accoutrements clattering and flashing in the sun. Meanwhile the camera had to wait until their warlike ardour was abated, and they could be made to understand that, when it comes to photographing, there is no need to howl and yell so desperately loud.

The Tibetans requested us to stay yet another day; that is, over the 20th September, that being one of their great holidays. This I agreed to gladly, because I wished to have a trip on the fjord. Selecting Khodai Kullu as boatman, I embarked and set out for the west; but no sooner did we get out into the open part of the lake than a westerly storm broke over it, and within a few minutes the lake was in violent commotion. We were, of course, driven back to our starting-point, and it was as much as the two of us could do, each wielding an oar, to keep the boat straight before the waves. The Tibetans gathered on the hillsides in a close-packed crowd and watched, motionless as statues, our battle with the Chargut-tso. Now the skiff disappeared from their sight, dipping into the trough of the waves; now she was lifted high on a crest, and hung there shivering and creaking amongst the flying spray. But within a very few minutes we were back to the shore, and after we had been swept in by a big wave, Khodai Kullu jumped out, while at the same moment the Cossacks dashed into the breakers, and between them they carried me high and dry up the beach, where the Tibetans flocked round to convince themselves that I was still alive. Later on in the day we had better fortune, and we remained out on the lake until dark. As we made our way home, the long line of bivouac-fires along the shore was quite like a festive illumination.

Next day we packed up and started for Ladak. After ordering the caravan to make for a suitable point at the west end of the lake, I once more took to the skiff, preferring my own company to the clatter and noise of the 500 Tibetans, and with Kutchuk for my boatman I started to

Our Camp on the First Island in Chargut-tso.

row up the Chargut-tso. We took warm clothing with us, and were provisioned for three days. Just as we saw the long black line of mounted men disappearing behind the mountains, a half gale sprang up in the west. But it was then too late to turn back; nor was there any protecting headland anywhere near. Our only hope was to pull for our lives to the nearest little rocky islet, of which there were two or three in the middle of the lake. Here we sounded a depth of 138 feet, but were unable to take any other soundings, owing to the violence of the waves. The "seas" kept breaking over us until everything in the skiff was wet. Slowly, slowly we approached the island, and, after what seemed an age, we got under its lee. Another spurt brought us to the shore, pretty well spent by our exertions.

After drawing our boat safely up out of reach of the waves, we proceeded to shelter ourselves behind her and a felt rug which we propped up. Fortunately there was plenty of fuel, and whilst Kutchuk lit a fire and prepared tea, I lay and read "Uncle Tom's Cabin." The wind howled and shrilled amongst the rocks, and the surf thundered against the cliff at the western end of the island. The gale still continued in the afternoon, and so long as it blew as it did we were prisoners. The sun sank bright and clear, and the deep shades of night settled down over our little camp, while the eastern shore was still bathed in light. But the shades climbed rapidly up the mountain sides; the highest summits glowed scarlet and red for a space, and then day became extinct; and after a while darkness reigned supreme, except for the wan light of a half moon. Kutchuk went off two or three times during the night to see if the gale had abated. At four we rose, but the wind was still blowing as hard as ever. As there were 9° of frost we made haste to build up a gigantic fire. I wonder what the nomads on the northern shore of the lake imagined that big glare was on the little island out in the Chargut-tso? We waited and waited. At length day broke in the east, making the mountain-crests stand out darker against the rapidly lightening background. All at once the sun burst above them, flashing like a jewel.

The storm, instead of waning, was increasing every moment. I mapped the island, and then sat and dreamed for hours, listening to the crash of the waves upon the cliffs of the island. Then we had dinner, and amused ourselves by gathering fuel, and then I climbed to the highest point of the island to bid good-bye to the setting sun. We prepared for our second night in our watery prison. The clouds thickened and raced on in the same wild wrack, while the moon sailed amongst them like a silver schooner. Again and again we studied the sky; again and again we went to the west end of the island, but always the lake was running just as high. I hoped, however, that we might make the next little rocky island before the night was over, and ere the moon set I took its compass-bearings.

At length the wind really did abate and the lake began to subside. We rowed along the southern face of the island, the rocky wall of which rose like a black spectre out of the waves, and then struck out into the open lake. The water was as black as ink, except where a belt of vivid moonshine danced across the dying waves, and the mountains which framed in the lake stood out like intense black etchings upon the general darkness of the night. Hour after hour we plied the oars. I sounded the depth; it was over 121 feet; land could not be near. Although I was able to read my instruments by the light of a lantern, I almost began to fear that we had passed the next island. If we had, then the broad western basin of the lake would be before us, and supposing the storm were to quicken up again, we should then be in a very perilous position. The moon had now set, and it was pitch-dark. But no, we are steering right; the depth is growing less. And before we were aware of it our little skiff was scraping on the rocks. We had not seen the island until we were actually upon it. We landed, and at once went to sleep.

When we awoke next morning it was still blowing hard. Must we actually spend another day on this little craggy islet, which was barely 350 yards across? And there was another source of anxiety: our provisions were running out. Then the storm quickened up into a full-fledged hurricane. A good thing we were not exposed to its fury! The narrow rift in which the Chargut-tso is situated appeared to act as a conduit for every storm and tempest in that region.

Yet within an hour the squall, violent as it was, had spent itself. The waves subsided to a gentle swell, the sun dipped towards the horizon, and the Chargut-tso was simply lovely. We pushed off, and Kutchuk began to pull hard, and very soon we reached the deepest part of the lake, about 157½ feet. We had already passed all the sheltering headlands and were entering the biggest reach, or fjord, of the lake, when the thunder again began to rumble, and we saw fresh storm-centres scattering rain and snow over the mountains to the north and to the south, though over the lake it was still clear, and the sun set amid a wreath of light fleecy clouds.

We were then steering for the southern side of the lake, where the cliffs descended precipitously into the water, when we saw a mass of steel-blue cloud rise threateningly above it. Its under side gleamed fiery yellow, as though it were passing over a conflagration. We knew well enough what that meant. But as there was no protecting headland in sight, our only chance was to pull against the wind and get under the shelter of the cliffs themselves, though they were still a long way off.

But the tempest burst upon us with startling suddenness. "Pull, Kutchuk, pull for your life." Every time our little craft pitched and her taut canvas struck against the oncoming wave, she shivered and groaned from stem to stern. Every moment we kept expecting to hear her canvas rend with a crack. We were pulling long, steady strokes and putting into them all the force we had stored in our muscles. The tempest, becoming concentrated into the narrow passage-way between the cliffs, increased in violence.

"Keep it up, Kutchuk! We are getting nearer! The danger is passing!" Then the breaking crest of a wave swept in all along the starboard gunwale, and the water began to wash backwards and forwards with every pitch and rise of the skiff. In came a second wave. We tightened our grip, till our knuckles whitened and the blisters burned. We literally lifted the skiff through the sea on our oar-blades. But things could not last much longer like that. The skiff was half full of water already, and the waves kept striking in over her bow. We must soon go to the bottom. "Get your life-belt ready, Kutchuk. And pull, man, pull. Perhaps she will keep up till we reach that cape."

"Ya, Allah," panted Kutchuk.

It was only by the most strenuous exertions and dogged persistence that we kept our craft afloat until we reached shelter and smoother water. We were within an ace of going to the bottom. In all the expeditions I have made on the Tibetan lakes I never came so near disaster as on that occasion. It is not to be recommended—a trip by night across an unknown lake in a violent gale, in a fragile canvas skiff, when the storm-clouds are being torn to rags by the wind, and the white-crested waves are tipped with silver by the moon.

We were so desperately tired that we flung ourselves on the beach, pulled the boat over us, and dropped off to sleep, in spite of the rain rattling all night on the canvas.

Next morning, favoured by splendid weather, we proceeded to the end of the Chargut-tso, traversed a very short connecting arm, and rowed out upon yet another lake. This we started to cross diagonally, keeping not very far from the shore. And fortunately for us that we did so, for ere long we were surprised by a fresh storm. But this time all our efforts were in vain. We were unable to make headway against the wind, and the waves carried us towards the shore, which luckily shallowed gently. The moment the skiff touched the bottom, over she went. We jumped out and drew her up on dry land, and then proceeded to wring the water out of our clothes and packages; and then, having spread them out to dry on the shingle, we lay and drowsed until our people came to look for us. And it was high time they did, for we were ravenously hungry.

The camp was jubilant when they saw us, for they had all given us up for lost. The Tibetans asked the Cossacks where I had gone to, and the Cossacks, without winking, swore that I had rowed to the south side of the Chargut-tso, meaning to seize the first horse I could, and ride straight to Lassa. The emissaries were in consternation. At once they sent off patrols to ride round the lake; but the patrols came back and reported that they had not seen a soul. All this while I was quietly smoking my pipe on the first island. Then they sent off several bands, each of about a score of men, to the south, in the direction of Lassa, but all by different routes; and these men had not come back when I made my entry into the camp, where Hlajeh Tsering and Yunduk Tsering gave me a most cordial and most effusive welcome. They were not the least bit annoyed at the anxiety and trouble I had caused them. We celebrated the occasion by a grand spread in their tent, and soon the images of their gods were but dimly seen through the tobacco-smoke.

Mohammed Tokta was worse; a camel had perished; and a Tibetan had died. We passed the corpse of the last on our way to camp; it was half devoured by vultures and wolves.

On the 25th September we said adieu to the emissaries of the Dalai Lama, after I had given them various presents, such as revolvers and ammunition, knives, daggers, mariners' compasses, and pieces of cloth. An escort of 22 men, under the command of Yamdu Tsering and Tsering Dashi, were to accompany us, and see that we obtained all we wanted from the nomads. I was sorry to part from Hlajeh Tsering and Yunduk Tsering, for I had spent three very pleasant weeks in their company. I bade them greet the Dalai Lama in my name, and tell him not to forget it, for we should meet some day.

## CHAPTER XXX.

### WESTWARDS TO LEH.

FROM this point to Leh, the capital of Ladak, was a distance of nearly 670 miles, and it cost us very nearly three months to cover it. Our caravan was in rather a pitiful condition; we had only 22 camels left, and all of them were a good deal spent. But we got on capitally with our escort, who helped us in arranging camp and in loading up when we started.

For the first few days we rode up the bank of the Boggtsang-sangpo towards the west-north-west. When you ride day after day in that direction up in Tibet the left side of your face gets so burned by the sun that the skin peels off, whilst your right cheek almost "burns" with the icy cold; your left foot is warm and comfortable, but your right is almost frozen.

Bright and clear flowed the river at our side. One day Shagdur lingered behind, and when he caught us up he flourished triumphantly above his head a string of splendid fish. After that we rested the 1st October beside the Boggtsang-sangpo, and putting the skiff together made such a glorious catch that for a couple of weeks we lived almost entirely upon fish.

On the 3rd October, taking Chernoff and the Lama with me, I climbed to the top of the dominating mountain of Erenak-chimmo. On our way back to rejoin the

The River Boggtsang-sangpo, Looking South-West.

caravan we came upon Hamra Kul lying in a hollow of the rocks, unable to move. He declared he could not take another step; so I ordered some of the Tibetans who were with me to look after him, and bring him into camp. Our caravan was now rapidly thinning away. The cold was intense, and the wind cut like a knife as we rode against it. It numbed us, it chilled us to the bone, it paralysed us. My men and the Tibetans were travelling on foot, though I had to keep the saddle myself, for I find that I am unable to walk when the altitude is more than 16,000 feet. One of the camels gave up and was left behind; I remained beside him, and, slitting open his pack-saddle, gave him the straw to eat. He ate it readily enough, but was unable to go much further before we had to kill him. After riding on a short distance I came upon two other camels which were unable to keep up with the caravan. The next invalids I came across were two horses in charge of Kutchuk; one was the horse I rode when we started from Kashgar two years before, the other one of those that Kamba Bombo gave me. Our next camp was very gloomy. Mohammed Tokta was no better, Almaz complained that he was almost blind, and Khodai Kullu was suffering from mountain sickness. We attended to their comfort as best we could, although very nearly half the caravan was now on the sick list.

Upon reaching the district of Setcha, 16,560 feet above the sea, we had to rest; for in the first place it was necessary to wait for the various men and animals that were lagging behind, and in the second place we were to be met there by the yaks which had been promised us, and consequently we had to divide up our baggage into smaller loads. The thermometer now dropped to half a degree below zero: winter had begun.

From this place I made, with Chernoff and the Lama and a small lightly-equipped caravan, a four days' ex-

Our Lama on the Left ; Yamdu Tsering and Tsering Dashi on the Right.

cursion towards the south, hoping to see something of the grand mountain scenery which lies around the massive, dominating, snow-capped mountain of Shah-ganjum. I had intended to prolong the excursion, although it was a forbidden region, and the Tibetans in desperation were clinging like leeches to our heels, but the condition of our horses was such that I durst not run any further risk.

At Camp No. CIII. Yamdu Tsering and his men left us, after I had given them revolvers and other presents, as well as, at their request, a testimonial to the effect that they had been civil and done their duty to my full satisfaction. In their place we were joined by another escort under Yarvo Tsering, with a fresh relay of yaks; all our animals were now travelling without loads. On the 18th October we struck the salt lake of Lakkor-tso, a lake which is drying up at such a rapid rate that its oldest shore-line is no less than 436 feet above the existing level.

On the 20th October a curious thing happened while we were on the march. Hamra Kul was bringing up the rear with two sick horses, when he came upon Mohammed Tokta in a pit by the roadside. The old man explained, good-naturedly, that he had grown tired of riding, and so had just rolled off his horse. Hamra Kul brought him along with him, and upon reaching camp his companions took the best care of him possible under the circumstances, and when I went and asked him how he was, the old man smiled gratefully. I gave him a bowl of milk, which he drank with pleasure. But when the sun rose next morning he lay stiff and stark in his furs, with his eyes tightly closed. Death had visited the old camel-driver in his sleep.

This made the fourth of my men who perished on this journey. After the last sad ceremonies were performed for the dead man, the caravan resumed its march towards the west. We still had 480 miles to go to reach Ladak.

Soon after that we came over a little pass to a fresh salt lake, which, like the preceding, was surrounded by magnificent mountains, with a broad belt of snow-white saline incrustations at their feet. When I reached the farther side of the pass, for I had remained behind to take some measurements, I found Hamra Kul sitting by the wayside with a couple of dying horses. One did reach

Laying out Mohammed Tokta.

camp; the other, a piebald from Korla, was quite unable to stand, so I had him killed at once. Then—but I cannot dwell upon all the misery of this part of our march. It will be enough for you to understand that a journey across Tibet is an unbroken succession of suffering for both man and beast. It is enough to make one weep tears of blood to witness all the wretchedness and misery that you have no means of preventing. Of the 45 horses and mules with which we started from Charkhlik, there were now only 11 left alive.

The temperature dropped to 2° below zero, while the wind, which never for one moment slackened, blew at the rate of 45 miles an hour. On the 25th October we had to kill a horse the moment we started. Six camels were on the sick list, and were left behind to follow the yak caravan, which travelled more slowly. Almaz, the sick man, was allowed to ride one of them. As it happened I had been delayed, and when I caught them up one camel had just laid himself on his side, with his neck and his legs stretched out; the butcher's knife soon released him from his sufferings. After a while a second was left, and a little later a third. Shortly after that it was the turn of the dromedary, until finally the beast that Almaz rode was followed by only one camel, namely, the mother of the little one that was born in Charkhlik, and which we were now feeding with bread. This left us with only 18 camels.

Next morning Sirkin and Turdu Bai rode back to see if they could bring in the three camels that had been left behind, or else kill them. They turned up at the next camp without them. The caravan was now followed by a troop of wolves, which feasted on our dead animals, and made the nights unholy with their howling.

On the 28th October we reached a pass which commanded a magnificent view to the west. It was like a transformation scene: the old Tibet closed behind us like a book, and a new world opened out before us. The feature that especially attracted us was the lake of Perutseh-tso. It was surrounded by glorious grass, and there we halted for four days, keeping ourselves warm and comfortable with a ring of big blazing fires day and night, for there was an abundance of brushwood. A horse, unable to digest the grass, died, and the mother of the little camel gave up when quite close to the oasis. This left us with only 14 camels. Here, Davo Tsering, our last chief guide, who

A Valley in Western Tibet.

all along had ridden at my side and willingly given me any amount of information, said good-bye, and went away with his men.

Upon reaching the western end of the lake Tsollo-ring-tso, where we reached the frontier of Rudok, we found seven tents and the governor of Chok-jalung awaiting us with a hundred armed men. That gentleman assumed great airs of authority and arrogance, and swore that we

Our Lama Quarrelling with the Leaders of the Yak-Caravan.

should not travel through Rudok, but would have to return the same way we came, unless we showed him a pass from the Dalai Lama. My Cossacks simply boiled with rage, and asked to be allowed to answer with their repeating rifles. But I took the matter coolly, and informed the governor that I would next day go back to Lassa, but at the same time gave him to understand that he must furnish me with a document to the effect that he had refused to allow us to march through Rudok. "Oh, yes, he would do

The Temple-Village of Noh.

that; he would willingly give me a writing, and more than that he would at once send a courier to Lassa; and if we would just keep quiet until the message returned, he would take what steps were necessary."

It would indeed have been an easy matter to have

A Chorten.

brushed this man's opposition aside, for we had four repeating rifles, two of them firing explosive bullets, whereas the Tibetans were only armed with heavy, clumsy, primitive muzzle-loaders. We had only to put ourselves under cover, and we could shoot them down, one by one, before ever they got within range; but it would have been cowardly and shameful to have used our advantage for such a purpose. Besides, my Cossack escort was not intrusted to me for the purpose of engaging in hostilities. In fact, it never for one moment occurred to me to use force. All this I explained to the Cossacks. But a plan did occur to me. It was this: we would return to the grazing-grounds of the Perutseh-tso and there build a fort of turves. Thence we would make excursions in the neighbourhood and live by hunting, and in the spring, when the

The Middle Basin of Tso-ngombo.

caravan had recovered, we would make another start for the Forbidden Land. This plan was, I confess, both interesting and tempting; however, it was never carried out, for the conceited governor changed his mind. He promised to give us yaks and provisions, and to let us travel through his province provided we did not visit the town of Rudok, and as I never had the least intention of doing that, the matter was soon settled.

On the 7th November the weather was splendid, and

the everlasting wind at last forgot to blow. The only thing to mar our enjoyment was that our escort began to quarrel with Shereb Lama, and called him a heathen dog for travelling about with "them there Russians!" The quiet priest grew so enraged that he let his riding-whip dance on the backs of the Tibetans, and I sent word to them that if they made any further disturbance we would stuff them into our boxes and take them home with us.

A View of the Western Tso-ngombo.

We saw no nomads in this region; nor was there a drop of water, until the Tibetans led us to the spring of Tsebu, where we spent the night. I have not yet forgotten that night in the wilds of western Tibet. It was so intensely cold, and at the same time so still, that we could almost hear the frost gripping hold of the earth. Nothing jarred upon the profound silence of the night, except the howling of the wolves and the monotonous footsteps of the night-sentries ringing against the icy ground. In the morning my water-ewer was frozen to the bottom, and the ink froze in my pen unless I sat leaning over a brazier. The temperature was now down to 16½° below zero, so that I did not wonder at the Tibetans wanting to go home to their own tents, especially as they wore no breeches.

Next day the little camel had to be killed. The strongest animals of all the caravan except the dogs were our two surviving sheep, Vanka, and one from Abdal. The Mussulmans would rather have perished of hunger than have killed these. After marching a few days further in the teeth of a killing wind, we reached a point where we were only 240 miles from Leh. This town I was anxious to reach at all costs before Christmas Eve, so that I might telegraph home to Sweden.

A Difficult Bit beside the Tso-ngombo.

On the night of the 20-21st November we had 18½° below zero, and the wolves were troublesome; and when our dogs began to howl in concert with them the night was made doubly hideous by their deafening chorus. We were now travelling beside the river Tsangar-shar, and on the 26th took a day's rest amongst some fine bushes. Here one of our horses tumbled into the river, and was only got out again with the utmost difficulty. But although we dried him beside a big fire, and wrapped him in felt rugs, he died a couple of hours later. On the following morning Li Loyeh reported that his horse was dead.

Converting the Skiff into a Sledge.

Later on that same day, Turdu Bai's old black horse dropped down suddenly dead, and was followed by the last of the horses that the Tibetans gave us. Of the stately caravan which started from Charkhlik half a year before there were now left only one horse, namely, that which I was riding, 13 camels, and five mules. Rather than make another winter journey through Tibet I would cross the desert of Gobi a dozen times!

Still struggling on, we at length reached the temple-

Carrying the Baggage across the Ice on a Make-shift Sledge.

village of Noh, with its bulb-shaped cupolas in red and white, its *chortens*, its flags and its gilded pinnacles. A little bit farther on we caught sight, from a pass, of the wonderful lake of Tso-ngombo, or the Blue Lake, then frozen over; it was long and narrow, and beset on both sides by rocky walls jutting out into it *en échelon*. Here we encamped, while the Tibetans pitched their quarters on a little island, whence their fires at night flashed a red glare across the dark transparent ice. From this place the chief of our Tibetan escort sent a messenger to Leh, so that when we reached the frontier between Tibet and Kashmir we might find everything we needed. I seized the opportunity to send letters to the British authorities in the town.

As we marched along the northern shore of the lake, zigzagging in and out at the foot of the cliffs, we met more than one trading caravan from Leh, the goods being carried on the backs of sheep. The route is difficult for camels; in fact some of the men had to go on first and level the road before we were able to advance with ours. Round one treacherous promontory we actually had to lead them in the water, while the Tibetans carried our baggage on the backs of their yaks, which surmounted the obstacle without serious difficulty.

On the 3rd December we were stopped by a far more difficult crag jutting out into the lake. The rocks shot straight down into the water, and the path, which climbed straight up them, was formed of slabs fastened into crevices; this made a tolerable pathway for men on foot, and for sheep and yaks, but was absolutely impassable for camels. What was to be done? Could we advance along the southern shore of the lake? "Impossible," replied the Tibetans. But as I did not implicitly believe them, I sent Chernoff to see if the ice would bear at a narrow place where it was frozen right across. He came back and reported that it would bear. I then measured the thickness of the ice in a series of cracks. If we led the camels round one by one, we might perhaps manage it. Nevertheless, when evening came, I sent Ördek across the lake on foot, to see what the southern shore was like, instructing him that, if he found it impossible to advance with the camels, he was to light a signal-fire. Meanwhile we waited on the northern shore, and very soon three big blazing

The Skiff on Lake Panggong-tso.

fires told us that the southern shore was as impassable as the northern.

However, it was not absolutely certain that the ice would bear the camels, and as I did not want to go all round the northern side of the mountains that were stopping our way, I set my wits to work. We had overcome worse difficulties than this, and there were now only ten camels left. Suddenly an idea struck me. There was an abundance of brushwood in the locality and plenty of dry poles. Why not make a ferry-boat, and convey the animals round one by one? But whilst we were considering the matter a way was opened for us. When we first reconnoitred the place, the lake showed open water, but during the first night a thin sheet of ice formed upon it; and twenty-four hours later the ice was two inches thick. Thereupon we made a big wide sledge out of the camels' pack-saddles, and as many of the men crowded on to it as would correspond to the weight of a camel. Then we pushed it round the promontory; but as the ice began to crack ominously, first one man jumped off in a hurry and then another, to the no little amusement of those who were dragging the sledge. The ice was as bright as crystal, without a single bleb in it, so that it was like walking on tranquil water, while far below we could see the dark-backed fishes gliding in and out amongst the algæ at the bottom. We could hear the ice-sheet clicking and crackling, and sometimes it sounded as though a projectile from a big gun were being discharged along it, the report dying away slowly with a long lingering whine in the far distance.

One day more we had to wait patiently and watch the ice growing thicker. Then before sunrise on the following morning we transported the whole of our baggage on the sledge round the interposing rocks, and after strewing about thirty sacks of sand on the ice, and so making a pathway for the camels, we led them round cautiously one by one, and fortunately got them all round without any mishap.

We marched for nearly a dozen days along the shore of this fairy-like lake and those of another, the Panggong-tso, a salt lake, the magnificent scenery of which my pen is all too feeble to describe. After almost superhuman exertions we managed to scramble over another tiresome projecting cliff, and on the 13th December finally reached the western frontier of Tibet. Here, to our indescribable

Gulang Hiraman and his Ladakis.

joy, we were met by a relief caravan of 12 horses and 30 yaks, which the governor of Ladak had sent to help us. It was under the leadership of two Ladakis, Gulang Hiraman, a comical, good-natured old man, who literally beamed with benevolence, and Anmar Ju, who spoke Persian, so that I was able to hold tolerable intercourse with him, thanks to my halting remembrances of the land of the Lion and the Sun. They brought with them sheep, flour, rice, dried fruits, milk, sugar, and corn for our animals. Thank goodness! Our sufferings were now over, and the relics of the caravan, which was actually on its very last legs, were saved. Here too the last tie that connected us with the wondrous and mysterious land of Tibet was severed, when we said good-bye to the escort which accompanied us to the frontier. At parting we gave to the Tibetans all the old cooking utensils we no longer needed, such as saucepans, cups, cans, etc., our old worn-out clothes, and a revolver, with all which they were immensely pleased.

But Tibet claimed yet one more of our veterans as toll for our passage across her inhospitable wilds. Yoldash spent the night as usual sleeping on the felts at my feet. At sunrise he got up, shook himself, and ran back up the mountains on the east, and—never came back again. Perhaps he thought—perhaps he still thinks, that I shall go back and fetch him.

# CHAPTER XXXI.

## A TRIP TO INDIA.—HOME.

AFTER we turned our backs upon the Panggong-tso, one of the most magnificent lakes in the world, I left the caravan and, taking with me Chernoff, Cherdon, and Anmar Ju, pushed on to Leh at a faster pace. Our route lay through Tanksi, with its picturesque temple, over the high pass of Chang-la (17,715 feet), past the temple of Jimreh and the temple of Tikkseh, beside the majestic Indus, which rolls its waters all the way from these wintry abodes to the warmer climes of the Indian Ocean. On the way I was met by a constant stream of messengers, bringing letters and telegrams. From the moment I set foot on British territory, I was overwhelmed with proofs of hospitality and kindness, which went on increasing day by day until I reached the capital of India. In Leh I found ready prepared for me a beautiful house, and a caravanserai for my animals and men, and heaps of letters from home. In reply to a telegram to His Majesty Oscar, King of Sweden, I received a most gracious answer; while another to Lord Curzon, the Viceroy, brought me an invitation to visit him and Lady Curzon at Calcutta.

I spent Christmas Eve with the good, kind missionaries at Leh. And although I did not understand one word of the Ladaki sermon which Mr. Ribbach preached, I have seldom been at a service that impressed me with the same degree of solemnity. The twinkle of the lights in the Christmas tree, and the soft, soothing tones of the organ—what a host of memories they awakened within me! How much I had to be thankful for!

On Christmas Day the caravan arrived, the last nine camels threading the noisy streets with shy and wondering eyes. At the same time I allowed Sirkin, who was longing to get home to his wife and children, to ride direct to Kashgar. But the rest of the caravan were to wait in Leh, whilst I, accompanied by Shagdur, paid a short visit to India. Two hundred and forty miles we had to ride to reach Srinagar, the capital of the Maharajah of Kashmir, and after that to drive 180 miles.

On the 1st January, 1902, we set off with a couple of attendants, all mounted on small Ladak ponies, and rode down beside the Indus, crossed the river, and at Kalachi we plunged into the mountain defiles. Our entry into the little town of Mulbekh was quite a triumph, for we were preceded by a procession of torch-bearers scattering clouds of sparks around them, and making the branches of the apricot-trees gleam out fiery red against the black sky. At Kargil we were welcomed by forty young girls in festal attire, who offered us various dishes of fruits and other delicacies. On the 9th we crossed on foot the Himalayan pass of Zoji-la, which, although only 11,485 feet high, is a remarkably difficult pass. This time there was indeed little danger; but a couple of months later, when we returned, it was decidedly ticklish work traversing the gorge, owing to the avalanches which kept constantly falling. After that we descended rapidly; but who can describe the lovely scenery of the last two days—the dark green woods, the picturesque villages with their happy people, the foaming rivers spanned by light, graceful bridges, with the glittering snowfields behind them, and above the whole the dome-like span of the turquoise sky?

The Temple of Tanksi.

On the 14th January the first *tonga*, or travelling cart, stood ready waiting for us outside the hospitable door of Captain and Mrs. Le Mesurier at Srinagar, with whom I had spent a couple of days that I shall not readily forget. From that city, 5,250 feet above sea level, we were driven at headlong speed down the winding rocky roadways, where nothing but a low breastwork of stone protects you from the abysses below, to lower and warmer climes.

One of the Courtyards of the Temple of Tikkseh.

Every half-hour we changed horses, a process which only took a couple of minutes, for the driver signalled his arrival beforehand by a melodious blast on a horn. It was quite dark when we drove through the long straight streets of Rawal-pindi. There was just an hour before the train left. The train! How strange it was to hear the shrill whistle of the locomotive after spending so many months amid the silence of the deserts and the solitude of the Tibetan wilderness!

The Town of Leh.

In Lahore I said good-bye to my old rags, and got a completely new rig-out from top to toe. Delhi, Agra, Lucknow, Benares! Wonderful cities that ye are, how gladly would I not see you again, for all too short was the stay I made on your historic scenes! At Benares I went on the river, and witnessed the thousands of pilgrims crowding on the quays and terraced steps, and bathing in the holy water at sunrise, in the hope to recover health and strength. Shagdur was amazed at everything he saw. One day in Lucknow, I obtained permission to stop an elephant, that I might feed him with sugar-cane, because my honest Cossack would persist in believing that elephants were machines, somehow or other related to the locomotive and the steamboat.

I reached Calcutta on the morning of the 25th January, and was met at the station by a vice-regal carriage, with four servants in scarlet and gold liveries, and tall white turbans. Another vehicle took charge of Shagdur and the luggage. We drove direct to Government House, where I was assigned rooms on the second floor. My bedroom had a separate balcony, shaded by an immense awning and perfumed by the palms in the park. From it I enjoyed a magnificent view of Calcutta, and beyond it right away to the jungles of the Hughli Delta. At night the vice-regal palace was simply a blaze of electric light. Two carriages were placed at my absolute disposal. Then a steam-launch carried me up the river to Barrackpur, where Lord Curzon generally spends the week-end with his family. The vice-regal dwelling at Barrackpur is beautifully smothered in greenery. Lord Curzon greeted me with all the warmth and cordiality of an old friend, and he introduced me to his charming wife. For ten days I enjoyed the delights of their hospitality, days which flew past all too rapidly, and which I count amongst my happiest and most valued recollections. At Government

House I had the honour to be present at a couple of state dinners and state balls, the magnificence of which equalled anything to be seen at the great Courts of Europe. What a change! For the past 2½ years I had been cut off from the world, travelling through the deserts and mountains of Central Asia, subject to every privation and hardship, and here I was now surrounded by the choicest refinements of civilization. Only a week or two ago I was painfully

On the Way up the Zoji-la.

struggling across the inhospitable wilds of Tibet at altitudes of 15,000—16,000 feet, with the thermometer down a dozen degrees or so below zero, where the *arkhari* and yak alone leave their footprints in the snow; whereas now I was strolling under the palms beside the Indian Ocean amid a scene bathed in light and warmth. Quite recently I was visiting in the dirty, reeking tents of the Tibetans; now I was being entertained in English drawing-rooms, amid flowers and entrancing music, by lovely ladies, and the most hospitable of hosts. The Tibetans had regarded me as a suspicious and dangerous individual; in India I was literally overwhelmed with the kindest and most flattering attentions.

I also received numbers of invitations to all parts of that wonderful land, amongst others to my old friend Colonel Younghusband, then Resident in Indore, and now leader of the British expedition to Tibet. But, however willingly I would have accepted, I could not forget the caravan that was waiting for me at Leh. All I could do was to give a peep in, as it were, while passing at one or two places. For instance, I spent four days with Lord Northcote, Governor of Bombay, and now Governor-General of Australia. It was like living on board ship at the extremity of Malabar Point, where the residency is situated, and where my verandah was surrounded on three sides by the sea. At Jaypur I was met by the Maharajah's carriage, and taken an interesting trip to see the ruins of Amber on one of his magnificently caparisoned elephants. At Jaypur all the houses are rose-coloured and the inhabitants dress in scarlet and red. The Maharajah of Kapurtala also invited me by telegraph to his castle, and His Highness himself acted as my guide when we made the round of the sights of Kartarpur on an elephant. He had four sons, lively, charming little fellows, who spoke English and French fluently, and thought it very strange that there should be a king in the far north seventy-three years old, for their own father was only thirty.

At Rawal-pindi I was rejoined by my faithful Cossack Shagdur, who had been attacked by fever in Calcutta, and had been sent north under the care of special nurses. The English doctors, and especially Colonel Fenn, the Viceroy's own physician, who had been unremitting in his attentions to Shagdur, afterwards received valuable presents from the Czar in return for the kindness they had shown to a Russian Cossack. Fortunately Shagdur recovered so far as to allow us to continue to Srinagar and Leh, but there he had a serious relapse, and when I started again on the 5th April, I had to leave him behind in the care of the missionaries. The sun shone bright and warm into his sickroom when I went in to say good-bye to him for the last time; but it was really very hard to part from him.

An Old Ladaki.

A year later I learned that he had reached Russian Turkestan in safety; but where is he now? God grant that he is still alive!

* * * * * *

At Kashgar I dismissed all my Mussulmans except Turdu Bai, who accompanied me to Osh, where I also left my dogs Malenki and Malchik in the care of Colonel Saitseff. At Chernyayeva Chernoff left me; while Cherndon and

# INDEX.